The
Brazilian Peasantry

SHEPARD FORMAN

New York & London   Columbia University Press
1975

LIBRARY OF CONGRESS CATALOGING IN PUBLICATION DATA

Forman, Shepard, 1938–
  The Brazilian peasantry.

  Bibliography: p.
  Includes index.
  1. Peasantry—Brazil.   2. Brazil—Rural conditions.
3. Brazil—Politics and government—1954–   I. Title.
HD496.F64   301.44'43'0981   75-16156
ISBN 0-231-03106-8

for *Leona*

моя сердитая ласточка

Preface

The personal and intellectual experiences which culminated in the writing of this book actually had their beginning over a decade ago and span my career, from Fulbright fellow to academic. The central argument has obviously matured in these later years, even as Brazil itself has undergone significant change. Nonetheless, a set of initial impressions have endured.

The first of these is of country roads and hemp bridges, São Julião wine, *linguiça* and *erva mate*, gaucho bravado, and hospitality—as I hitchhiked through the hills and pampas of Rio Grande do Sul with James Algeo and Gordon Burgett in the summer of 1961, then a National Defense Foreign Language fellow at that university. I stayed on for a year as a Fulbright fellow, through the resignation of Janio Quadros, the first obvious machinations of the military, and the ultimate assumption of a limited presidency by João Goulart.

The impressions of that wonderful and hectic year are recorded in a genuinely naive article, "Up from the parrot's perch," in a book appropriately entitled *Young Americans Abroad*. A number of fellow fulbrighters-turned-academics shared and helped to form some of these early impressions: Diana Siedhoff, James Burnham, Robert Price, and the late Bob Shackleford. Patricia Bildner was the kind, devoted, and sympathetic administrator of the program who encouraged me to roam freely. Those were the years of Zi-Cartola and the Estudantina, popular clubs where it was possible to absorb much of the style and rhythm of Brazil in the gaiety of a thumb-stomping samba or in the pitch and sway of a snug *gafieira*. I was intoxicated by the *samba urbano* of Ismael Silva, the nostalgia of Dolores Duran, the *samba canção* of Herivelto Martins, and the beat of the *escola de samba da Mangueira* as it found its way out of the hills and into the popular clubs of downtown Rio de Janeiro.

If I'm not mistaken, it was in one of those clubs, or strolling along Avenida Atlantica, that I met Charles Wagley for the second time. The first was in a course at New York University, when I was taking a master's degree in Brazilian studies and history. It was in his course on social anthropology that Brazil as a nation first came alive for me, and it was Charles Wagley who helped orient me to Brazil *in loco* as well. At a time when the Fulbright Commission was demanding that I come in off the streets to attend a rather dull class in history, he insisted that I join him and Cecília, his wife and collaborator, in Bahia. I did so gladly, although with considerable sadness at leaving behind a family of Brazilians who had become and remain extremely important to me. Lívia Cavalcanti, Julia Pessoa, and *o capitão* had really shown me what Brazil was about, from the royal palms on Paissandú to the *umbanda* cult on the *cais* (docks).

Bahia was another universe. I studied anthropology at the Universidade da Bahia with Dr. Thales de Azevedo, whose wife, Mariá, and delightful family helped introduce me to Brazilian folk culture. It was with them that I launched my first candle-heated balloon and ate my first manioc cake at a festa de São João. Maria David and Paulo Brandão took me on trips into the interior and argued with me about Brazilian politics and economics. I met Russell and Cherie Hamilton, who introduced me to Bahia's artistic and literary colony and to *condomblé* and *capoeira*. I wandered the Pelourinho, the *mercado modelo*, and the streets and alleys of the upper and lower city with Antonio Vieira and Clovis de Sá. Elena Bremgartner and Herman Naiser eventually took me to practically every church in the city. Hans Greve, Sr. Damião, and Miudinho opened up an entirely new world to me in Armação Saraiva, where I went frequently to see the *pesca de xareu* and to watch Damião dance for Iemanjá, the goddess of the water.

For nearly two months I traveled the Transnordestina with the Wagleys in their Willys Rural. We picnicked throughout the sertão on *quitute,* sardines, and guaraná, visiting market towns, pilgrimage shrines, countless villages, and all of the major urban centers of the Northeast. I discovered the peasantry and met their organizers at a bloody confrontation in Surubim, Pernambuco (Forman 1963). I sailed on my first jangada and began to formulate the research project that would culminate in my Ph.D. dissertation (Forman 1970).

In the meantime, Charles Wagley invited me to apply to Columbia University's anthropology department where, he said, I could learn some anthropology to help me order the array of impressions with which I had been presented. I returned to Columbia in the fall of 1962 to begin my graduate studies, first on a Korvette Fellowship and, later, on several National Defense Foreign Language Fellowships. There were a number of faculty members and fellow graduate students there whose influence is to be found in the pages of this book. Obviously, and I hope to his liking, the book is a tribute to the teaching and writing of Charles Wagley. His student and friend, Marvin Harris, became my teacher and friend, and what I have learned from him should be readily apparent to all. I was also intrigued by Abe Rossman's seminar on social organization and discussed it and related ideas nearly every night at the West End Bar with Ralph Hollaway. Janet Siskind, Stanley Regelson, Susanne Hanchett, Victor Novick, Nan Pendrell, Robert Shirley, Susan Kaufman, Riordan Roett, Ken Erickson, Paul Mandell, and Roger Newman are but a few of my contemporaries who shared my interests either in anthropology or in Brazil during my two years of residence at Columbia. In addition, I had the privilege of meeting there three distinguished Brazilian scholars—Anísio Teixeira, Octavio Ianni, and Florestan Fernandes—from whom I have learned a great deal.

In the summer of 1962, I had my first opportunity to teach about Brazil in a Peace Corps Training Program at the University of Florida in Gainesville. For me, perhaps the most significant thing about that program was the fact that it brought me into contact again with Russell and Cherie Hamilton, who helped to enrich my first teaching assignment and rekindled some of my memories of Bahia. Fabio Barbosa da Silva helped me to put a number of ideas in perspective. I am also grateful to the Peace Corps trainees in that and subsequent programs at the University of Wisconsin (Milwaukee) and the Experiment in International Living, Brattleboro, Vermont, for practical reflections on my experiences in Brazil that they elicited. I am particularly appreciative of the fact that those programs brought me into repeated contact with a number of insightful and interested ex-volunteers whom I had first met in my travels in Brazil: Dick Pozzini, Steve Keyes, Bob Bachus, and Stephanie Smith.

In the summer of 1963, I returned to Brazil as field assistant in the Columbia-Cornell-Harvard-Illinois Summer Field Studies Program. Along with a number of undergraduates, we conducted three months of research in coastal villages to the north of Salvador. I myself lived in Arembepe, a community known to me by the previous work of my friend and colleague Conrad Kottak and his wife, Betty. Arembepe is the site of Conrad's dissertation research and his forthcoming book on Brazil. I was privileged to work there with Joseph Kotta, Niles Eldridge, and Janice Pearlman. Libby Thompson lived and conducted research in the neighboring village of Jauá, providing me with a point of comparison that ultimately fed into the formulation of my dissertation proposal. It was during that summer in Arembepe that I acquired my first goddaughter, baptized Maria do Passeio since she was born en route to the hospital in my jeep. The very next day I was introduced to mourning ritual when a man, whom I also agreed to transport to the hospital, died en route.

From 1964 to 1965, I conducted dissertation research in the northeastern state of Alagoas, returning to Columbia University to write up the results of that research in 1965–66. While due acknowledgements are made in the dissertation (Forman 1966) and subsequent book (Forman 1970), some names must be repeated and additional ones mentioned here. Dr. Theo Brandão continues to have my deepest admiration as a person and as an intellect. Would that every researcher could have such a willing and brilliant intellectual companion ready at hand while in the field! Again, neither this nor subsequent research in the Northeast could have been undertaken without the hospitality of the Tercio Wanderley family. I am ever grateful for their help and their friendship. My colleagues Christopher Tavener and Diana Brown influenced in many ways my ideas about life in rural Brazil. Rosemary Messick contributed in innumerable ways to my knowledge of Brazilian politics. Daniel Gross has been a stimulating and encouraging critic. It was largely on the basis of my dissertation that Columbia University Press invited me to write this present book, and I thank Robert Tilley, then assistant Director of the Press, for his patience and his encouragement.

In 1966, I began teaching in the Department of Anthropology at Indiana University. I am grateful to a number of colleagues there, particularly Robert Birrell, Robert Burks, Chiao Chien, Paul Doughty, Jerry Mintz, and John O'Connor, for their comments and criticisms as this book began to take shape. Much of the original format was developed in classes I taught on peasant society and Brazilian culture, and I am grateful to my students there for bearing with me. One merits special mention: Marc Hoffnagel, a fine Brazilian historian, contributed to the field research on marketing systems in the Northeast, undertaken with Joyce Riegelhaupt in the summer of 1967, on grants from the Agricultural Development Council and the International Affairs Center at Indiana University. While at Indiana, I met Eric Wolf for the first time, when he came to lecture on peasant revolutions. I hope that he will recognize his influence and appreciate my admiration. About that same time, I met Paulo Freire, whose friendship I cherish. He has helped to transform my thoughts about Brazil in a number of important ways.

Joyce Riegelhaupt cannot help but find some of her own thoughts in mine. We have been friends, compadres, colleagues, and collaborators for a very long time. A thick file of correspondence dates back to the mid-1960s, and the seeds of many ideas are sown therein. We conducted research together in the Brazilian Northeast in 1967, and many of my own

thoughts matured in the course of that joint endeavor. The results of that research appear in an article in *Comparative
Studies in Society and History* (Forman and Riegelhaupt 1970),
which also comprises the first half of chapter 4 of this book. An
early version of chapter 2 was also written together (Riegelhaupt and Forman 1970). This book, as a whole, stands as a tribute to her good judgment and sound criticism. In some sense, I
would like to think of it and her own forthcoming book on the
Portuguese peasantry as part of a continuing collaborative effort. Edward Riegelhaupt has been a source of energy and commitment for us all.

The manuscript was laid aside in 1969, the year I left Indiana
University to undertake post-doctoral study at the University of
Sussex's Institute for Development Studies, under a grant from
the Social Science Research Council. Although I did not add to
the manuscript during that year, many of the ideas developed in
the course of my readings in economics and anthropology undoubtedly entered into the subsequent writing. Many of these
ideas were worked out in discussions with Jeremy Swift—
ecologist, economist, and humanist, a gifted man for whose
friendship I am particularly grateful.

Upon my return from England, I began teaching at the University of Chicago, where this book has been brought to completion. Grants from the University's Committee for the Comparative Studies of New Nations and the Committee on Latin
American Studies enabled me to conduct further research on
rural politics in Brazil in the summer of 1971 and to spend a
part of the summer of 1972 working on the manuscript. A
number of colleagues at the University of Chicago have contributed to it in one way or another. John Coatsworth, Friedrich
Katz, and Philip Schmitter have discussed various parts of the
manuscript with me and offered excellent commentaries. I have
benefited considerably from interaction with younger colleagues in the Workshop on Comparative Social History. Lloyd
Fallers has been a source of confidence and inspiration. Raymond T. Smith and Bernard S. Cohn have been influential in
ways which they probably do not know. Ralph Nicholas, above

all, has known what the endeavor has been about. I am grateful for his interest and his help. Innumerable students in several courses and seminars have listened to and commented upon parts of the manuscript—in particular Stephen Soiffer, an extremely sophisticated and insightful critic, who undoubtedly in his own research on peasant ideologies in Northeast Brazil will extend our knowledge far beyond its present state. Robin Shoemaker was an industrious and highly competent research assistant who helped in the preparation of the bibliography.

Finally, I am most appreciative of the opportunity to have lectured to a class of students in the Programa de Posgraduação em Antropologia, of the Museu Nacional, Quinta de Boa Vista, in Rio de Janeiro, during the summer of 1971, and especially to Professor Roberto da Matta, who made that possible. The Brazilian students there are doing serious and significant research, and their discussions of my work and my ideas were very helpful to me. I am particularly grateful to Professors Moacir Palmeira, Neuma Walker, and Amaury de Souza for a number of points and clarifications. Moss Blackman attended our discussions and contributed in important ways to them.

An unemployed Ph.D. in oriental art history who prefers anonymity, forced by the cutbacks in educational funding to accept work not quite suited to her real talent, patiently and expertly typed the manuscript. She deserves the credit, if not the glory.

En fim, to the Brazilian people: Venceremos—se Deus quiser.

Shepard Forman
July 1973

Contents

Chapter one–
Introduction

In April 1962, I attended a meeting of the peasant leagues on the outskirts of a small town in the drought-ridden interior of the Brazilian Northeast. Just prior to the start of that meeting, I interviewed an elderly peasant, hoping to understand some of his problems and also to discern the extent and significance of the then much-publicized peasant political movement that had begun to stir fears of a Cuban-style revolution in the Brazilian backlands. "Sim, Senhor," responded the old man when asked if he had ever heard of Francisco Julião, the acknowledged leader of the Peasant Leagues. "He is the Prince of Life who is going to give us the means to live." "Have you ever heard of Fidel Castro?" I asked the poor sharecropper. "Não, Senhor," he replied. "Have you ever heard of Cuba?" I pressed on. "Yes, Sir. My neighbor has a little transistor radio, and it said they were fighting a war over there. Who won that war anyway?"

At the meeting that followed, the hired guns of local landlords opened fire on the group of peasant men and women that had gathered in the town square to listen to the Peasant Leagues' youthful organizers. In the indiscriminate shooting, several persons were wounded, and a twelve-year-old boy died from a bullet in his head. From that time on, through ten years of study and teaching about Brazil, I have pondered the elderly peasant's question. I have wondered who might win the Brazilian war against the poverty, illiteracy, and disease that plagues the overwhelming majority of the rural population. I have wondered if the peasants, in a revolutionary fervor, would rally against an agrarian structure that has dominated Brazil for four centuries and that continues to manifest an extraordinary influence in governmental affairs even today. That is, I have questioned whether the many development schemes and foreign aid programs might not raise up the mass of people before they themselves rise up at tremendous cost—and probably to no avail.

Now, this last consideration certainly seems unlikely at a time when an entrenched military dictatorship has bridled the masses and seeks to harness them to the national purpose of "Transamazonian development." Still, this developmental panacea, like the others offered up as palliatives for the nation's masses, holds out greater promise for agrarian and industrial elites than it does for the peasants and agricultural laborers themselves. My travels and research in Brazil in 1971 suggest to me that, some seven years after the military coup d'état promised to reintegrate the nation along the lines of "Order and Progress," integration of the peasantry is yet to be achieved, if by that we mean the full participation of the masses in the economic and political affairs of state. The peasant toiling in the fields or walking the long, dusty road in search of some new field in which to toil is surely aware of the accomplishments of economic development and growth that have marked the post-1964 Brazilian "revolution." Nonetheless, he is also aware of the increased discrepancies that make ever starker the hardships of his life in the Brazilian countryside.

There is in Brazilian society a peculiar "dualism," not of separate systems in isolation, or in tense confrontation, nor even in some odd time warp, but of segments related symbiotically over time in ways that make the peasant an integral part of national life, even while limiting his full participation in that "good" life. This is not just a complicated way of saying that the Brazilian peasant is essentially a second-class citizen. It frames the dilemma that I seek to clarify in subsequent chapters of just how the peasant is enjoined to produce for a system in which he does not really share.

In this book, I will explore the social, economic, political, and cultural dimensions of this dilemma in the interest of placing the variety of peasant types in proper perspective in contemporary Brazil. I want to pull them out of the shadows of Brazilian history where they have been cast and clarify their role in the development of the nation. Now, to do so requires a particular perspective and a special strategy. It means, at the outset, that I must present the Brazilian peasantry in all of its diverse manifestations as simply one set of constituent elements among many in a complex but unitary social system. The multiple elements, or segments, that constitute this system are related in ways which determine both their individual character and that of the system as a whole. Moreover, the relations between and among these sets of elements and certain historical events redefine and condition the character of the segments *and* the whole at given points in time, thereby providing us with a series of new configurations—that is, "epochal systems," such as the colonial, the imperial, and the republican—which, in some instances, help to mark out the temporal aspect of our study. More importantly for the present undertaking, however, is the fact that the dynamics of these complex interrelationships alter the very nature of the relation of the part to the whole—in this case, the relation of the peasantry, either differentiated or generally defined, to each of these systems—thereby constituting a set of *integrative processes* that are amenable to both historical and ethnographic research, as I hope the following chapters will show.[1]

Now, I do not for a moment pretend that I can examine here the totality of the integrative processes in this complex social system. In the chapters that follow, I will focus exclusively on the manner by which those segments of the population which I designate collectively as the peasantry [2] have been related to other population segments and to particular social, economic, political, and cultural phenomena over time. That is, I am concerned in this volume to know how the peasantry has been rendered a part of the Brazilian social system and not with the actual workings of the totality itself.[3]

To facilitate this undertaking, I will examine the processes of integration in each of these several domains in turn. That is, I will pursue separately the social, economic, political, and cultural dimensions of peasant integration in the Brazilian social system. Strategically, and as a heuristic device, this will enable me to follow changes in the condition of the peasantry and their mode of integration into the regional and national system along several axes, thereby allowing for some simplification and, hence, greater clarity in the exposition of precisely what these historical processes are. Obviously, the separation of these domains is artificial, since the dimensions along which integration takes place are articulated in multiple ways in a unitary process.[4] Thus, for example, in the reality of the Brazilian sociocultural system, it is impossible to examine politics without reflecting upon social stratification and ideology, just as the study of social stratification and ideology requires a grounding in economics and the agrarian structure. Together, these domains comprise an extremely complex "feedback" system, only a brief glimpse of which will be provided here.

The complexity of this system, as we shall see, transcends the constraining bounds of time and place. It demands that this study remain essentially unbounded by communities or even groups of people as strictly defined entities in favor of a more fluid approach to the processes of interaction among sectors of the population in an extremely far-flung system. This suggests, of course, a significant departure from the usual anthropological choice of both temporal and spatial unit of study. To begin, since our very subject—the Brazilian peasantry—emerges in a variety of forms out of a set of processes identifiable in the historical record and is further differentiated and changed as these processes are themselves transformed, it can neither be defined a priori nor simply located in a specific time and place. That does not mean that a local and contained history cannot provide us with considerable insight into a particular expression of this complex social phenomenon, nor that a single ethnographic case cannot be elucidating and even provide some explanation of the more general phenomenon.

It does mean that the full array of peasant types that color the

Brazilian landscape constitutes a part of a rural socioeconomic and political system which is itself part of a more encompassing social and cultural system. Studies in peasant societies now explicitly take cognizance of this fact. Thus, it is increasingly recognized that local histories and national histories are not the same, and that it is often necessary to gauge the events of the one in terms of the other. For example, it is conceivable that an event of significance for the nation as a whole may not effect immediately and directly the lives of local villagers, although this is generally unlikely as the following chapters will doubtless show. It is far more likely that a local event, say a short-lived rebellion like the revolt of the fishhawkers in the remote village of Coqueiral, Alagoas, in the late nineteenth century, never enters into the pages of national history although it might be seared into the imagination of the local masses through the lore transmitted generation after generation. The point that I wish to make here is that, over and above the importance of their meanings for their immedate constituencies,[5] these local occurrences must be measured against other regional, national and even international events.

The socioeconomic and political relations that define the variety of peasant types over time are actuated amidst certain conditions prevalent in specific localities, but they must, in turn, be understood in broader historical perspective. Thus, to plot the events of the fishhawkers' revolt, in which female vendors allegedly chopped off the heads of eight policemen from the municipal seat, who had come to enforce new and repressive regulations regarding the sale of fish, would have limited utility in the present context. It makes a delightful story: how Maria Maloquia led the charge of the fishhawkers and, according to local legend, squatted to urinate in the mouth of the police sergeant when he pleaded for water—but the event itself tells us almost nothing, and the analysis of it little more. We could extract from it some statements about the structure of relations in the local community and reactions to administrative fiat in the raising of taxes and the localization of the market place. It could, perhaps, even serve as a case for further, limited generalization. But it could not do much to clarify the problem at hand, that is precisely what is the nature of the system in which this seemingly isolated act took place.

To know the answer to this larger question requires us to examine the overall structure of production and market relations in the nation itself and, only then, how these might affect the extent and significance of political action in specific localities in rural Brazil. That is, we must first elaborate in a general way the actual power relations, codified in the state and modified at the local level, before we can appreciate how local events, such as the fishhawkers' revolt, are generated and precisely what they mean. In short, to understand the nature of peasant integration in Brazilian society, history must be made to work for us, not merely by providing the backdrop for a particular village or group of people, nor even for the elaboration of specific situational sets of events, but by becoming the dynamic field in which particular events and relations are seen to transpire.

It is precisely this that I attempt to do, with varying degrees of success, in the three explicitly historical chapters in this book. In chapter 2, for example, I describe the emergence of a diversified peasantry out of the complex of local socioeconomic relationships which were generated in the context of a commercial, export-oriented, land-grant system.[6] The question of integration is brought most clearly into focus in chapter 4, however, where I examine the sets of economic processes which define both market relations and changing land-tenure and land-use patterns in rural Brazil over time. In both of these chapters, I try to present local historical patterns in their relation to the regional, national, and international events which clearly affect them, whether these be the deliberate policies articulated by the colonial administration, the vagaries of sugar prices on the world market, or the processes of urbanization and industrialization within Brazil itself. In chapter 5, I discuss in rather explicit terms the need to examine the interrelationship between exogenous historical events and ideologies and particular historical discontinuities and their effect upon various segments of the population and the relations between them. Speci-

fically, I intend there to demonstrate how local political events
and behavior articulate with regional and national political processes in each of the historical epochs in which the Brazilian
peasantry has played a decisive part.

To accomplish this task, of course, I must chart a rather difficult course between the macro- and the micro-, the general
and the specific, the national and the regional, now sketching a
broad picture of the Brazilian peasantry, later elaborating dis-
tinctions based on details from my own field research and other
ethnographic and documentary accounts.[7] In order to provide a
comprehensive picture of the rural laboring classes in Brazil, I
am forced out of the confines of the little community and into
the large and significant body of data which is now available in
official and unofficial documents, national statistics, sociological, economic, and political studies, and even literature, folk-
lore, and the arts. Anthropologists have long been aware of the
futility of attempting to understand such a broad and variegated
segment of the population as the peasantry by describing the
style of life in a single rural community. While there is undoubtedly a wealth of detail to be culled from the various eth-
nographies of village life in rural Brazil, these also provide us
with a bewildering array of rural peasant types, with no simple
way to make sense of this variety. One could, I suppose, sum up
all of these community studies in the hope of providing a comprehensive framework out of which an ideal peasant subcultural
type could be molded and into which it could then be recast
whenever the empirical referent were needed.[8] However, the
simple description of an ideal peasant type would not do justice
to the complexity of the changing Brazilian agrarian system as
described in the pages of this book. Moreover, the community
studies that were undertaken in the 1940s and 1950s throughout
Brazil, informative as they are, do not provide the materials for
a clear and decisive picture of the past or present condition of
the Brazilian peasantry. Nor, in all fairness, were they intended
to do so. They were largely concerned with describing the style
of life within the type of community selected for study (usually
a rural town or city) and not with the ways in which the rural

laboring segment of the population (only partially represented in these little communities) articulates with other population segments in the nation as a whole. In the chapters that follow, but especially in chapter 3, I will elaborate on the internal structural differentiation among Brazilian peasants that results from the abundant forms of labor exploitation which together comprise the basis for this complex agrarian system.[9]

To continue with the immediate question of the appropriate unit of study, however, the complexity of the Brazilian agrarian system presents us with yet another significant problem. In addition to its substantial degree of internal differentiation, the Brazilian peasantry is also highly diversified regionally, a reflection no doubt of the interaction between particular historical and ecological factors. As innumerable writers have pointed out, Brazil is a nation characterized by extreme regionalism and regional extremes. Yet, the rich body of literature on Brazilian regions and regionalism that has been so helpful in demonstrating the complexity of that vast nation now contributes to obscuring the fact that Brazil is facing a national crisis with regard to a national segment of its population. The previous emphasis on regionalism in Brazilian social studies may well have been a reflection of an earlier reality, when regional claims to privilege dominated a weak imperial regime and when, in the First Republic, local agrarian interests exercised a powerful voice in a loose federation of hegemonic states, a subject I will describe at some length in chapter 5. At least since 1930, however, and certainly since the 1964 military coup d'état, Brazil has been governed by a strengthened central authority, that mediates between closely integrated structural segments of a modern nation state in which the regions have become strikingly interdependent. I am impelled, therefore, to focus my attention not so much on regional differences from the perspective of a micro-study of one small segment of the Brazilian peasantry, but on the structural and cultural similarities that define agricultural labor as an inclusive category in relation to the nation as a whole, a point to which I will return in chapters 3 and 6.

This book, then, is about peasants and agricultural laborers throughout Brazil, although it relies a good deal on data drawn from my own field research in the Northeast region.[10] The oldest and once the most opulent region of the nation, the Northeast is now an area provoking national and international concern because of its general state of underdevelopment and human misery. A region of impressive latifundia encroaching on the life chances of a land-starved peasantry, it typifies the most significant problem of a nation that soon must make a desperate and *honest* search for solutions.[11] For the human tragedy that bares itself so starkly in the Northeast is not confined to that region alone, but extends itself throughout the Brazilian hinterland. This agrarian crisis, with its debilitating effects upon a whole nation, can neither be masked by the affluence of a privileged few nor be presented as a regional crisis. The peasant problem is not a northeastern problem. It is a national disgrace, intricately tied to the periodic successes of the various export crops that have dominated all of the regional and national economies of Brazil for most of its history and also to the more recent growth of cities and industry, as I shall observe in chapter 4. Only once the extent of the national problem is established and there is a firm commitment to confront it, can solutions be sought that might well take important regional and local differences into account.

Quite clearly this agrarian crisis and its solution have a great deal to do with the manner in which the various segments of the agricultural labor force are integrated into national economic and political processes. To simply say that we must look beyond the confines of the little community is not to comprehend the dimensions of this problem, because by so doing we only recreate the conceptual and methodological dilemma that has plagued anthropologists working in peasant societies ever since Kroeber first defined our universe of inquiry as constituting "part societies with part cultures" (1948:284)—i.e., the precise nature of the relationship between the part and the whole. For a generation of anthropologists this dilemma has been resolved by focusing down on the "linkages"—patron-clients (Wolf 1966a, 1966b; Foster 1963, 1965); culture brokers (Wolf

1956; Geertz 1960); hingemen (Redfield 1960); mediators (Silverman 1965); networks (Barnes 1954; Cohn and Marriott 1958; Beuchler and Beuchler 1971); quasi-groups (Mayer 1966); or agents (Nash 1965)—through which the specific locality is tied to the nation.[12] Now, I do not wish to deny that the structures through which the peasant is involved in national affairs are linked interstitially in ways which themselves help to define the peasant segment of society. That is, politically, economically, socially, and culturally, there are individuals or groups of individuals who mediate between the peasant and national institutions and who stand at critical junctures in the lines of communication, often limiting the peasants' access to them.

Nonetheless, in focusing our attention on these junctures, these *means of articulation,* per se, anthropologists have in effect merely described the points at which community and nation—still conceived as separately analyzable systems—are joined, thereby tending to ignore or slight the crucial fact that these newly defined units of study are themselves simply the agencies of broader historical forces playing on the social system. For example, "patron-clientship" has proved to be a useful conceptual tool for describing an important set of dependency relationships in agrarian societies. As I point out in chapters 3 and 5, it provides the content for an analysis of the dynamics of interclass behavior in rural Brazil. However, to concentrate on the internal dynamics of these exchange relationships to the neglect of the changing context in which they transpire obscures the fact that patron-clientship is little more than one *mode of integration* between social classes, the form and content of which varies considerably over time (Silverman 1965; Scott 1972a, 1972b).

Essentially, most of these studies of mediatorial agents are only variations of incursionist philosophies, which describe a village or a set of villages in the ethnographic present and then pinpoint the instruments of social change—roads, markets, electricity, literacy—through which the larger society begins to effect the local transition from "traditional" to "modern." [13] It hardly need be stated that this outside-in trajectory of the ties that bind community to nation is far too narrow to account for the complex of relations which define the changing Brazilian agrarian system. Once again, we must look neither to communities or groups of people (as defined entities or units) but to processes of interaction in which the peasant not only *receives* wisdom, commodities, benefits, and other items which "infringe" on him from the outside and to which he must adapt, but in the course of which interdependent segments of a unitary social system act upon each other in recognizable, reciprocal ways. For example, it is insufficient to point out as is usual in anthropological studies of this type that the peasant is tied to the market by a need to sell produce for cash with which to purchase needed consumer goods and services since it is in the nature of the attachment to the marketing system, and to wider sociopolitical systems, that both the peasant sector and the agrarian system itself are defined.

It is quite clear to even the most casual observer that the Brazilian peasant is integrated into a system in which he only partially shares. He is at once a commodity producer for the market and a consumer of a wide variety of goods, some produced locally and others filtered back to the countryside from the principal manufacturing centers of the nation. The organization of peasant economic life represents a carefully balanced response to this dual role as producer and consumer.[14] Needless to say, this balance is a precarious one, and shifts markedly as commercialization proceeds in the countryside. Nonetheless, it is the nature of market involvement rather than the simple fact thereof that is critical in determining outcomes at the local level.

There has been some speculation about the degree of involvement of peasants in the market economy (Wolf 1966:41ff.; 1968:xiv; Dalton 1967a:75; 1967b:156–57; Miracle 1968; Wharton 1963). On the one side, there are those who view the peasant as essentially market-oriented, gearing his production decisions to price information, demand schedules, and the like. On the other, there are those who argue that the peasant is primarily a subsistence farmer who interacts in the market place only to fulfill his immediate household needs. In the latter case, it is assumed that in the ideal-typical peasant society, the agricultural smallholder moves back and forth between subsistence and limited production for the market with a surefootedness which ensures him both survival and security. The penetration of the market economy into the countryside then results in the breakdown of the traditional institutional framework and subsequent peasant disaffection.[15]

In the Brazilian case, the catallactic effects of commercialization are not so easily pinpointed. In the first place, the transitional nature of the Brazilian economy makes a baseline definition of a self-reliant peasantry elusive. The Brazilian peasant has always been tied to a monetized economy, as I will demonstrate in chapter 2. Since the colonial period, his production has been directed in one way or another to the export-oriented sector of the economy, either through growing commercial crops directly or through supplying foodstuffs to growers through rural markets. In addition to the labor requirements imposed on large monocultural estates, there were innumerable instances of legislation over the production and distribution of needed foodcrops which make apparent the kinds of demands to which the peasant was forced to adapt.

In point of fact, it is difficult to ascertain an ideal time in the historical past when the Brazilian peasant's participation in the market arena was determined *solely* in terms of his own household consumption needs. The peasant undoubtedly traded or sold part of what he produced in order to obtain those necessities of life which he could not produce himself. He relied on family labor and the reciprocal labor of neighbors and friends for the planting and harvesting of crops. Insofar as the basic portion of his produce was consumed at home and only the surplus was traded at the market place, we could say that he "subsisted." Security for his person and property and the economic well-being of his family were insured just so long as he was able to maintain control over the land he farmed. Even today, the peasant engaged in the production of foodstuffs on land he controls himself is able to revert to a "subsistence" pattern of production if necessary. For example, when demand for a commercial crop lags, when prices fall sharply on the international market, or when inflation cuts deeply into his purchasing power, the peasant is able to tighten his belt and subsist, for a time, on his own produce.

This ability to control the processes of production and to work out strategies which most closely conform to a peasant's needs becomes more difficult, of course, in situations in which agriculturalists engaged in the production of export crops like coffee or sugar cannot easily convert their landholdings to immediately consumable foodcrops. It is precisely in such situations, when the peasant's security is threatened because he is no longer able to make the best decisions concerning the utilization of his land, or when he is unable to compete for land on the open market (which occurred as a generalized phenomenon in Brazil in the 1950s and 1960s, but also in a number of specific previous instances), that he is most likely to express his individual discontent in a public way. It is not simply that the inclusion of the peasant in the market economy transforms him into a revolutionary. Rather, overriding tensions are generated and radicalization is likely to occur when there is an explicit threat to his means of livelihood and sense of security. This is not a matter of the *degree* of market involvement per se, but rather a reflection of the particular structure of relations of production and exchange which characterize a local, or regional, or national economy in place and time, a process of peasant *economic integration* which I will examine at length in chapter 4.

There is little question that the basic organizing principle in the peasant sector of the economy is the maximization of security and the minimization of risk. In a previous study, I analyzed the strategies which account for the differential acceptance and rejection of innovations in the peasant raft-fishing economy of the Brazilian Northeast (Forman 1970). I found that these peasant fishermen made their calculations in terms of a work-energy production ratio that promised them maximum returns for efforts expended.[16] Their total inputs into the fishing economy were a reflection of their expectations of return, calculated according to the needs of their families, the members of which contributed in no small way to the maintenance of traditional economic patterns. The expectation of return could, and often did, have a monetary referent. However, considerations of return for labor expended were based on buying power for household consumption needs rather than on the acquisition of cash for purposeful reinvestment in an expanding business enterprise.

These Brazilian peasants did make rational calculations consistent with market principles, although their decisions were also based on a variety of ecological, political, social, and cultural factors which comprised their total environment. Rather than the dual set of operations which characterize the family-run business enterprise, in which the owners invest labor and capital in their firm which, in turn, seeks to maximize its independent advantage in terms of profit margins and capital for reinvestment, the peasant's undifferentiated household unit was geared to a system of savings and credit, which was essential for the maintenance of the traditional economic system. These two economic types, the peasant household and the firm, represent different sets of value orientations, obviously determined by their place within the general economic system. Both are attached to the market but in different ways and for different ends. Each has a cultural set of standards to which production is, in some sense, geared, but the one is to security, the other to profit maximization.[17]

The Brazilian peasant is caught up in an enveloping commercial system that eventually will undermine the character of the peasant sector of the economy. The peasant is forced to sell his produce to obtain cash for the purchase of innumerable manufactured products that quickly become part of his consumer wants. Urban demands for increased production and for a steady supply of agricultural produce add to the domestic pressures which condition the peasant's productive inputs. In order to satisfy the nation's needs, the peasant is asked to increase his on-farm productivity, and he sometimes relies on hired wage labor to help in the production of his cash crops, a fact which reduces his real income. In order to satisfy his own and his family's wants, he increasingly is induced to seek outside additional income, often by assuming the role of market middleman. All too often the meager earnings from slash-and-burn and hoe agriculture, combined with limited access to a resource base, force him to sell his own and his family's labor on the market.

Undoubtedly, these processes of integration become more acute as modernization occurs. Urban populations and industrial enterprises make pressing demands upon the agricultural sector which the peasant is ill-equipped to meet. There follows, as I will demonstrate in chapter 4, a restructuring of market relations which instigates changes in the system of land tenure and land use as well. At its worst, increased concentration and consolidation of landholdings take place, and the peasant loses his land. At best, through his involvement in the market economy the peasant is subject to a wide variety of economic controls. His decisions regarding production come to be affected as much by the urban and industrial sector of the economy as by local demands and his own consumption needs.

The encroachment of the ever-expanding latifundia on independent smallholdings and the socioeconomic arrangements between landlord and tenant or sharecropper infringe substantially on the peasant's productive strategies. The smallowner must fight to compete in the market arena and often falls victim to the excesses of the middleman. The sharecropper is told what crops should be grown and when and at what price they will be sold. The tenant farmer is subject to the will of the landlord who limits his tenure, the choice and placement of his crops, his right to breed livestock, and the numbers and kinds of fruit trees he can plant. The peasant is further affected by legislation which controls the distribution of his product. He is heavily taxed, required to buy licenses and pay fees, and even told where to sell his crop and at what price. These matters will be discussed at length in chapter 3. The important point to be made at the moment is that these controls are not merely the capricious whims of the landlord, the mayor, or the tax collector, but are the rational decisions of men in power in a socioeconomic and political system in which land, labor, and capital are all commodities to be traded on the market and used to their best advantage.

Of course, it is possible to emphasize the processes of economic integration in the definition of a peasantry to the neglect of important cultural criteria, as Charles Wagley recently has pointed out (1968:20).* A peasantry, as a socioeconomic phenomenon, can be found in many contemporary and past societies, and it is easy to identify a set of structural regularities that have some cross-cultural validity (Bloch 1966:446; Wolf 1966a). However, in my view a peasantry should also be examined contextually, that is, within the particular sociocultural milieu in which it is embedded and which gives it its peculiar character. For example, the Brazilian peasantry emerged out of a particular set of historical circumstances, as a by-product of a developing internal and external marketing system. It has been integrated into the Brazilian nation by means of a hierarchical set of relationships maintained by explicit social and economic sanctions as well as by more subtle demands on expected behavior. It is, therefore, incumbent upon us to include a broad range of sociocultural data in our study of the peasantry.

Certainly, a study of the Brazilian peasantry would be incomplete without exploring the range of dependency relationships which characterize Brazilian society. By this I do not mean only the exploitative relationships assumed within the usual definition of a peasantry, but also, for example, the ways in which the peasant himself uses patron-dependent relationships as part of his adaptive risk-reducing strategy. Any broader discussion of peasant behavior in Brazil requires a clarification of the socioeconomic *and* cultural aspects of these patron-dependent relationships, which afford the peasant protection, expose him to national culture, but also deprive him of the

* When I refer to "culture" in this volume, I am referring to the shared symbols and meanings that inform behavior (Geertz 1966b) and not simply to the behavioral manifestations which have generally been the focus of attention of ethnographers working in Latin America.

possibility of individual growth and meaningful participation in the affairs of state.

These dependency relationships are class relationships, sometimes interethnic ones, the significance of which are often lost in the formality of many class analyses and in the rigidity of many sociological accounts of systems of stratification. In chapter 3, I will examine these relational aspects of social class, particularly the ideological component expressed in the notions of submission and obligation, in order to clarify the precise nature of interclass behavior in rural Brazil. In chapter 5, I will demonstrate how the form and content of these dependency relationships are altered in the course of Brazilian political history, and examine the various forms that recent peasant political experience has taken as peasants and agricultural workers have been recruited en masse into supra-local peasant leagues and rural syndicates.

Yet, precisely because all of these relationships are overlaid with a set of conventionalized understandings regarding proper behavior in interclass situations, a discussion of their cultural dimension is also necessary, if we are to fully apprehend the crucial difference between the extent and significance of peasant political action. In rural Brazil, the overt symbols of status are readily apparent—perhaps not to the degree of the Indian caste system or the gross diacritical markers of Andean South America. Still, they are recognizable: the sun-parched figure of the Brazilian peasant clad in rough white cotton and straw hat, clutching his bush knife, his bare feet shifting ground, as head lowered, he addresses his *patrão*, "Sim, Senhor. Não, Senhor," with that characteristic tone of resignation that borders on revolt. However, in addition to identifying this peasant way of life with its distinctly Brazilian flavor and describing the attitudinal differences that distinguish peasants from other national subcultural types, we must also be able to describe the manipulation of cultural codes and symbols by the various segments of the social system. For only by so doing, can we begin to explain the more subtle forms of social control that are pressed upon the peasant (like "knowing one's place" or "waiting on the will of God"), or how peasants themselves transcend their traditional behavior patterns and expectations in adjusting emotionally and intellectually to changing institutional contexts.

The very study of the world's peasantries has been propelled by divergent national ideologies, mainly concerned with development (Shanin 1971:11). Yet, in our quest to understand our subject as object, the interrelationship between these dominant ideologies and the masses' own belief systems has not been pursued at any length. In chapter 6, I will explore the place of popular religion in the formation of a peasant ideology and its significance for political action in rural Brazil.

Religion is a basic fact of peasant life. The Brazilian peasant shares only partially in the formal Catholic religious system which itself has come to have a peculiarly Brazilian stamp. Nonetheless, he has incorporated this Catholic tradition, or elements of it, in a meaningful way into his own religious belief system, which includes aspects of Afro-Brazilian and Amerindian religious practices and beliefs and an individual reflective mysticism that personalizes an otherwise gaudy and noisy collective religious experience. That is, formal Catholicism provides a set of institutionalized beliefs and meanings and a system of ritual acts which fulfill the social needs of the rural masses. It also contributes to a comprehensive popular belief system which intersects with social structure in such a way as to provide the peasant with a profound and often unyielding personal outlook on his relationship to other men, to society, to his saints and his God, in a sense, to life in general. It is necessary, therefore, to look past the famous shrines, the saint's day processions, household prayer meetings, and spirit possession in order to fully appreciate the peasant's communion with a religious ideal. Among Brazilian peasants there is a deep sense of resentment and outrage at the humiliating condition of their lives. As we shall see, the resignation which allows for the passive acceptance of this condition and the devastating action which it sometimes engenders both derive their strength from the popular religious system. By examining the range of integrative processes that make the peasantry an integral part of the Brazilian social system, then, this book also undertakes a tentative explication of that fundamental relation between culture and social action.

Chapter two –

Beyond the Masters and the Slaves: A Peasantry in Brazil

Portuguese settlement in Brazil was based from the earliest times on the development of export-oriented commercial agriculture. The production of sugar for the expanding European market in the sixteenth century established a plantation economy which continues, although in a considerably different form, to the present. The agricultural labor force was originally supplied by large numbers of African slaves and, later, by freedmen tied to the plantation through a variety of tenure arrangements.[1] In addition, numerous small holdings developed in support of the larger, export-oriented commercial enterprises, whose business it was to provide a growing internal marketing system with much-needed foodstuffs and other primary produce. Thus, alongside the Brazilian plantation system, there developed early on a peasant sector comprised of small owners, tenant farmers, and sharecroppers, who served as both commodity producers and a labor force within that system, as well as suppliers of foodcrops to it.

This early commodity production (of export crops for the external market and foodstuffs for the plantations and the growing urban centers) marks the emergence of a peasantry in Brazil. While certainly overshadowed by the dominant export-oriented sector of the rural economy, peasant production for the internal market nevertheless has been an important commercial activity since colonial times. Indeed, the popular characterization of

Brazilian agrarian history in terms of extensive landholdings, masters and slaves, and production for the European market is inadequate for any understanding of the present agrarian crisis in Brazil. The slave plantation that has been projected both forward and backward as prototypical of the Brazilian social system from colonization until the onset of the industrial era actually had its fullest expression in the nineteenth century (Lockhart 1972:12–13). The colonial socioeconomic system was very complex, and probably the economy of the land grant was focused not primarily on the exploitation of sugar, but instead designed to produce income for the Portuguese Crown—from whatever source.

Although the slaveholding monocultural fazenda (the Brazilian plantation system) has come to exercise economic, political, and social hegemony over the nation during four centuries, it was not—and is not—a total picture of the way of life in rural Brazil.[2] From the beginning of colonization, the Brazilian export economy was crosscut by a network of other economic ties, which gave rise to a rather involved domestic economy. In the words of historian Richard Morse:

Complementing and making possible this (external) commerce . . . was an internal movement of jerked beef and other foodstuffs, hides and cash commodities in transshipment which has only a modest place in colonial statistics, yet which inconspicuously served to articulate those very regions which production for export appeared to isolate one from another. (1962:168)

Undoubtedly, the institution of slavery left an indelible mark on the Brazilian sociocultural system. Its incumbent traditions of patronage and paternalism have come to characterize the entire system of socioeconomic relations in Brazil.

However, it is also important to understand the types of relationships which existed in Brazil apart from the system of slavery.[3] As early as 1711, Antonil was to write:

Even though slavery engraved a fundamental image on plantation society, the slave labor force hardly extended throughout the totality of the productive system. There persisted on the sugar plantations sectors that functioned on the basis of free labor. In this way, subsistence agriculture should have been the most important sector, or, at least, that which offered the best conditions for permanency and stability, notwithstanding the existence of a reduced number of negro slaves who could participate in it. (1967:60)

From the outset, too, slavery began to relinquish its own product to the free labor market. Incomplete as they remain, historical data indicates that a large free peasant population existed early in the colonial period and was engaged in a lively internal trade.[4] The change over from a slave to a nonslave plantation system between 1888 and 1889 occurred with little, if any, alteration in structural relationships in the Brazilian countryside, indicating that the transition from slave to free labor was well under way before abolition. Work patterns remained largely the same, only now a system of debt and credit effectively tied the freed black man (with limited resources and nowhere to go) to the land. After abolition, the ex-slave, already locked into Brazilian colonial society and necessary to its continued economic growth, remained an integral part of the agrarian economy and expanding urban artisan trades.

Generally speaking, abolition did not seem to have wide-ranging effects on the overall Brazilian economy at the time, which suggests to me that historians might do well to turn their attention away from discussions of slavery in Brazil and look instead to an examination of the total agrarian system of which slavery was only one part. Such an approach could help us to understand the nature of the socioeconomic relationships both between masters and slaves and landlords and peasants as responses to a complex economic system dominated by the export-oriented latifundia.

The highly enterprising Portuguese Crown had two principal interests in the development of a Brazilian colony in the expanding European market of the sixteenth century—the administration of the territory and commercial exploitation. Both of these ends were accomplished through the granting of large landholdings, called *sesmarias,* to favorite subjects of the Crown. These sesmarias were a tried and tested form of territorial expansion and administration that had been used by the

Portuguese as early as the fourteenth century in their recon-
quest of peninsular lands from the Moors. Originally intended
as jurisdictional rights and sets of privileges over conquered
lands and their resident populations rather than as rights in
property per se, these sesmarias became in colonial Brazil extensive latifundia, subject to commercial performance requirements set by the Crown and to royal regulations regarding obligations between settlers and the land grantee (Johnson
1972:205ff.). Cultivation, for the most part, was directed toward
export crops, principally sugar, a commodity with which the
Portuguese were already quite familiar. A sugar economy existed on the island of São Thomé as early as 1493, where it was
maintained by a population consisting of exiled convicts and
Jews who refused to abjure their faith.

It was not unreasonable, then, for Lisbon to assume that a system of land grants could be transplanted in the New World
without expending substantial Crown funds or sustaining a loss
to Portugal's hard-pressed labor force. It was not anticipated
that these economic and political units would provide for a
rather smooth transition to local control by landowners rather
than centralized control by Crown officials. Furthermore, it
could hardly be foreseen that the recognition of property rights
in slaves as opposed to jurisdictional rights over resident native
populations (as in continental Portugal or Spanish America)
would establish early on an economic rather than a legal-political relationship between landowner and laborer, thereby setting the pattern for the fundamental form of social control that
has since characterized rural Brazilian social structure.

Portugal was already well acquainted with the economic vir-
tues of slavery, and she quickly adjusted to its social vices in
Brazil. Notwithstanding, the sesmaria was a radical ecological
adjustment with no precedence in the small farm economy of
Portugal itself and only slight resemblance to the "classic"
slave plantation that would develop in Brazil in the nineteenth
century. To begin, the principal wealth to be derived from
sugar was in its processing and transshipment, not in cultivation
per se. At the center of the land-grant institution stood the

engenho, an animal-driven mill for the crushing of cane. These were highly capitalized operations, which often utilized slave labor obtained through the consignment of processed sugar to a merchant slaver.

Because of costs involved in maintaining a resident slave population, the colonial period never supported extensive plantations with hundreds of imported slaves. While up to fifty slaves might be employed at a single engenho, the production of sugar on satellite holdings demanded the labor of perhaps ten to twenty slaves, certainly no more. Innumerable smaller landholdings supplying sugarcane to the mills often operated with as few as one or two slaves, and some, of course, operated with none. In all of these instances, actual production of sugarcane for the milling operations was undertaken by less fortunate settlers, who bought or rented lands from the sesmeiros. In this way, the large landholdings did not long constitute a monolithic form of agricultural exploitation. According to Canabrava:

"The division of old sesmarias through the sale of land, possibly under financial pressures, gave the less fortunate settlers the opportunity to set themselves up among those who subsidized the production of the mill" (1967:47).

The land grants were further broken up by landowners who subdivided their estates into smaller holdings which they rented to individual farmers (Castro 1966:98). So it was that absentee ownership helped to demarcate the outlines of a peasant society early in Brazilian history as the following sixteenth-century account describes:

The system of renting to the small colonists then began. Now we have the agent of Dom Alvaro subdividing his grant among the colonists, so creating a class of tenant farmers contributing much to the owner's prosperity. It was precisely this class that was the first form of free labor in Brazil, side by side with slave labor . . . (cited in Castro 1966:96–97)

Within a relatively short span of time further adjustments in the system of land tenure became necessary, both for the supply of sugar cane to the mills and of foodstuffs to a growing population. By the eighteenth century, smaller properties called *datas de terra* began to be distributed, primarily to colonists from the Azores, for the purpose of practicing diversified agriculture based on family labor.[5] These *datas de terra,* or peasant farms, were encouraged in order to solve the problem of internal food supply in an export-oriented agricultural system, a problem that vexes the Brazilian government even today.

Throughout its history, then, the Brazilian agrarian system has been comprised of a diversified labor force organized in a variety of tenure arrangements.[6] Peasant farmers, variously known as *lavradores, moradores,* and *foreiros,* had different socioeconomic ties to the *senhores de engenho* (lords of the sugar mills). An adequate history of these land tenure patterns is yet to be written, but the general manner in which a Brazilian peasantry emerged can be reconstructed from a number of sources. Writing about the types of arrangements for supplying sugar to the mills in the seventeenth century, A. P. Canabrava states:

We must not forget the lavradores who occupied themselves in subsistence agriculture, also contributing to the plantation economy. Whether on their own land received in grants or on lands rented from the plantation, they prepared their plots of manioc and raised some cattle, using these products when necessary to complement those for which they labored in the manufacture of sugar. (1967:48)

The lavrador was a small, independent planter with a significant role in the sixteenth-century sugar economy. He planted sugarcane on his own land and sold it to the engenhos (steam-driven sugar mills), which were required by law to process it (Canabrava 1967:45–47). The term *lavrador* was alternatively applied to a sharecropper on a large plantation who paid neither rent nor fees. He ". . . was permitted to build a house, maintain other lands, at times to have a slave, but his main obligation was to plant cane for the owner of the engenho" (Diegues Junior 1959b:106–7).[7]

The morador also resided on engenho lands in the early colonial period.

The *morador* was not obliged to plant the cane; at first, he was a person to whom the owner of the estate gave a piece of land on his property, helping him to build his house and plant *roças* (swidden plots) of greens, vegetables, corn, beans, sweet potatoes and yams; in return, he was subject to the payment of a fee, which not all the owners collected as it was generally a small sum. Rather, the owner received from the *morador* food crops which were considered more as a gift than a payment. (*ibid.*, 107)

The moradores, however, were not merely food suppliers; they constituted a labor reserve for the sugar industry and were required to give several days of work, either at low pay or free, to the senhor de engenho (Andrade 1964:79). As we shall see, such exchange relationships took on a decidedly different aspect in the twentieth century, as the internal market for foodstuffs in Brazil became more commercialized and as the exigencies of export-crop production required more stringent exploitation of labor.

Foreiros are still another segment of the Brazilian peasant population with roots deep in the colonial past. *Foreiros* originally rented marginal lands from the senhores de engenho on which they grew subsistence crops. In addition to the low rent which they paid, they performed corvee labor during the harvest and planting seasons. The importance of this arrangement grew with the development of the cotton economy (Andrade 1964:109), and today we find temporary renting arrangements in which the landowner receives only a small annual sum in rent but a significant commitment of labor in the clearing of virgin lands.

In addition to the development of these regular tenure patterns, squatters began to move out from the coastal regions and settle in the vast areas of the Brazilian hinterland during the seventeenth and eighteenth centuries (Diegues Junior 1959a:21). The Brazilian geographer Josué de Castro describes the situation in the following way:

Rural masses in increasing numbers were flooding onto uncultivated private or public lands. It was these waves of squatters—or intruders, as they were called—that hastened the downfall of the land grant institution . . . . the squatters ushered in a new phase in Brazilian agrarian life . . . The squatters' struggle for land engendered a new capitalist peasant form of ownership. (1966:103)

Castro attributes the abolition of the land-grant system in 1822 to the situation created by the squatters, who made apparent the need for a system of legal tenure and set the stage for the transition from sesmaria to fazenda, the large-scale, privately owned plantation which is the predominant form of landholding in Brazil today.

It would be useful at this point to present a demographic history of Brazil; however, there is limited material for the colonial period; and the first official census for all of Brazil appears only in 1872. Historians have not as yet examined tax, legislative, or land records; nor wills, Church, or other documents for land-tenure data for the colonial period; and the published primary source material is slim. What data we do have, however, clearly attests to the existence of a sizable free peasant population in colonial Brazil. Dauril Alden, describing sources for the study of population in eighteenth-century Brazil, gives partial statistics for the numbers of slaves as opposed to freedmen in the 1770s, indicating that, save for Rio de Janeiro, the percentage of slaves in the overall population was generally less than one quarter (1963:197). In like fashion, a province-by-province study of censuses undertaken in the nineteenth century points consistently to a far larger proportion of freedmen to slaves, regardless of any discrepancies which might exist in each of the individual estimates under review (Silva 1951). In his examination of the local histories of a number of northeastern states in the same period, the Brazilian geographer Manuel Correia de Andrade notes that the percentage of slaves in the population of the Northeast was never particularly high (1964:95–98). Comparative data gathered for the Northeast provinces in the mid-nineteenth century by the English editor William Scully confirms this view (1866). At the same time, a review of census materials for a number of localities in the *capitania* of São Paulo in the early nineteenth century demonstrates a considerable preponderance of agriculturalists without slaves as compared to those utilizing slave labor (Willems 1970:34–35, 39).

My own research into the emergence of a peasantry in the northeast state of Alagoas also indicates that in the nineteenth century the majority of rural dwellers in that region were free peasants. The population figures fail to specify the occupations of the people—whether moradores, foreiros, or squatters—but comparison with the above-cited sources suggests that my own data is representative of conditions in other regions of the Northeast and, with some modifications, throughout Brazil.

In 1847, a statewide census calculated the population of Alagoas as 207,294 of whom 39,675 were slaves (Diegues Junior 1949:153). A more detailed 1837 census for the *comarca* (district) of Penedo lists a population of 82,590, of whom 22,045 were white, 32,694 were free mulattos, 4,531 were mulatto slaves, 10,113 were free blacks, 10, 876 were black slaves, and 2,331 were Indians. The population of the city of Penedo, a small port on the São Francisco River from which sugar and cotton were shipped to the northern province of Pernambuco, numbered no more than 4,000 inhabitants (Gardiner 1848:95). The total slave population of both the city and the countryside amounted to only 18.6 percent at a time when sugar and cotton production were in ascendancy in the area, suggesting that the vast majority in the countryside were peasants. Similar population statistics also hold for the county of Guaiamú in Alagoas which, during 1871, some eighteen years before the abolition of slavery, had a total population of 17,117, of which 78 percent were freemen and only 22 percent were slaves. This free majority was engaged in the production both of sugarcane for the engenhos and foodstuffs for a lively internal market.

During the sixteenth and seventeenth centuries, the município of Guaiamú was an economic satellite of the expanding sugarcane fields of the province of Pernambuco. From it, cattle and agricultural produce were sent to Olinda, the provincial capital, and dyewoods and hardwoods were supplied to the Portuguese Royal Navy (Andrade 1959:40; Almeida Prado 1941:445–46). By the beginning of the seventeenth century, an "agricultural highway" existed for the transport of goods from the city of Penedo, on the São Francisco River, along the Alagoan coast through the county of Guaiamú north of Olinda, the provincial capital.

Large-scale exploitation of sugarcane began in the county in the eighteenth century and spread so rapidly that it was necessary to place the forest resources under royal preserve. Peasant land use in Guaiamú and the surrounding counties were soon restricted to the arid coastal areas, as provided for in a royal decree of 1798. This decree stated that "The lands more or less concentrated adjacent to the sea as well as those bordering on all woodlands judged to be useless for the Royal Navy will be set aside for the agriculture of the people" (Vilhena 1921:804–5). The heavily furrowed plots now abandoned on the worn-out tablelands attest to the intensified agriculture which was practiced at that time. A nineteenth-century account describes the county as ". . . extremely fertile and containing various sugar mills whose inhabitants annually harvest rich crops of all forms of foodstuffs and transport them to the capital and other parts of the province." This same account also indicates that Guaiamú was ". . . a refuge for the inhabitants of the interior during the droughts and . . . one of the rich bread-baskets . . . supplying manioc, beans, corn, oil, and sometimes even fruits . . ." to the metropolitan centers to the north (Espindola 1871:236–37). These products reached their destinations through the Northeast's internal marketing system, comprised of a vast network of *feiras*, or weekly marketplaces.

Peasant populations such as those described briefly above are evident throughout the pages of Brazilian history,—although all too often between the lines. For example, the eminent Brazilian historian Caio Prado Junior writes in his important study, *Formação do Brasil Contemporâneo*, that the agrarian population of colonial Brazil was comprised of three elements: masters, slaves, and an "inchoate mass of humanity," a *populacão vegetativa*, which lacked in social and economic organization and lived on the furthest margins of Brazilian society. According to Caio Prado, the masters and the slaves

are well-classified in the hierarchy and in the social structure of the colony: the former are the directors of colonization in its various sectors; the others, the working masses. Between these two neatly defined categories involved in the work of colonization, exist a number, growing with time, of unclassified people, useless and maladapted; individuals with more or less uncertain and undependable occupations or with no occupations at all. (1957:279–80) [8]

This mass of people, comprised of ". . . freed or runaway black and mulatto slaves, semi-acculturated Indians, mestizos of all color gradations and categories . . . even whites, pure whites . . . including those torn off from illustrious Portuguese family trees," were a large and growing segment of the population. Referring to Couty's *L'Esclavage au Bresil*, published in 1881, Prado writes

In Couty's time, he calculated them at nothing less than 6 million, or half of a total population of 12 million. The proportion would be less among the 3 million people at the beginning of the century; but even still it would certainly comprehend the immense majority of the free population of the colony. (*Ibid.*, 80)

Of this "immense majority," some subsisted in remote areas of the nation. Others took refuge under the wing of some powerful landlord. Still others, "the most degenerate," according to Caio Prado, lived by *vadiando*, or simply "hanging around."

In my view, a closer examination of the historical materials available to us will reveal that this peasant population was highly articulated with Brazilian society at large. In his admirable reexamination of early nineteenth-century census materials from the *capitania* of São Paulo, anthropologist Emilio Willems describes a considerable degree of social and occupational differentiation among rural colonial populations. Although arguing for the subsistence nature of agriculture at the local level, Willems notes that, "All these local systems produced commercial crops for foreign and domestic markets . . ." (1970:32). From my perspective, there is no reason to believe that the mass of free agricultural labor in colonial Brazil differed in any decisive way in social and economic organization from the peasant populations described in the Introduction or, for that matter, from those we find in a distinctly more integrated fashion in contemporary Brazil. The peasant in colonial Brazil was organized into family regimes which produced commercial crops for the export market and foodstuffs for home consumption, selling his surpluses at local market places and supplementing his income through a variety of handicraft occupations. He lived in small villages, hamlets, and plantation towns and neighborhoods scattered throughout the vast countryside. He acknowledged the priest, paid homage to his saints, and offered labor and allegiance to some member of the landowning class in exchange for a parcel of land to farm. He was, historically, the same dependent being.

A number of early travel accounts provide us with firsthand observations which suggest the form of economic organization of the free laboring majority in these rural towns and villages in colonial Brazil. Further studies in colonial history could undoubtedly aid us in the reconstruction of the social and political organization of these peasant communities. In his *Travels in Brazil,* published in 1816, Henry Koster describes innumerable rural settlements producing foodstuffs for sale at the local market places. For example, he

. . . entered the long, straggling village of Paratibe, with manioc lands and plantain and tobacco gardens intermixed with the houses. The inhabitants are mostly laboring free persons, white, mulatto, and black. The houses are built on each side of the road at intervals, for the distance of one mile. . . . several sugarworks are seen, and great numbers of small cottages; the passing of the country people with loaded horses, carrying cotton, hides, and other articles, the produce of the country, and returning with many kinds of wares, salt, meat and fish from Recife, may almost be called continual. (1966:27)

In one of his many references to an internal trade in food products, Koster writes that "The trade with the interior is considerable, and particularly on the day of the market, which is held weekly, the bustle is excessive" (*ibid.,* 102).

A slightly later account by the Englishman, James Henderson, describes each province and its principal villages in terms of the numbers of inhabitants and their occupations. Henderson's account demonstrates that, at the beginning of the nineteenth century, the majority of small hinterland communities were growing foodstuffs, some for home consumption but much of it also destined for the network of local market places. Recounting his visit to the southern parish of São Gonçalo d'Amarante, Henderson explains that "Its members produce a large quantity of *farinha, feijão,* and Indian corn, with the superabundance of which, as well as that of coffee, sugar and *casacha,* much specie is introduced into the district" (1821:97). Somewhat to the north ". . . is the parish of St. Nicolau . . . being planted with mandioca, rice and coffee, but principally with the banana fruit, which introduces annually seventy thousand crusades, arising . . . from the industry of the whites, who exceed the number of negroes . . ." (*ibid.*). Arriving in the Northeast, Henderson passed through Pilão Arcado, a town created in 1810, which is

well situated near a small hill upon the margin of the São Francisco, its only resource for water, and whose greatest inundations always visit it with some injury. The church, dedicated to St. Antonio, is new, and solidly built with bricks and lime. The houses are generally earth and wood, and many of them covered with straw. It has three hundred families, which are increasing, and, with those of its vast district, comprise five thousand inhabitants, who cultivate mandioca, maize, vegetables, good melons, and watermelons, upon the margin of the river. (*Ibid.,* 378)

It was undoubtedly the produce of peasant communities such as these which supplied the weekly market at the São Francisco river town of Propriá, so well described by yet another English traveler in colonial Brazil, George Gardiner:

This town has a market each week on Saturday . . . The preparations created quite a stir, to be seen throughout the previous day, but especially in the late afternoon when produce for sale arrives without end, brought along the river in canoes or overland on horseback from the interior. . . . [I went to see] the type of articles displayed for sale, finding them unexpectedly varied, but comprised principally of foodstuffs and clothing. Among others of less importance, we noted an abundance of . . . manioc flour, salted beef, large fish . . . loaves of brown sugar . . . honey in pouches, fresh meat, bananas, soap, shoes, better fabrics and simple cottons, rope made from fibers, tobacco . . . clay kitchen utensils . . . (1849:97–98)

Since early colonial times, then, the Brazilian peasant has been a seller of foodstuffs in local market places. While the greater part of peasant production was surely for home consumption, the setting aside of surpluses for sale marked the beginning of internal commercial activity in the Brazilian countryside. The peasant's entry into this commercial arena was instigated by a chronic shortage of foodstuffs in an export-oriented economy, which led him (and in some instances, the slave) to sell a part of his crop at the neighboring plantation, in the nearby town, and even in the growing coastal cities.

There has been speculation that this direct flow of nonbulk goods from a large number of producers to a limited number of consumers was primarily a series of horizontal transactions conducted by trade and barter. However, all of the early travel accounts make clear that the produce was being sold for cash, and there are more than passing hints that at this time there were already merchants engaged in the wholesale buying and bulking of food staples in growing hub cities in the hinterland. Warehouses operated by wholesalers did exist in urban centers along the coast during the colonial period, and we can assume that the difficulties of transportation and communications between these coastal cities and the widely scattered hinterland suppliers necessitated a multiplicity of market places.

The role of the peasant as middleman in this market arena has never been very secure. As early as 1807, a report on the state of agriculture and commerce in the province of Bahia disclosed that peasants were prohibited from selling in the places they judged most advantageous and that numbers of middlemen were excluded from open competition in the marketing system. The report to the governor states that, "Consequently, the few who are lucky enough to be able to buy, and sell, enjoy a de facto monopoly over this important branch of subsistence of the people . . ." (Brito n.d.:77). Moreover, the commercial activities of peasants were strictly controlled and the marketing of certain produce was legislated as to both locale and price. The same report states that

The wretched cultivator of manioc, grains and vegetables, who deserves our commiseration for his poverty, is denied the liberty of selling his produce where the market is most receptive, despite considerations of fairness, and the public interest, and the clear laws. . . . and peasants because of their suffering, and losses, lose their will to return [to the market] with another load, and spread their discouragement

throughout the countryside, thus disheartening other potential entrepreneurs. (*Ibid.*, 60, 61)

A full discussion of the development of these market places
and the concurrent integration of peasants in regional and national marketing systems will follow in chapter 4. My reason for
introducing the subject here is simply to clarify the nature of
peasant economic organization in colonial Brazil. Whether or
not the rural Brazilian social system falls under the rubric or
feudalism, capitalism or some other variant of a larger economic
system is continuously debated in the economic histories of
Brazil.[9] There is even some disagreement over whether or not
there are peasants in Brazil (Caio Prado 1957; 1966:118 et passim). In part, the confusion stems from problems of definition
and the projection onto Brazilian peasant life of models and
descriptions developed for peasants in other times and places.

It is, perhaps, unnecessary to point out that the peasant as a
social type existed long before and continues long after the advent of feudalism in Europe. Historically, peasantries are found
in feudal, capitalist, socialist, and other socioeconomic systems.
Each of these systems is a peculiar constellation of socioeconomic, political, and cultural elements, which gives its peasant
sector a unique character. The crucial factor which distinguishes the peasant societies of the contemporary Third World
from those of the past is precisely the way in which the rural
sector of the economy articulates with the nation at large.[10] In
the Brazilian case, the critical component is the effect of national and international commercialism at the local level. The
arena in which this commercialism is played out is the regional
and national marketing system.

The rural marketplace in Northeast Brazil and elsewhere may
still resemble the periodic fairs of medieval Europe in its carnival atmosphere, but the institutional arrangements by which
these distributive systems operate are vastly different. In feudal
Europe, the landlord had liens on peasant production for the
maintenance of his estate, which essentially operated as a
closed system. In the capitalist world, on the other hand, the
marketing system is the crucial juncture at which the peasant

economic subsystem and the larger economy are joined. It is the complex internal distributive arrangement for the transfer of foodstuffs and manufactured goods in contemporary societies. The equilibrium of the estate as a boundable socioeconomic entity is no longer the question. Now entire national and international socioeconomic systems depend upon peasant subsystems for their "equilibrium." In this sense, too, contemporary peasant societies are not "part societies," "part cultures," nor are they anachronistic segments of "dual economies." Peasant societies are part and parcel of national and international economic systems, and the peasants themselves serve as commodity producers and consumers of goods vital to the continuity of these systems.

Viewed in this way, and with reference to the total Portuguese economic system, the peasant economy in colonial Brazil bore only passing resemblance to feudalism.[11] The colonial economy of Brazil developed as a special adaptation to ecological conditions on both sides of the Atlantic Ocean at a time when mercantile-capitalism was replacing feudalism in Europe. To begin at the national level, the institution of vassalage, the relationship of homage and fealty binding lord and vassal in medieval Europe, cannot be found in the colonial Brazilian context. In colonial Brazil, land grants—which comprised only one of several possible forms of fief in tenth- and thirteenth-century Europe (Ganshoff 1961:112ff.)—were made to hold and exploit the land for commercial purposes, rather than simply to reward loyalty and service to the Crown. The landlords turned to the Court in Lisbon more for the pleasures of urbane life than to demonstrate fealty to the Crown or signal their obligation for military support. The sesmarias could not be inherited and, theoretically, could be taken away if they were not made commercially viable, although a distant Portuguese Crown hardly exercised close control over Brazilian landed estates. Again, these estates did not represent a closed self-sufficient system, but were oriented toward export-crop production for the external market.

Likewise, at the local level the relationship between landlord and tenant in colonial Brazil did not represent a feudal relationship. The peasant in colonial Brazil was not tied to the land by any legal restrictions on his movement, but rather by poverty and economic dependence that limited his freedom. Then as now, there are two distinct aspects of the socioeconomic bonds that characterize these superordinate/subordinate relationships in Brazilian rural society: patron-dependency and landlord-tenancy. The two should not be confused.

1.) Landlord-tenancy relationships are written and nonwritten contractual relationships based on monetary exchanges or on fixed values in the exchange of labor for rights in land. The rights and obligations of both landlord and tenant in this exchange of land for labor are clearly stipulated. Aspects of more generalized social exchange, i.e., noblesse oblige and loyalty, are superimposed upon this basic economic transaction. What often appear as social arrangements in rural Brazil are, in effect, economic arrangements, elaborated within the context of plantation life. By enveloping temporary commercial arrangements within social bonds,

2.) Patron-dependency serves to reaffirm, legitimize, and justify authority between broad structural categories that extend far beyond the individual, local economic dyad. Hence, despite extraordinary peasant mobility from farm to farm, certain general socioeconomic patterns *appear* to persist and predominate. Nonetheless, while patron-dependent relationships characteristic of the colonial plantation system exist and may resemble feudal relationships in certain social-structural aspects, the economic basis for such ties in Brazilian peasant society are found in agricultural labor arrangements. The kinds of landlord-tenant/patron-dependent relationships which existed in Brazil historically, and exist today, are not the result of feudal relationships at all. They follow from the labor arrangements that prevailed on the commercial export-oriented plantation, as opposed to the self-sufficient feudal estate.

In sum, the peasant in Brazil has historically operated within an expanding capitalist system where land, labor, and product all have a market. He has been the small-scale producer supplying foodstuffs and labor to the dominant export-oriented sector of the economy. This description of the Brazilian peasant as part and parcel of an on-going commercial system has obvious implications for agricultural development and social change in Brazil. In my opinion it is a misreading of Brazilian history to assume that the agrarian problems that beset the country can be traced to the presence of either a feudal system or a new world slavocracy.[12] Instead, what we see today is the rapidly increasing commercialization of agriculture and its effects as it alters the role of the peasantry—from small-scale producers to rural proletariat.

The fundamental problems in rural Brazil are tied to the manner in which, historically, a capitalist export-oriented economy has been provisioned by a peasant sector. Current social tensions arise from the strains inherent in such a system. Social change is not new to rural Brazil; changes have been occurring continually over the last four centuries. The weight of their intensification and the concomitant developments in transportation and mass communications have only made the problems seem more immediate.

Chapter three –

The Nature of Integration 1: The Social Dimensions of the Agrarian Crisis

There is an agrarian crisis of tremendous proportions in contemporary Brazil. On the one hand, it is an economic problem concerning land tenure, land usage, and the supply of foodstuffs and other commodities to the Brazilian nation. On the other hand, it is a social problem involving the interpersonal relations of man to man. It is, moreover, a political problem not only because it involves the allocation of power and public policy regarding the disposition of resources, but also because it demands an end to the insufferable condition of a great mass of humanity.

This agrarian crisis is hardly a new one. It has existed for centuries, as we shall see, and is only now made more immediate by the heightened pace of socioeconomic change. For as the Brazilian nation moves steadily along the path of industrialization and urban growth rates far outpace those of rural areas, demands on the agricultural sector increase. These demands are reflected in the production, distribution, and consumption spheres of economic activity, all of which are undergoing increased commercialization with concomitant changes in the general profile of the agrarian structure.

In 1950, some 33.2 million people, or approximately 64 percent of the total Brazilian population, lived in rural areas. Of these, nearly 30 million people, or 57 percent of the national population, were directly dependent upon agriculture for their livelihood (CIDA 1966:56). Despite ten years of steady industrial and urban growth, over 50 percent of the population of the nation was rural in 1960, and today Brazil is still an essentially agrarian nation. These figures notwithstanding, the agrarian crisis that Brazil now faces does not follow from absolute population pressures on the land nor from natural limitations on the availability of land which, in theory, is plentiful. Large areas of the nation, such as Amazonas and the extensive northern and western frontiers, are greatly underpopulated, and only now is systematic attention being given to their exploitation. Even along the coast where the bulk of the Brazilian population is concentrated, land resources are often underutilized. For example, there are approximately 3.8 million farm properties in Brazil, occupying some 350 million hectares, but this represents only about 40 percent of the total Brazilian land mass. Less than 20 percent of this total land mass is being effectively utilized in agriculture (IBRA 1967:36).

In essence, the agrarian problem in Brazil reflects the unequal patterns of land distribution and the favored position of the latifundia in the competition for land and labor among the different sectors of the rural economy. The dominant land-tenure and land-use pattern throughout Brazil was and is that of the large estate engaged in the production of commercial crops for the export market. The well-known boom crops—sugar, coffee, cotton, cocoa, rubber—continue to prosper in the particular regions of Brazil where they once had their heyday. Their spheres of influence may have diminished on the international market, but they still dominate large areas of rural Brazil, and each major region of the nation boasts its own export specialty. For example, sugar is paramount in the humid valleys of the Northeast and São Paulo, expanding relentlessly into the surrounding tablelands where it gobbles up the small farms in its wake. Likewise, coffee is "king" in the western reaches of São Paulo and Paraná, and the frontier of development now reaches far into the neighboring country of Paraguay. In addition, new

commercial crops like sisal and coconuts, which were intended
to help democratize the agricultural system, also require extensive plantations and have come to occupy large expanses of land
in response to new market pressures.

The literature on rural Brazil usually describes this domination of export crops on large estates as simply an outgrowth of
an archaic system of land tenure and land usage. The latifundia
are viewed as an inherited evil of the colonial system of land
grants, and rural poverty is explained away as a legacy of slavery. However, the present system of land tenure and land use in
Brazil is not merely a throwback to a previous socioeconomic
order, but rather a response to contemporary economic realities.
Even in the colonial period, the large estates were intended to
be viable economic units in a far-flung capitalist system of agricultural exploitation for an international market, as we have
seen in the preceeding chapter.

The small farms that grew up around this dominant export-
oriented agricultural sector, supplying plantations as well as the
burgeoning urban centers with foodstuffs and other primary
produce, are an important part of a dynamic economic history, a
study of which will reveal the accelerated processes of peasant
integration in the national and international economic system
over time. Indeed, the two currently interconnected trends of
increased concentration of landholdings [1] (CIDA 1966 passim;
Diegues Jr. 1959a:38) and the proletarianization of the rural
masses follow demands that are now being made in the national
and international market economies, a process of rationalization
that will be discussed in detail in the next chapter.

The most recent cadastral survey undertaken by the Brazilian
Institute of Agrarian Reform (IBRA) demonstrates the extreme
imbalance in the system of land tenure and land use in Brazil.
According to IBRA, 76 percent of the properties registered in
Brazil belong to smallholders, or minifundiários, who operate
family farms with less land than is necessary to absorb the total
labor force of four adult family members and thereby guarantee
family subsistence.[2] These 2.5 million uneconomic properties
are crowded into a total land area of only 40 million hectares,

Table 1. Number, Total Area and Cultivated Area of Declared Farms by Size, 1967

Size of Farm (in hectares)	Number of Farms	Percent of Total	Total Area Held (hectares 1,000)	Percent of Total	Cultivated Area (hectares 1,000)	Percent of Total
Under 10	1,202,663	36.3	5,568	1.8	3,316	2.3
11–100	1,728,303	51.5	57,101	18.6	27,516	17.8
101–1,000	375,879	11.5	105,852	34.5	52,189	34.5
1,001–10,000	39,276	1.0	97,355	31.7	42,144	30.4
10,001–100,000	1,628		35,973	11.7	11,847	13.7
over 100,000	27		5,401	1.7	1,854	1.3
TOTAL	3,347,776	100.0	307,250	100.0	138,866	100.0

Source: IBRA 1967.

less than 14 percent of the total land area registered as private property. In sharp contrast, a total land area of some 32 million hectares is held as private property by only 150 large land-owners, or latifundistas, each of whom owns more than 100,000 hectares, which are for the most part unexploited and held mainly for speculative purposes (1967:vii, passim).

Yet, the inverse relationship between the proportion of total area cultivated and the size of the farm unit as represented in Table 1 does not adequately represent the extent of the agrarian crisis in Brazil. Emphasizing the gravity of the situation, Frank estimates that in 1950, 62 percent of the people dependent upon agriculture for their livelihood were landless agricultural workers. If those whose land was not economically viable are included, the number of de facto landless agricultural laborers climbs to 81 percent (Frank 1968:249). The situation is essentially the same today.[3]

It is clearly a mistake to characterize the entire Brazilian agrarian regime in terms of these grossly discrepant categories. Between the two extremes of minifundia and latifundia, there are numerous medium-size family farms and many highly efficient estates operated with wage labor and a variety of share-cropping and tenancy arrangements.[4] Nevertheless, an examination of Table 2 demonstrates that the minifundia/latifundia syndrome still prevails throughout Brazil, where the tenure system is strikingly uniform despite considerable regional ecological variation (CIDA 1966:84–85). The only notable contrast appears in the distribution of frontier land in the north and central-west where there are proportionately fewer small properties. Over 70 percent of these land areas are concentrated in estates of more than 1,000 hectares, obviously reflecting the exaggerated extent of land speculation and underutilization of land resources in the two regions.

While the Brazilian agricultural census shows a large increase in the number of small farms and thus a reduction in the average size of farms in the decade after 1950, the overall pattern remains essentially the same. The increase in acreage of small farm units is accounted for by the establishment of many tiny plots of under 10 hectares on marginal lands primarily in areas of new settlement, a figure clearly offset by the much more extensive land areas which are being organized into fewer, large estates.[5] Table 3 presents data on changes in the distribution of properties by size between 1920 and 1960.

Some writers do stress a trend toward fragmentation of landholdings in Brazil (Schuh 1970:149). However, it is hard to determine to what degree the supposed break-up of large estates is a legal fiction. Although some farms are undoubtedly divided up over time, there is a prevailing tendency in the Brazilian landed class to operate properties as single economic units after inheritance, although for tax purposes these are often recorded as separate plantations belonging to a number of individual heirs. Furthermore, multiple farm ownership by single families is not accounted for in the agricultural census (CIDA 1966:90ff.), particularly when properties are located across county lines. If any trend toward fragmentation is evident in Brazil, it bespeaks a very long process indeed, and as the CIDA study notes, "It is no consolation for a sharecropper or a landless worker in 1963 to know that in another 250 years all farms might have become substantially smaller" (*ibid.*, 101).

The three-year plan elaborated by the Brazilian government in 1962 recognized that the greatest impediment to agricultural development lay in the unequal distribution of landholdings and the subsequent underutilization of agricultural resources (Brasil: Presidência da Republica, 1962). In truth, a socioeconomic system in which access to strategic resources such as land, labor, and credit is a function of a landowner's ability to manipulate the social and natural environment simply perpetuates the discrepancy between haves and have-nots.

The majority of smallholders in Brazil farm with inadequate resources and, as a result, productivity is sharply curtailed. As has been noted previously, some of the large plantations in Brazil are highly commercialized operations utilizing the most modern agricultural methods. Nevertheless, 73 percent of all farms in 1950 employed human labor exclusively. They used hoes, bush knives, and axes as their only equipment. At that

Table 2. Number and Percent Total Area Held of Declared Farms by Size and Region, 1967

Size of Farm (in hectares)	North		Northeast		East		South		Central-West	
	Number of Farms	Total Area Held (%)	Number of Farms	Total Area Held (%)	Number of Farms	Total Area Held (%)	Number of Farms	Total Area Held (%)	Number of Farms	Total Area Held (%)
Under 10	10,209	0.2	321,373	2.3	387,573	2.5	467,089	3.4	16,419	0.1
11–100	32,559	5.4	292,223	18.4	504,001	25.8	823,562	34.2	75,958	3.8
101–1,000	11,622	17.4	89,021	43.6	125,501	46.1	94,696	35.9	55,039	22.4
1,000–10,000	3,668	41.1	7,606	29.3	7,145	21.5	7,413	22.1	13,444	46.9
10,001–100,000	223	21.7	185	6.2	156	4.1	142	4.3	922	25.0
over 100,000	16	14.2	1	0.2			1	0.1	9	1.8
TOTAL	58,297	100.0	710,409	100.0	1,024,376	100.0	1,392,903	100.0	161,791	100.0

Table 3. Changes in the Distribution of Properties by Size and Number, 1920–1960

Size of Farm (in hectares)	1920 Number (1 million)	1920 Area (hectares 1 million)	1940 Number (1 million)	1940 Area (hectares 1 million)	1950 Number (1 million)	1950 Area (hectares 1 million)	1960 Number (1 million)	1960 Area (hectares 1 million)
Under 10	463.9	15.7	654.6	2.9	710.9	3.0	1,499.5	5.9
10–100	158.0	48.4	975.4	33.1	1,052.6	35.6	1,494.5	47.7
100–1,000	24.6	65.5	243.8	66.2	268.2	75.5	315.1	86.3
1,000–10,000	1.7	45.5	26.5	62.0	31.0	73.1	31.2	72.8
over 10,000			1.3	33.5	1.6	45.0	1.7	52.7
TOTAL	648.2	175.1	1,904.6	197.7	2,064.6	232.2	3,349.5	265.5

Source: IBRA 1967.

time only 27 percent of all farms used draft animals, and 82 percent of these farms were located in the southern part of the country, a fact which emphasizes the extent to which paleotechnology (Wolf 1966) characterizes the greater part of Brazilian peasant agriculture. A full 78 percent of all farms had no plows, and 98 percent had no tractors (CIDA 1966:76–77). Only some 116,000 agricultural establishments had electric power, and half of these generated their own on diesel engines adapted to that purpose (Schuh 1970:170). The major portion of land under cultivation was cleared by the slash-and-burn technique, which is often claimed to be detrimental to the soil and which, in any event, fails to effectively clear a plot of stumps or other incumbrances, making both planting and harvesting difficult. Very few peasant farms utilize either fertilizer or new seed, since neither is generally available.

When a peasant is willing to add to his input in order to increase production, he tries to do so by committing additional labor to larger areas of land, rather than by attempting to employ capital to intensify production on existing plots. Of course, little capital is available to him for investment, and almost no credit exists either for the replacement of equipment or for innovation. A number of state and federal extension agencies such an ABCAR (Associação Brasileira de Crédito e Extensão Rural) exist,[6] but they mostly offer seed and demonstration plots to larger farmers and give virtually no loans of cash or equipment. To date, they have worked mainly with well-to-do farmers or with agricultural colonies; the peasant sector has hardly benefitted from their expertise.

During the year in which I did field work, I never saw the state extension office open in the county in which I resided. The extension agents did maintain a farm for demonstrating the use of fertilizer on sizeable coconut plantations, but no fertilizer was available for purchase within a fifty-mile radius. There were some credit and loan agencies, but the limited amounts of money that they controlled was given to local elites. For example, the Banco de Produção de Alagoas announced in 1967 that it would give loans to small- and medium-size farmers in the Brazilian Northeast at one percent interest per month. When a farmer initiated a request for a loan, an extension agent made a study of his resources and determined the possibility of his being able to pay back the loan from his earnings on the cash advanced rather than from other sources of income. Theoretically, no collateral was required and a farm of any size could make a request, provided the land was owned by the applicant. This stipulation immediately excluded sharecroppers, renters, and the majority of landed peasantry who operated minifundia and could not guarantee an immediate return on the loan. In effect, the only loans available to the majority of these peasants were those forthcoming from a patron or from cooperative savings and loan associations, which sometimes operated at the village level, but which limited their cash outlay to "replacement funds" (Wolf 1966) and death benefits.

Not only do the size of plots and the lack of modern technology curtail productivity on peasant farms; the quality of the soil and the length of tenancy also pose problems. Soil in Brazil is generally not of outstanding quality, being low in nutrients and high in acidity. The best land is owned as large estates and is highly underutilized, being held either in pasture or in forest as a speculative hedge against inflation. Intensive agriculture is carried out by the minifundiários, who thus bear the burden of production of foodstuffs on marginal lands for a nation whose overall population grows by more than 3 percent annually. While production of foodstuffs seems to be keeping pace with population growth, the increases actually follow from the expansion of small plots into areas of new settlement, rather than from improvements in yields on existing farms, a situation which adds to the logistic difficulties of food supply, since these new areas are often not integrated into on-going marketing structures. Even when good land is made available to peasants, usually in order to clear forested areas desired by landowners for commercial crop production, the temporary tenure arrangements offered to the peasants encourage the systematic investment of neither labor nor capital (a problem which will be discussed in greater detail below).

Perhaps the most salient feature of the agrarian crisis in Brazil, however, is the set of dependency relationships engendered by the inequities in the system of land distribution; that is, by differential access to the most strategic resource in the economic system. The dominance of export crops on large plantations in the various regions of the nation has given rise to a number of land-tenure patterns and different production arrangements in which the landless worker or smallholder subjects himself to the hegemony of the landlord.

In the course of time and under diverse ecological pressures, there developed on the Brazilian landscape a seemingly endless variety of peasant types engaged in a broad spectrum of economic activities.[7] There is, for example, considerable overt divergence in the life styles of the vaqueiro of the Northeast, the cattleherder on the pampas of the South, the rubber collector in the Amazon, the smallholder in the Agreste, the raft fisherman and coconut gatherer along the coast. Notwithstanding, from a sociocultural point of view, there are also many similarities among these rural types; each works as a commodity producer and a laborer for a member of the dominant upper class; and each shares the same view of his life chances in the prevailing agrarian system. As Bernard Siegel notes:

Regardless of region, each is a variation of the rural *caboclo*. Each has a status in a traditional set of interpersonal relationships whose structure is determined by the nature of the economic activity to which he is devoted. The form which these take varies from region to region and from economic activity to economic activity. All of these various regional arrangements are, broadly speaking, similar (1955:399).

In a strong indictment of the Brazilian landed class, CIDA suggests that each of these rural forms results from the landowners' attempts to maintain control over the land and to make favourable labor arrangements:

. . . *Latifundistas* have astutely adjusted the terms of employment to fit their own needs by trying to maintain an adequate and dependable supply of labor, by protecting themselves against rights and claims of the worker against the land or against them, and by keeping labor disoriented so that it doesn't become a threat to the existing structure of ownership (1966:195).

TYPES OF RURAL LABOR

The CIDA study adopts the position that all peasant tenure arrangements in Brazil should be seen as forms of utilization of a labor force by a dominant landholding class.[8] Each type of rural laborer is viewed as a variant of a wage-laboring class with different rights and obligations, all of which weigh heavily in favor of the landlord. For example, sharecroppers and tenant farmers are said to be subject to unwritten contracts in which neither the size of the plot nor the actual labor requirements are specified. The landlord exacts a maximum expenditure of labor from a land-hungry peasantry, which receives only meager recompense either in money or in kind for working the land.

. . . there emerges in the various areas of the country a general pattern of systematic disregard of the rights of the rural workers from the 'tenant' to the migrant laborer, of consistent evasion of labor legislation, of disrespect for the economic and personal well-being of workers and an undisguised attempt to defraud them at every possible turn (1966:297).[9]

In my view, it is absolutely necessary to distinguish between (a) the economic arrangements made by wage laborers and landowners on the basis of cash payments for labor services rendered and (b) the quasi-legal relationships entered into by sharecroppers and tenant farmers who are tied to a landlord by some contractual arrangement, written or unwritten, involving rights to land. Theoretically, peasant producers can allocate agricultural resources to their best advantage when they have some semblance of control over the land they farm and their own labor, although this does not always happen in practice. The same is not true of wage laborers, who are alienated from production decisions and simply exchange their labor for cash. Furthermore, sharecroppers, tenant farmers, and smallowners each react differently to the pressures of the market, either internal or external, as do wage laborers whose livelihood is primarily affected by the export trade. Most important for our subsequent discussions, each of these rural peasant types has basically different needs which they seek to fulfill by making different political demands.

As we shall see in the discussion of peasant political participation in Brazil in chapter 5, there was a notable failure to
achieve unity among agricultural laborers in the tumultuous
years between 1946 (the founding of the first peasant league)
and 1964 (the Brazilian military coup d'etat), largely because of
the fundamental differences among these Brazilian rural types.
Decisive collective action on the part of all peasants could only
be achieved by a program so broad as to span the variegated
needs of all agricultural workers. Such a program was not forthcoming, and a rather tenuous unity was forged only among the
leaders of a variety of discrete rural movements.

Before each of the peasant types in rural Brazil are described,
however, it is important to clear up one basic problem. From a
strictly empirical perspective, any neat typology of agricultural
labor, broken down into separate categories of tenant farmers,
sharecroppers, and wage laborers, is quite insufficient in the
Brazilian context. There is, of course, a tremendous intermixing
of economic roles among Brazilian peasants, a phenomenon
which results from the exigencies of low earnings and limited
economic opportunities on the small farm. For example, a single individual may own a small plot and be a renter, a sharecropper, an employee, and/or a wage earner at the same time on
different agricultural properties.[10] He, or a member of his
household, may also be engaged as a market middleman, selling
his own crop and those of his neighbors at the local marketplace; or as an artisan, working in wood, leather, straw, metals,
or a host of other local handicraft products. With the rapid de-
cline in cooperative forms of labor exchange, the Brazilian peasant often hires wage labor for clearing and planting and, in turn,
sells his own labor when work on his own land is completed.
This is particularly true among minifundiários, whose plot is too
small to employ all adult family members full time.

There is, further, a great deal of mobility within the agricultural sector, that is, among different kinds of farming operations,
so that tenants and sharecroppers in the mixed-farming zone of
the Northeast migrate to the humid coastal valleys to cut sugarcane during the harvest season (Furtado 1965a:49). There even

is seasonal migration from the Northeast to the coffee plantations in the central-south. Nevertheless, although an individual peasant may have to enter into these multiple tenure arrangements in order to satisfy the economic demand of his household, one of these economic roles clearly dominates his outlook, and he will time and again state a preference for one over the other.

TENANCY

Although tenants represent only a small proportion of the total agricultural population of rural Brazil, as represented in Table 4, tenancy is nevertheless an extremely important category of agricultural labor. For example, it was the dislocation of dependent tenants by landowners, no longer satisfied to exchange their land for rent and services rendered, which led to the rapid growth of peasant leagues throughout Brazil in the 1950s and 1960s as we shall see in chapter 5. There are, of course, many large rental properties rightfully included in the category of "rural businesses," which are defined as viable estates producing commercial crops with hired labor. However, the great majority of tenants are smallholders, or minifundiários, who are assigned a piece of land in exchange for a cash payment and the inevitable promise of additional labor service on the estate.

These tenancy arrangements vary considerably from region to region and among the various crops. For example, there are some instances of rent being paid entirely through labor service, although such commitments are rarely desired by the tenant, himself. In São Paulo state, transactions involving more than 20 hectares of land require at least 50 percent of the contract price to be paid in cash in advance, the rest being paid in cash or in kind after the crop has been harvested and sold. Sugar mills in the Northeast often rent out land for a percentage of the crop in addition to a cash rent.

The amount of rent payments on land are, of course, a function of the land value, which is determined by quality, productivity, and proximity to urban markets or rural industries. In

Table 4. *Socioeconomic Stratification of Brazil's Farm Population (Labor Force), 1950 (in thousands)*

Socioeconomic Group	Farm Families		Farm Workers	
	Number	Percent	Number	Percent
Latifundistas (producers):				
Owners	45.5		135.1	
Tenants	1.7		4.9	
Occupants	.9		2.6	
Mixed form of tenure	1.4		4.1	
Producers with administrator	47.9		142.6	
Total	97.4	1.8	289.3	2.3
Producers of medium-sized multifamily farms:				
Owners	579.4		1,871.8	
Tenants	22.5		71.8	
Occupants	29.7		96.5	
Mixed form of tenure	12.3		40.4	
Producers with administrator	50.7		163.8	
Total	694.6	12.9	2,244.3	17.8
Producers on family farms:				
Owners	647.2		1,886.2	
Tenants	58.8		171.9	
Occupants	75.8		221.3	
Mixed form of tenure	11.9		35.3	
Producers with administrator	13.4		40.0	
Total	807.1	14.9	2,354.7	18.7

Administrators and technicians in farms of above three groups:				
Administrators	112.0		112.0	
Technicians and special workers	162.4		165.2	
Total	274.4	5.1	277.2	2.2
Underprivileged farm people:				
Producers on minifundios:				
owners	(265.7)		(648.2)	
tenants	(98.8)		(240.2)	
occupants	(93.4)		(227.8)	
mixed form of tenure	(3.8)		(9.1)	
producers with administrator	(3.4)		(7.9)	
Total producers	465.1	(8.6)	1,133.2	(9.0)
Workers:				
Administrators and special workers on minifundios	(6.4)	(.1)	(6.5)	(.1)
sharecroppers	(800.6)	(14.8)	(1,245.6)	(9.9)
permanent workers			(1,420.9)	(11.2)
temporary workers	(2,258.6)	(41.8)	(2,308.4)	(18.2)
other workers			(1,333.2)	(10.6)
Total workers	3,065.6	(56.7)	6,314.6	(50.0)
Total Producers and Workers	3,530.7	65.3	7,447.8	59.0
All families or workers	5,404.2	100.0	12,613.3	100.0

Source: CIDA 1966:132.

remote and marginal areas of the nation, rents are often quite small, sometimes as little as a few cents per tarefa (a land measure in several northeastern states, which varies between 3,052 square meters in Alagoas and 4,350 square meters in Bahia). Invariably, however, the number of work days the tenant is required to donate in service to the landlord places a heavy burden on the peasant. This institution, known as *condição* or *cambão*, is common throughout Brazil and in practice serves to exact a much higher rent from money-poor tenants. Although it was originally intended as a form of corvée labor for the maintenance of "public" facilities, such as roads and reservoirs, it soon degenerated into a blatant form of unpaid labor for commercial crop production on private plantations.

The exiled leader of the Brazilian Peasant Leagues, Francisco Julião, emphasizes the critical importance of the corvée labor requirements for tenants in the establishment of the first league on the plantation Galileia, in Pernambuco state:

The custom was to pay on December 8 of each year the rent or fee stipulated by the landowner. Moreover, the renter was obliged to give a certain number of days in free labor to the owner when he so demanded. The number of days varied according to the will of each *latifundista*. They were never fewer than four nor more than fifteen in that region. These unpaid days are called *cambão* in the Northeast. The renter was not obliged to render the *cambão* in person, save when the landowner insisted either capriciously or in order to disgust the renter and throw him off the land. He could send a son or pay a third party to fulfill this hateful obligation. The landowner insisted that the *cambão* was a tribute given to benefit everyone, since it was intended to clean the streams and reservoirs or maintain the roads and other services of the property. But what should have been the rule was transformed over time into the exception, since the renters ended by working jointly with paid day laborers in the preparation of the fields, in planting, cleaning, and collecting the harvest. It will be said that the number of days demanded was very few in a year's time. The problem was not in the number of days, but in the humiliation and shame that working against his will, without pay, for a landlord to whom he paid rent in money for his plot, signified to the peasant. Of all of the demands imposed on the peasant in the Northeast, we have no doubt in asserting that the *cambão* is that which weighs least upon him materially, but most touches his honor, which most shames and humiliates him. For this reason, the *cambão* was made the spark that lit the consciousness of the peasant in the Northeast and transformed him into a political animal (1968:86).

There can be no doubt that the contract terms are always favorable to the landowner, who may even dictate which commercial crops will be planted and when. Decisions regarding the cultivation of crops grown for subsistence or for sale at the local market place are usually left to the tenants themselves. However, these are subject to certain restrictions, such as the prohibition against planting crops or fruit trees with a long growing cycle, which would tend to indicate a long period of tenure for the tenant. Likewise, tenants are forbidden to graze animals on rented lands, lest their animals compete with livestock the landowner has pastured there.

In all cases, the tenant's on-farm decisions are conditioned by the length of tenancy stipulated in the contract, but subject to a constant threat of summary eviction. The peasant leagues and other rural associations have recorded innumerable complaints of outright eviction which are rarely, if ever, brought to court. Peasants have little recourse when they are ordered off the land by the hired guns of the rich, who emphasize the immediacy of their demand by destroying crops and sometimes houses. In no instance does a landowner allow a tenant to remain on the land for any length of time approximating ten years, when laws of usufruct would give that tenant permanent rights.

One of the more satisfactory tenancy arrangements, described by Diegues Jr., exists in the cacao-growing region of southern Bahia state:

The owner gives the worker a piece of land, generally from 20–50 tarefas which the worker is to clear and return to the owner five or six years later, planted in cacao trees. During this period the contractor may use the land for the temporary planting of manioc, beans, or corn, the profits belonging to the worker. At the end of this period, the contractor receives a stipulated remuneration for each tree of cacao planted. He has no other right over the land he has cultivated. (1959b:118)

The rental contract is one of the best ways for a landlord to arrange for the clearing of forested lands which he intends to incorporate into the cultivated areas of his estate. From his perspective it has considerable advantage over a system of wage labor. In essence, the tenant is forced to pay for the right to work and feed himself and his family. The lands made available for clearing are ever more distant from existent settlements, thereby increasing the logistic difficulties which already face the peasant. He is not allowed to construct a house or even temporary living quarters on the land, but must travel many miles, often on foot, to farm a small piece of land which hardly produces sufficient yield to afford him a marketable surplus.

All too often the rental contract is offered very late in the season, after the landowner has determined his own production needs, thereby requiring the tenant to hire wage labor to help him clear the land in time for his own planting. Cash for paying wage labor is usually obtained by selling charcoal made from the trees that are felled and burned, in a time-consuming process which also delays the planting of food crops. The charcoal is sold on a share basis, with the tenant required to give a 50 percent share of the profits to the landlord. He then plants a small crop, not laid out in neat rows but scattered among the tree stumps and rocks which did not yield to fire, and rushes to harvest it before his tenancy expires at the end of a single year.

In some instances, the poor tenant does not even last the year. I recorded one particularly grievous incident in the northeastern state of Alagoas in 1967, in which an old man rented 4 tarefas of land for a modest $40,000 cruzeiros (approximately $20 at that time). The unwritten rental contract provided that he clear the land and utilize it for a single harvest. It took the tenant approximately twenty days to clear each tarefa, or better than three months' labor in the total clearing operation, plus another three to four weeks to plant his crop. Unable to harvest the crop in time by himself and with no money to hire outside labor, he was finally forced to sell the unharvested manioc to the landowner for $150,000 cruzeiros. The four tarefas of land ultimately yielded 200 *cuias* of manioc flour (7 *cuias* in a sack), or just under thirty sacks of flour, valued at $10,000 cruzeiros per sack. The owner of the land, then, received a net profit of $190,000 cruzeiros, plus over four months' free labor and a plot which was cleared and ready for plowing. He had no expenditure for harvesting the manioc or preparing the flour, both of which were accomplished by corvée labor provided by other tenants. The old man, on the other hand, received a total of $110,000 cruzeiros in compensation for over four months' labor, less than half the minimum daily wage of $2,000 cruzeiros in this region.

Why does a peasant subject himself to this kind of tenancy arrangement? Simply because there are no other alternatives available to him in a nation in which land resources are tightly controlled and agriculturalists need land to feed their families. Land in Brazil is in short supply, not because of any immediate limitations in absolute quantities of cultivable land, but because access to land resources is strictly limited. No wonder that peasants go to the extremes of planting coconut palms in tidal lands in the eminent domain. If they cannot own the land, they can at least claim possession of the trees and the few fruits thereof. And others, still more desperate, eke out a dismal existence gathering crabs and other crustaceans found in the mangrove swamp.

One retired fisherman I knew could not find a plot of land to rent, so he built up a small half-acre island in the mangrove swamp by packing mud up against the encroaching tidal waters. He planted a few ears of corn, some watermelon, and a bit of manioc, which he watered each day by carrying gourds over three miles from the fresh-water well in the village. He arrived at his plot by crossing several bridges that he had constructed from old logs. Taking me to see his "farm" one morning, he paused on top of one of these logs and, pondering the ground, asked, "Why do you blow up bridges?" "We do that," I responded grimly, "because my country is at war and the army wants to keep the enemy from crossing them." "If they come here and blow up my bridges, then I'll have to be your enemy," he said, and moved off into the swamp.

SHARECROPPING

Sharecropping is another significant category of agricultural labor in Brazil although, again, sharecroppers represented only 14.8 percent of the farm families, or 1.2 million individuals (9.9 percent of the total number of farm workers) in the total Brazilian agricultural labor force in 1950 (CIDA 1966:132). Sharecropping arrangements are common in the production of numerous crops, such as cotton, rice, beans, manioc, corn, coffee, sugar, in the herding of cattle, and in the fishing industry (Forman 1970). Specific arrangements vary from region to region and from crop to crop.[11]

In one sense the sharecropper may be viewed as a salaried worker, who receives a piece of land and a portion of the crop he grows or the proceeds from its sale in return for his labor on someone else's property. A one-half share, called *meiacão*, is common. However, arrangements involving thirds, fourths, and even fifths occur. The assigned portion of the crop goes to the landlord or to a designated third party and the time for the sale of the crop and its price are predetermined. The size of the share is affected by a number of factors including the extent of capital inputs on the part of the landowner in preparation of the soil, provisioning of seed, and the loan of machinery or other equipment. Not infrequently, the quality of the soil, expected yield, and market price also influence the sharecropping contract. Still, there is evidence that the size of the share may also vary with the availability of labor. Stuart Schwartz (1973:154ff.) provides data which indicate that the sharecropping contracts between sugarcane growers and mill owners were part of a broader factor market even in the seventeenth century. The share demanded by mill owners fell from one-third or one-fourth in the late sixteenth century to one-fifth and even one-fifteenth or one-twentieth by 1680, when the falling price of sugar and the rush of labor to the gold mines of Minas Gerais sharply reduced the numbers of available farm hands.

It is important to note that sharecropping arrangements extend beyond the production of commercial crops. Oftentimes, some part of the worker's own food crop also will be shared with the landowner. This is particularly true in the case of manioc, up to one-tenth of which is given to the owner of the *casa de farinha*, the tiny and primitive millhouse where the tuber is ground and toasted to make flour. Even less to his advantage, the landowner's cattle often is grazed on the sharecropper's plot, and he is obliged to give them his corn husks as feed without compensation. Frequently, a sharecropper's contract, whether verbal or written, fails to specify the size of the plot being ceded to him (Caldeira 1956:40–41), the size always being adjusted down to the landowner's advantage after the crop has been planted. As in the case of rental contracts, a *con-diçao*—literally "condition"—is specified, requiring the sharecropper and members of his family to give a number of days' labor without remuneration in the service of the landlord (Candido 1964:82).

Although tenant farmers enjoy a relative freedom of choice regarding the cultivation and sale of foodcrops, they must pay a fixed cash rent regardless of yield. Sharecroppers, by contrast, prefer to pay in kind rather than in cash since the actual amount of a share adjusts to the size of the harvest. The tenant receives nothing but a plot of land, which he is often required to clear. He must provide seed and tools himself, and his usual term of tenancy is short. In fact, in some cases a one-year rental contract accomplishes the landlord's objective of clearing the land; the relationship is then converted to a share arrangement for the cultivation of a commercial crop. In the sharecropper's case, however, the owner of the land is prepared to and usually does make a requisite number of inputs upon relegating a plot of land to the peasant. Of course, the greater the number and kind of inputs on the part of the landowner, the larger will be his share of the crop. Furthermore, the landowner's initial financing of seed and fertilizer creates greater indebtedness on the part of the sharecropper, since the landowner charges high interest rates for cash advanced, in addition to the agreed-upon share of the crop. Because the landowner's goal in the sharecropping arrangement is the steady production of a particular crop rather than the clearing or leasing of land, the sharecropper can extend his tenancy on the land, at least as long as the landowner continues to derive an advantage from his production.

Whether this places him in a favored position or not vis-à-vis the tenant farmer, the plight of the sharecropper is serious as noted by the Brazilian geographer, Manuel Correio de Andrade in his vivid description of *meieiros* (sharecroppers who pay one-half of their yield) engaged in the production of rice along the banks of the São Francisco River. Each cropper takes charge of between 5 and 10 tarefas of land. Because they need food and have no salaries, they are forced to take loans from the landowner at 6 to 10 percent interest per month, the interest payment being exacted at the time of harvest from the meieiros' share of the crop. They are required to care for the paddy for three months between planting and harvesting and are also responsible for cleaning and husking the rice, which can be done either by hand or by machine. In order to use the landowner's machine, however, the sharecropper must pay rent on a per kilo basis in addition to the salary of the man whom the landowner assigns to work the machine. At the end of four or five months, when rice cultivation is completed, the sharecropper moves off to a rented plot where he grows beans and corn, paying 20 percent of the harvest profits to the landowner (1964:132ff.).

The CIDA study again makes the point that the sharecropper, like the tenant, is not an independent worker, but a hired wage laborer. To quote, the sharecropper is

. . . only a hired worker whose salary is paid under conditions which differ only in some details from those of other salaried workers, without however affecting otherwise the "employer-employee" relationships. It is highly doubtful that one can speak therefore of him as "having possession of the land," except perhaps in highly theoretical terms. *In practice, it would seem that the landlord wishes to tie the worker only to the enterprise, but certainly not to the land* (1966:217).

It does seem clear that the sharecropper is a dependent agricultural worker, perhaps even more so than the tenant farmers, but the labor arrangements are not necessarily the same as they are for salaried workers. In fact, the system of sharecropping that we find in Brazil today is perhaps best characterized as a highly adaptive employment mechanism in a money-poor economy, since it requires little, if any, cash outlay on the part of landowners.

Furthermore, there are instances which suggest that sharecropping might be a transitional form of wage labor. Thus, cowboys in the Northeast are monthly wage earners who also receive a one-fourth share of the stock at the end of each year. In this case, the sharecropping system is obviously intended as an incentive to maintain stocks at high levels. Of late, however, the share system has been abolished in cattle raising in certain regions of the Northeast, owing to the increased value of "high bred" cattle, and the cowboy now is paid entirely in cash (Andrade 1964:164). The small group of sharecroppers in São Paulo state studied by Candido likewise represents a transitional socioeconomic type which is being seriously threatened by the concentration of landholdings in the coffee economy. The sharecroppers on the coffee estates described by Candido were formerly smallholders who tended to become wage laborers (*colonos*), paid on both a piece and share basis (1964:163).

The differences between sharecropping and simple wage labor, even transitional forms like colono arrangements, are made clear in CIDA's own description of labor arrangements in the coffee economy. For example, the colonos of the coffee zone of São Paulo and Paraná traditionally receive a specified amount of money per 1,000 trees cared for, a plot for subsistence farming (2.4 hectares for every 2,000–10,000 trees), some coffee for home consumption, and pasture for animals and hogs. They work as daily wage earners but receive less than the minimum wage, earning extra money during the harvest season for each bag of coffee collected. They also get a house, firewood, light, water, and sometimes milk at discount prices. According to CIDA, the number of sharecroppers and colonos still exceeded the number of simple salaried workers in São Paulo in 1960

(1966:259–60). As we shall see in chapter 5, these sharecroppers and colonos were to have a decisive role in radicalization of the peasant political movement of the 1950s and 1960s.

WAGE LABOR

An increasingly large proportion of rural agricultural laborers in Brazil are salaried workers, numbering some 1,550,000 people out of a total of over 12 million (IBRA 1967:62). They are engaged primarily in the production of export crops in the fields and mills that dominate the countryside. These salaried workers produce coffee, sugar, cacao, and other export crops, and increasingly they are also to be found on the food-producing *roças*, or plots, of smallholders. They do not fit into a simple category of "rural proletariat" since work contracts vary widely from place to place and carry with them a variety of subtenancy arrangements, as in the case of the colonos described above.

There are at least three major types of wage-labor arrangements in rural Brazil. In some instances, a worker is allotted a small plot of land on which he can raise his own subsistence crops. By a presidential decree of 1965, every rural worker in the sugarcane zone is entitled after one year of continual service to have up to 2 hectares of land near to his house, "sufficient to plant and raise livestock to an extent necessary for his and his family's subsistence" (SORPE 1967). In other cases, a worker is given a house on plantation lands but no land to farm. The Rural Labor Statute of 1963 provides for the maintenance of "adequate" housing for rural workers and for rent deductions from salary in the amount of 20 percent to cover the costs thereof.[12] There is, finally, the wage worker who resides in rural towns and villages and enjoys only a wage relationship with the plantation. This latter type is often called a *camarada* or a *trabalhador braçal* (day laborer) and would most closely approximate a rural proletariat.

The CIDA study draws a picture of hired labor in the rural Northeast as

. . . an array of low wages, hard work, deception of workers, extortion and usurious interests, hunger, inadequate housing, insecurity, instability and migration. Granted the severity and hardship of the area's dry seasons and prolonged drought, the conditions of life and work which are man-made are harder (1966:270).

Without in any way denying the miserable inequities suffered by plantation workers in the Brazilian Northeast, I would suggest that the norm is somewhat higher than the CIDA study would admit, or at the very least that some plantation owners do have a greater sense of social responsibility toward their employees. Certainly, plantation workers have a higher general standard of living and more security than the increasing numbers of day laborers who are now employed by peasants themselves to clear land and produce foodstuffs.

At the sugar mill in the region of my own research, for example, all of the plantation workers are resident except for a small supplementary migrant labor force, hired during the harvest season. Each worker is given a house and a small plot of land on which to plant subsistence crops. Mill workers live in the plantation "town," and field hands are scattered about in small neighborhoods on the numerous plantations which comprise the mill's total operation. Both mill workers and field hands receive the established minimum salary for the region, and they enjoy the fringe benefits to which the law entitles them. A doctor and dentist visit the mill town once each week, and medical services and medicines are dispensed free of charge. A very handsome rural school is supported by the mill owners and is ably administered by the wife of one of the owner's sons, who is resident manager of the mill. This school is particularly well-run compared to most in rural Brazil, and the children seem to be receiving a decent education. The rate of literacy in the mill town itself is considerably higher than in surrounding rural towns and villages.

The residents of the mill town have a sense of community not shared by the field hands in the outlying plantation neighborhoods. The priest comes from the municipal seat to celebrate mass at the mill's chapel at least once a month. A football team, supported by the mill, plays each Sunday against teams from the neighboring communities. A social center and movie house operate daily. The mill owners loaned money to a local resident for the establishment of an ice-cream parlor and a hotel and restaurant. There is only one store in the town. It is privately owned by a man who pays rent to the mill, and there is no question of a high-cost mill store to which plantation workers are continually indebted. Housing improvements have been made on all mill properties, and there is a program underway to furnish every house on mill property with "a tile roof, a toilet, and a radio." In addition, the mill provides electricity to the town; new power lines from the hydraulic dam at Paulo Affonso Falls are being extended to all of the satellite plantation neighborhoods.

Still, the situation of these wage workers is anything but ideal. The mill reaches out and dominates every aspect of the workers' lives. Only people employed by the mill are resident on mill property; when their newlywed children apply for housing they must wait until there is certainty that the young husband will be employed somewhere on the plantation before it is assigned. In fact, the marriage is often delayed until housing—hence, employment—is obtained. The up to 2 hectares of land provided each worker is really inadequate to supply sufficient foodstuffs to workers, although they are encouraged to plant, provided with seed and fertilizer, and helped to raise goats which provide milk for their children. The raising of sheep, which feed on sugarcane, is strictly forbidden. The mill owners or their agents select political candidates for local office and attempt to arrange votes for them, as well as for candidates selected for state and national offices. The role of the sugar mill in the political life of this município will be discussed at length in chapter 5.

Before proceeding, however, something should be said about the oft-made comparisons between the urban and so-called rural proletariat in Brazil. It should now be clear that the rural salaried worker, who is himself engaged from time to time in sharecropping or tenant farming or whose family members are part of a more generalized peasant sector of the economy, differs in many crucial respects from an urban proletariat. This is true not only in work habits, specifically as regards the allocation of time, but also in terms of his overall attitude toward the place of work as part of a more enveloping social ambience. To a certain degree at least, these differences will account for the difficulties that Brazilian leaders encountered in attempting to apply an urban trade-union model to rural syndicalization.

Generally speaking, a wage worker is an individual who is assigned particular tasks during a specified period of time for which he receives a cash recompense and certain stipulated fringe benefits. In an industrial setting, his wage and these fringe benefits are his principal incentives to work. His employment tends to be separated out and differentiated from other primary attachments such as family or religious affiliations. The quest for security that delineates nuclear and extended families as operative economic units in the peasant sector is not so salient a characteristic of the urban environment. The industrial wage earner rarely makes decisions regarding the production or distribution of the commodity he produces. In effect, he makes no decisions regarding the allocation of productive resources beyond his initial decision to offer his labor at such a time and place and for a particular wage, although, of course, he does have some control over his own rate of output. Instead, most production decisions are made by management, regardless of the consumption demands of the worker's family, which are taken into account on the peasant farm. The manager himself is part of a differentiated authority structure in which teachers, policemen, and bureaucrats all function in separable areas of daily life to which the urban wage earner learns to accommodate himself. His behavior vis-à-vis the manager of a firm does not necessarily coincide with his behavior toward other superordinates in this differentiated authority structure. This, of course, is not the case on the traditional sugar plantation in the Brazilian Northeast where the multiplex roles of the patrão were not always clearly distinguished. It is precisely the changing patterns of authority and the disjunction in expected forms of interclass behavior that led to increased politicization in the Brazilian countryside in the 1950s and 1960s.

In rural Brazil, wage work must be examined as part of a more generalized system of interrelationships between ecology, social organization, and the distribution of rewards in the society. Wage work, even in the highly modernized, corporately-owned sugar mill described above, is not nearly so alienated from the total socio-cultural milieu in which the worker lives as in the case of the urban factory worker. The rural worker does not conceive of his "job" as a separable aspect of life, apart from family, religion, education, recreation, or even politics. To begin, wage work on a plantation or in a mill town is often closely tied to production for one's own use on small plots of land that are assigned as part of the work contract. The worker's family is the operative economic entity which functions as an undifferentiated production and banking unit. Through the total earning capacity of members of the family, the rural wage earner establishes credit in the local shop and sometimes manages to save, just as in the peasant household. Furthermore, the family bears a joint, as opposed to individual, responsibility toward the employer, with whom the rural wage earner invariably tries to establish a patron-dependent bond. Finally, as we shall see, the undifferentiated authority structures of rural Brazil are part of a general system of stratification in local communities in which the individual both works and resides, and his behavior in the face of authority tends to coincide in the social, religious, political, and economic aspects of his life.

SOCIAL STRATIFICATION, SOCIAL PROCESS, AND SOCIAL MOBILITY

BRAZILIAN CLASS SYSTEM

The variety of tenancy and labor arrangements which result from differential access to land resources in rural Brazil leads inevitably to a ranking of occupational statuses, as well as to a more general discussion of what Lloyd Fallers has appropriately termed the "primary and secondary structural and cultural aspects" of social stratification.[13] Brazil is, by any measure, a highly stratified social system. Yet, the description of a static social structure based on the delineation of two socioeconomic groupings, corresponding broadly to national upper and lower classes, recast as latifundiários and minifundiários [14] does not stand up in the light of empirical investigation. As we have seen in chapter 2, a two-class system was not adequate as a description of the social system in colonial Brazil when social differentiation was already taking place, and it certainly does not adequately describe the Brazil of today where we find considerable intermediate ranking between the upper and lower echelons of rural society. Power and privilege in rural Brazil *are* derived from wealth, invariably measured in acreage, but they are not the exclusive purview of a dominant landowning class standing in stark and exploitative opposition to an undifferentiated mass of peasants. Power—in fact, in perhaps its rawest form—is also wielded, to varying degrees, by various intermediaries in the system who do not have the status of the rural gentry but who have access to them and, thus, to a relative share of strategic resources. Such privilege helps to differentiate these intermediaries from the masses of lower-class rural Brazilians, but it does not justify lumping them in a clearly definable middle stratum between rich and poor, as is so often done in the literature on social class in rural Brazil. To be sure, differences in standards of living in the countryside are measurable, and some lines can be drawn between strata to mark off local upper, middle, and lower classes. Furthermore, a segment of a national middle class comprised of civil servants, commercial elites, and even some richer farmers might well be emerging in rural Brazilian communities. Nonetheless, to simply create a broad residual category—by whatever criteria—for those who do not fit at either extreme of the social herarchy still does not do justice to the complexities of this dynamic social system.

In his *Introduction to Brazil*, Wagley (1963) delineates the traditional upper class of landed gentry and local elites; the traditional lower class of rural workers and peasants; the new rural proletariat of agricultural wage workers; the emerging middle class of white-collar workers, civil servants, and salaried professionals; and finally, the new upper class of industrial entrepre-

neurs. He provides us with some very useful insights into the
relationships between these various segments of the nation's
population and with a genuine feeling for the changes currently
taking place within the complex social mosaic that crisscrosses
the Brazilian landscape. Most importantly, he makes us fully
aware that to talk about social stratification in rural Brazil is to
deal with only one segment of a more encompassing stratifi-
catory system, in which all of these segments are ultimately
linked.

This does not mean simply that there is a static correspondence between rural and urban social strata so that a landowning elite, an improverished peasantry, and an intermediate
group fit schematically into the upper, middle, and lower strata
of the pyramidal structure of the national system as shown in
Table 5. Rather, it means that the social differentiation that is
now taking place in rural Brazil increasingly reflects the
changes that are occurring in the nation at large. It means that
the social, economic, and political components of the rural
"subsystem" articulate in rather precise and identifiable ways
with the on-going social, economic, and political processes of
the nation-state. It also means that the degree of openness or
closedness of the rural social system and thus, the possibilities
for social mobility and change are dependent upon a wide variety of factors that may not become apparent in the bounded
study of a local community. In fact, it requires us to turn our attention away from local communities and local social structures
and to seek to understand the precise nature of integration between local and national units. That is, the internally differentiated peasantry, artisans, day laborers, local shopkeepers, and
market middlemen, who are all part of the enormous Brazilian
underclass resident in rural areas, are subject to demographic,
economic, and political changes that occur within the nation at
large.

In like vein, it appears that since the military government
seized the reins of power in 1964, the landowning elite and
some rural industrialists have become, perhaps more than ever
before, the critical underpinnings of a national political system

that seeks widespread support throughout the countryside for the centralization and legitimization of its authority. Following along this same line of thought, we can hypothesize that in many, although by no means all, rural communities civil servants, who together with commercial elites and even some richer farmers are now thought of as part of a growing national middle class, might come to comprise a network of communications and control that is vital to the propagation and maintenance of that system of authority.

These and other questions concerning social structure and political integration will be taken up at length in chapter 5, where I will examine closely the sets of transformations that lead from patron-dependency (when the peasant or rural worker is forced to enter into a set of exchanges with a given patron) to patron-clientship (when the peasant is presented with a choice, however limited, among potential "benefactors" who offer him differential returns for services rendered) (Hutchinson 1966; de Kadt 1970:23). For the present, it is necessary to lay the groundwork for that discussion by describing the "relational aspect" of social stratification in rural Brazil, that is, the interactional processes between and among differentially placed members of the social hierarchy.

To the extent that I will focus on the interactional aspect of the "dyadic" ties as between patron and dependent,[15] I do not mean to imply that there is no utility to a class-based mode of analysis. On the contrary, I view patron-dependency as perhaps the most salient aspect of a rigid system of social stratification, one which provides the content for an analysis of the dynamics of interclass behavior in rural Brazil. For, as we shall see, it is within the context of this relationship that the peasant's or rural worker's assessment of his relation to a class of superior beings begins to take shape.

Now, to describe the internal dynamics of patron-dependent relationships is, in some sense, to run the risk of merely describing the content of a set of linkages which are nothing more than the *means* of articulation between particular individuals in a social system at a given time. To understand that phenomenon

Table 5. Brazilian Social Classes, in the Community and in the Nation

NATIONAL	CIDA	VINHAS	HUTCHINSON	HARRIS	WAGLEY	FORMAN
Upper	Large-size multifamily farms	Latifundia	Aristocracy	Not present	Not present	Landed aristocracy; rural industrialists
			Local upper class	Brancos-ricos (white-rich)	First-class (Os Brancos- The Whites)	Local bureaucrats; commercial elites
Middle	Medium-size multifamily farms	Rich peasants		Class A		Agriculturalists
			Local middle class	Class B1		Shopkeepers; peasant middlemen
	Family-size farms	Middle peasants				Smallholders
Lower				Preto-pobre (Negro-poor)	Second-class (lower-class town dwellers)	
	Minifundia	Poor peasants		Class B2		Sharecroppers; tenant farmers
			Local lower class		Farmers (rural lower class)	Artisans
		Rural proletariat		Class C	Collectors (rural lower class)	Day laborers

Sources: Wagley 1952:146; CIDA 1966; Vinhas 1963.

diachronically as a *mode* of integration between social classes which varies over time, on the other hand, requires that the exchanges which characterize patron-dependent relationships be examined within the most encompassing socioeconomic and political context in which they transpire. As the foregoing discussion should have made abundantly clear, it is within *that* context that the content and form of the exchanges themselves are determined and ultimately made to change, as for example in the aforementioned transition from patron-dependency to patron-clientship.

For the purposes of the present discussion, suffice it to say that controlled access to land requires Brazilian peasants to seek ties with persons who are more advantageously placed within the stratification system. In the absence of any kind of legal institutional framework that supports their claims within that system, peasants are forced to subject themselves to patrons who can facilitate access to strategic resources and who offer them some measure of security and protection. I have already stressed that these relationships are rooted in the agrarian class structure and, specifically, in the limited access to land.

While it is obviously the most critical resource in an agrarian society, land is not the only item to be exchanged, and exchanges do not occur only between individuals drawn from the extremes of the social hierarchy. As Wagley himself notes:

A *patrão* was not always an actual employer. Landholding peasants might be tied to a storekeeper through debts or past favors. Frequently the local political boss, the *coronel* (similar to a Kentucky Colonel) was a sort of *patrão* to his followers, who had received favors and expected future favors. A lower-class worker without a *patrão* of one kind or another was a man without a protector in time of need. The *patrão* provided some measure of social security—generally the only form available to the worker. (1963:107)

In other words, there are any number of strategic resources such as credit, capital, medical aid, information, etc., in addition to land, that are exchanged between individuals who might actually stand in relatively close proximity to one another on an objectively measurable social scale. Yet, the differences in the quality of these various kinds of exchange relationships are many, and the degree of harmony in interclass relations is often in direct proportion to the relative social distance between the parties involved.

It should be pointed out here that not all of the above-mentioned socioeconomic classes will be represented in every rural community, although a discussion of dependency relationships can, I believe, be generalized to practically all of them in which a rural lower class is found in one form or another. For example, a traditional upper class will be confined to the areas of plantation agriculture in the coastal humid valleys of the Northeast and around Rio de Janeiro and São Paulo, and the local middle class will be found only in those municipal seats that boast a governmental bureaucracy and a lively commerce. Most community studies in Brazil have been undertaken precisely in these rural administrative and commercial centers where access to elective and appointive offices and to investment opportunities clearly elevate some individuals above the rest. However, I would argue that even where such obvious social hierarchies are not in evidence, there are ranked differences among local residents, some of whom may have access to special privilege through a patron or who may be distinguished from the others by virtue of the simple fact of literacy (see, for example, Kottak 1966). Whatever the case, the interactional processes by which individuals in these communities are socially, economically, and politically integrated into the nation as a whole are essentially the same as in the municipal seats in which the formal institutional linkages established through government offices, churches, schools, clinics, market places, and police constabularies have been pushed to the forefront of our analyses. They are to be located within the sets of dependency relationships which are the most fundamental aspect of social class in rural Brazil. As Charles Wagley explains:

For most of this rural lower class, economic security and social well-being are conceived as flowing from the paternal ministrations of the local elite. Everyone should have a *patrão* (1963:106–7). . . . this "*patrão* complex" is not a thing of the past. It is still the basic form of relationship between people of different social classes in most of the communities of northern Brazil, and it is far from extinct in São Paulo and even in the extreme South. (*Ibid.*, 107–8)

In my previous study, *The Raft Fishermen: Tradition and Change in the Brazilian Peasant Economy* (1970), I described in considerable detail the system of incipient social stratification infringing upon the village of Coqueiral, município of Guaiamú, in the Brazilian Northeast, in which none of the political and civil offices located in municipal seats were to be found. Nonetheless, power and privilege were highly evident, concentrated in the hands of a few local "bigwigs" who had ready access to landowning and commercial elites outside of the community. For example, when the long arm of syndicalist organization reached into the village from Rio de Janeiro during the regime of President Getulio Vargas in the 1940s, the president of the newly established fisherman's guild was selected from among the few residents who had direct connections with a highly placed patron in the municipal seat. In the ensuing years, political spoils and nepotism have enabled this individual and his kinsmen to consolidate a political base in Guaiamú, as the local representatives of the ruling party in the município. He proceeds to ride roughshod over the entire community, virtually unchallenged by a rival tied to the local political opposition.

The important point to be made here is that even this tiny village of 852 people, who eke out a poor existence on the sea and on marginal agricultural lands, is neither homogeneous nor socially static, although it may well appear to be so from the outside. Rather, its social structure is comprised of a network of dynamic socioeconomic interactions that ramify through extended-family households, among neighbors, across villages to the municipal seat, and to the sugar mill beyond. The horizontal linkages between kinsmen, neighbors, ritual friends, coparents and godparents are explored in *The Raft Fishermen,* where I demonstrate that the quest for security and minimization of risk are the basic orienting principles in the elaboration of these local social bonds.

At the same time, a hierarchy of relationships based on access to outside sources of political power and wealth, oriented around the quite different principles of submission to authority and obligation to meet debt, was operative in every aspect of village life. Large-scale sugar planters and, in particular, the owners of the sugar mill in the interior of the valley, stand at the apex of this social hierarchy, exercising economic and political hegemony over the município as a whole. A "middle stratum" is comprised of a group of smaller landowners, lesser bureaucrats, professional men, and tradesmen who are resident in the municipal seat but dependent for their well-being upon the good will of the planter class. The lines of authority then descend through the village power brokers to the rank and file of the villagers themselves.

The successful manipulation of these vertical linkages, through a pervasive system of debt and credit relationships, determined who had access to local productive resources and technologies, who took advantage of the possibilities for innovation and change, whose houses were electrified, and whose children had places in which of the municipal or village schools. It even conditioned, to a large extent, who attended the occasional masses that were celebrated in the village church. In short, patron-dependent relationships permeated virtually every aspect of social and economic life—even in this community where the extremes of the general Brazilian system of stratification were not immediately in evidence (Forman 1970).[16]

Precisely because patron-dependency is such a pervasive aspect of social class, it should be examined within specific situational contexts. That is, it is not reasonable to characterize the entire system according to some ill-defined relationship in which noblesse oblige is meted out by a patron in abundant measure in exchange for a dependent's manifestations of loyalty and support. On the contrary, if we are to understand the nature of interclass relations in rural Brazil, we must know in each instance exactly which resources are controlled and by whom and how access to them is structured.

The foregoing description of land tenure and labor arrangements in rural Brazil exemplifies, in general terms, the one kind of patron-dependent economic bond—i.e., the exchange of land and/or a share of the crop between landlords and peasants. At the same time, however, it is important to emphasize that I am not describing, even in that instance, an economic exchange-relationship exclusively. Such a system cannot be understood one-dimensionally. Rather, it is necessary to pay careful attention to both the material *and* the nonmaterial content of these exchanges as they affect the quality and extent of social relationships.

As we have seen earlier, there are two distinct aspects of the asymmetrical socioeconomic bonds that characterize Brazilian peasant society. The first and most fundamental is decidedly economic. However, superimposed upon the basic contractual relationship between peasant and landlord or debtor and creditor is a set of understandings regarding the rights and obligations of each party to the exchange which, following Peter Blau (1964), we might best indicate as the "social exchange" dimension of these labor arrangements. Eric Wolf has referred to these relationships as "manystranded, dyadic, and vertical coalitions," stating further:

Such a relation involves a socially or politically or economically superior person in a vertical relation with a social, political, or economic inferior. The tie is asymmetrical . . . At the same time it is manystranded. The two partners must be able to trust each other; and in the absence of formal sanctions a relation of trust involves a mutual understanding of each other's motives and behavior which cannot be built up in a moment, but must grow over time and be tested in a number of contexts. . . . Hence, patron-client relations involve multiple facets of the actor involved, not merely the segmental single-interest of the moment. (1966a:86–7)

In point of fact, this mutual confidence resides not so much in knowing the intentions of the actual parties to the specific exchange as in a shared set of expectations about proper behavior in interclass interactions which is projected onto the particular relationship itself.

Hierarchy is a fundamental tenet of Brazilian social life. It is evident in a variety of deference patterns, such as the elaborate set of terms of address, that mark out and define an individual's place in the social system. Actual position in this system is determined, once again, by proximity to the locus of power, usually associated with ownership of land. It is also conditioned by a number of other factors including occupation, education, place of residence, family affiliation, and, not the least, race. (Wagley et al. 1952) [17] Rural Brazilians are quick to recognize the social differences that these criteria establish between themselves and others, and they behave in inter-class situations according to well-accepted standards deemed appropriate to their rank. A wealthy or educated man is referred to as *doutor* by Brazilian peasants, who receive the simple form, *você*, in return. When addressing a member of the upper class, a Brazilian peasant will invariably lower his gaze, hat in hand, and shuffle his feet in an embarrassed mockery of his own humility. He will defer to the landowner, the shopkeeper, and the tax collector in countless ways, accepting that it is right and proper for him to do so, as long as proper behavior is reciprocated in turn.

PATRON-DEPENDENCY

More to the point, throughout his life the Brazilian peasant or agricultural laborer *submits* to a series of acknowledged disequal relationships in which he *obligates* himself in a variety of ways that were discussed in terms of the various labor arrangements at the outset of this chapter. Obviously, this repeated behavior is born of necessity, but it is nurtured by a set of general propositions about submissiveness to authority and obligation to meet debt, which give the sociocultural content of particular patron-dependent relationships its peculiar efficacy. Reinforced by a congruence of ideas drawn from a number of domains, but particularly the religious, patron-dependency thus provides the set of understandings that become the ideological underpinnings of the class structure.

While surely not balancing out the inequities in the actual transmission of goods and services, patron-dependency does, at the individual level, mitigate the harshness of the contractual exchange for the peasant and helps to alleviate some of the tensions that the constant realization of loss might otherwise build up in him. By defining a peasant's place in the social universe and asserting the general correctness of asymmetry in socioeconomic relationships, it also proffers an explanation of individual misconduct for the incorrectness of particular behavior on the part of a "bad patron," thereby militating against inter-class conflict and helping to maintain the status quo. That is, when faced with the abuses of patronism, the peasant is led to seek out a better patrão rather than faulting the *system* itself. In short, by enveloping temporary economic arrangements within social bonds, patron-dependency reaffirms, legitimizes, and justifies the authority of the landed class as a group despite the tenuousness of the contractual bond between individual dyads.

The patron's demands on his dependents are few and so straightforward as to bring into sharp relief the fundamental asymmetry of even the social exchange dimension of these relationships. In all cases, deference goes up; directives come down. Beyond the economic requirements stipulated in the land-for-labor exchanges and the additional services rendered by dependents, a number of generalized expectations exist. The patron expects and receives loyalty, obedience, and dependability from those in his charge. In chapter 2, I observed that Brazilian peasants are constantly establishing new patron-dependent bonds in the wake of their extraordinary farm-to-farm mobility. Nonetheless, such mobility does not diminish the need for their faithful adherence to the person whose employ they are in at the moment. Loyalties can be transferred, but the worker's obligations must be met first.

The patron's word is law and not to be questioned. His will is done, because it is believed to be right and proper to do so. Any act of defiance is cause for dismissal regardless of whatever contractual agreement might exist and, when "reason" fails, the patron always has recourse to the will of God, the Law, or, in the last resort, to the force of his hired guns. Notwithstanding, his most important asset is his reputation, and therefore, in some sense the most important task his dependents can perform is to enhance his reputation by spreading the word of his "goodness" throughout the countryside.

In this way, patronage also becomes the medium of competition in a system in which power and privilege are clearly monopolized. At one level, it provides the basis for economic competition among landed elites for a mobile labor force (Johnson 1970:39), facilitating the acceptance of disadvantageous contracts on the part of peasants and rural workers without the bargaining for better terms which might otherwise occur. At another, the patron who wants to participate in the highly-charged rural Brazilian political arena needs to be able to muster the support of a large and loyal coterie, upon which he can depend in disputes and which he can mobilize for votes. While this claim of loyalty produces the immediate effect of aligning individuals across class lines into factions comprised of a patron and his "following," it also opens the way for that transition from dependency to clientship.

It is axiomatic that a good patron must *command* respect and deference if he is to build up a "following." The ideal patron is a rich and powerful figure who can and does protect his dependents and intervenes for them in their dealings with the world at large. While his attitude toward them more often than not contains a degree of condescension, he is expected to treat them with affect and respect, and, at least traditionally, to solidify the assumed social bond by accepting the additional obligations of godparenthood, a ritual undertaking that further serves to assert the correctness of the asymmetrical bond, as we shall later see. He is expected to be concerned with their health and well-being and with that of their families, loaning them money and even providing them with food and medical aid when need arises. He might also facilitate the education of their children, and, occasionally, a really good patrão will recognize a viable commercial opportunity for a dependent and help him to get started in some limited entrepreneurial activity. In point of fact, direct intervention is not always necessary since the guardianship of a truly powerful patron can afford protection and a degree of privilege to a dependent simply by virtue of the association betwen them, some of the patron's "presumed charisma" falling on those close to him.[18]

To be sure, a member of the traditional upper class has an élan which sets him apart from other men. Nonetheless, a measure of the prestige and deference accorded any man, irrespective of his ultimate wealth and power, is the correctness of his behavior in actual, observable interchanges with his dependents. It is not simply the assumption that patrons are *supposed* to act in prescribed ways that entitles them to deference, but the fact that they *do* so act. Stories about proper and improper behavior on the part of social superiors circulate throughout local communities and the surrounding countryside, making and breaking the reputations of the *bom patrão*. For example, the birthright of the scion of a traditional landowning family will assure his assignment to the upper class, but he will be judged, as will his family over time, by his ability to maintain the reputation that they have built up in many years of interaction with the local peasantry. By the same token, a member of a fallen "aristocracy," bereft of land, stripped of political power, and maintaining a standard of living only slightly above the peasantry, is still accorded deference because "he has not forgotten how to treat people."

On the other hand, new commercial elites who have come to replace members of the traditional upper class in positions of power in many rural communities are constantly compared negatively to the old "patriarchs" (Johnson 1972; Gross 1970), and local bigwigs who substitute for absentee landlords in administrative functions on plantations or fill power vacuums in communities without resident elites are despised and feared by their peasant compeers (Forman 1970), largely because they fail to fulfill the peasants' expectation of what proper behavior should be. As I explained in *The Raft Fishermen,*

A landowning elite, which was formerly resident in the village, moved away when cattle raising and salt production ceased. They have been replaced by local "bigwigs" who have come to occupy a position of power within the village. *Os grandes do lugar* (the big men of the place), as they are called by the fishermen, have filled the vacuum left by the traditional local patrão. Born in the village of lower-class families, they actually stand just above the peasant fishermen in status, although, for the most part, they have managed to earn a better living than the fishermen, and they maintain a standard of living slightly above the norm. As a group, these bigwigs bear closer resemblance to the town-type subculture of the county seat than they do to the local peasant subculture (Wagley and Harris 1955:438). In Coqueiral they are, so to speak, the 'biggest frogs in the pond.' Although they attempt to emulate the upper-class townsmen, the local bigwigs have highly limited social mobility. Like the peasant whom they tend to disdain, they, too, are continually in debt, to the sugar planters for their land or to the tradesmen in the city, as a result of overextended patterns of consumption. These debts tie them to the village. . . . The status of the local bigwigs is largely dependent on their identification with the traditional power structure in the county at large. It is through such identification that they exert a tenuous, indirect control over the local fishing population. . . . [they] maintain their position by pretending to have greatly outdistanced their peers in the village and by making themselves useful to the real sources of power in the county. A rudimentary knowledge of reading, writing, and simple arithmetic helps them to differentiate themselves from the lower class, from which they themselves have arisen, and which they constantly and publicly malign. More often than not, it is the local bigwigs who perpetuate the myth of the lazy, ignorant, and uncooperative peasant. Whereas the relationship between the peasant and the traditional elite is rather paternalistic, characterized by a high degree of dependency and trust, peasant ties with local bigwigs are built upon and maintained through fear. Although the lower classes live in the hope of change, the bigwigs view the maintenance of the status quo as vital to their own interests (Forman 1970:34–36).

Tensions often run high in rural Brazil, but between the most proximate segments of the social system rather than between upper- and lower-class groupings strictly defined. In point of fact, it is not class conflict but intraclass antagonisms at the local level that most frequently results from the changing social and economic structures in the countryside. Increased absenteeism on the part of traditional elites, accompanied by the depersonalization of both administrative functions and economic interactions in a rapidly commercializing system, often lead to the brink of potential hostilities. Yet, peasant enmity is rarely directed toward the ruling class. Generally speaking, peasants respect and admire the traditional patrons, whose positions in the social system are so lofty that they can only be held in awe.

However, they despise and fear those of their peers who shouldered them aside and now look back mockingly.[19] Peasants might question the behavior of new and traditional elites alike, but only when their superiors fail to perform in time-honored ways. In brief, it is not the expectation of favor that breeds contempt, but rather the competition for favor in a situation of limited social mobility. As Harris has written:

> To imagine that the situation we have been describing is an instance of an economically-based general 'class struggle' would be a severe distortion of the facts. There is no sense of oppression in class 'B' or class 'C', because the fundamental justice and correctness of the principle of rank and of the major ranking gradients are believed in by all members of the community. Nothing in Minas Velhas is more stable and more tenacious than the belief that some people are better than others, and that the best deserve and get the best (1952:77).

Although this system is sometimes judged to be unfair, it is largely held to be immutable. The peasant occasionally questions the correctness of his position as perpetual underling, but more often than not he resubmits to authority and prepares to meet his obligations, like Fabiano, the cowherd adrift in the drought-ravaged Northeast in Graciliano Ramos' brilliant novel, *Barren Lives:*

> In the division of stock at the year's end, Fabiano received a fourth of the calves and a third of the kids, but as he grew no feed, but merely sowed a few handfuls of beans and corn on the river flat, living on what he bought at the market, he disposed of the animals, never seeing his brand on a calf or his mark on the ear of a kid.
>
> If he could only put something aside for a few months, he would be able to get his head up. Oh, he had made plans, but that was all foolishness. Ground creepers were never meant to climb. Once the beans had been eaten and the ears of corn gnawed, there was no place to go but to the boss's cash drawer. He would turn over the animals that had fallen to his lot for the lowest of prices, grumbling and protesting in distress, trying to make his meager resources yield as much as possible. Arguing, he would choke and bite his tongue. Dealing with anyone else he would not let himself be so shamelessly robbed, but, as he was afraid of being put off the ranch, he would give in. He would take the cash and listen to the advice that accompanied it. He should give thought to the future, be more careful. He would stand there with his

mouth open, red-faced. . . . Suddenly he would burst out:
"Talk, talk! Money goes faster than a race horse, and people can't
live without eating. Ground creepers were never meant to climb."

Little by little the boss's brand was put on Fabiano's stock, and
when he had nothing left to sell, the backlander went into debt. When
time came for the division, he was in the hole, and when accounts
were settled he received a mere nothing.

This time, as on other occasions, Fabiano first made a deal regarding
the stock, then thought better of the matter, and, leaving the transaction only half agreed upon, he went to consult with his wife. Vitória
sent the boys to play in the clay pit, sat down in the kitchen, and concentrated, lining up different kinds of seeds on the ground, adding and
subtracting. The next day Fabiano went back to town, but on closing
the deal he noted that, as usual, Vitória's figuring differed from that of
the boss. He protested, and received the usual explanation: the difference represented interest.

He refused to accept this answer. There must be some mistake. He
was not very bright, that he knew. Anybody could see he was. But his
wife had brains. Surely there was some mistake on the boss's paper.
The mistake couldn't be found, and Fabiano lost his temper. Was he to
take a beating like that his whole life long, giving up what belonged to
him for nothing? . . . To work like a slave and never gain his
freedom?

The boss became angry. He refused to hear such insolence. He
thought it would be a good thing if the herdsman looked for another
job.

At this point Fabiano got cold feet and began to back down. All right,
all right. There was no need for a fuss. If he had said something wrong,
he was sorry. He was ignorant; he had never had any learning. He
knew his place; he wasn't the cheeky kind. He was just a half-breed.
He wasn't going to get into any arguments with rich people. He wasn't
bright, but he knew how to show people proper respect. His wife must
just be mistaken, that was all. In fact her figuring had seemed strange
to him. But since he didn't know how to read (he was just plain ignorant) he had believed his old lady. He was sorry and he wouldn't make
a blunder like this again.

The boss calmed down and Fabiano backed out of the room, his hat
dragging on the brick floor. Once outside the door he turned around,
fastened the rowels on his spurs, and stumbled off, his untanned
leather boots clumping on the ground like horses' hoofs.

The basic discrepancy that so plagues Fabiano does not go
unnoticed by the masses of rural workers in Brazil, who recognize that the exchange relationships into which they are forced

to enter with patrons are clearly inequitable. It would be quite wrong to assume that some compensatory level of satisfaction accrues to peasants who continually get the "short end of the stick." Simply because they utilize the resources meted out to them by patrons [20] and participate in the social transactions that accompany the basic economic exchanges does not mean that they do not see the fundamental disadvantage in their position compared to that of the patron to which they can never hope to aspire. Values in exchange are not always commensurate, and individuals do question relative worth in exchanges.

It is true, of course, that each party to the patron-dependent relationship is deriving different benefits from the exchange. The patron seeks to maximize economic and political gain. The dependent seeks to maximize security. Each elaborates a strategy in the exchange relationship designed to meet these goals. Yet, inequities exist and are clearly perceived by both patrons and dependents. The important question then becomes how the disadvantage to the dependent is explained and rationalized so that the advantage to the patron can be justified.[21] There exists in rural Brazil a set of understandings about proper behavior in inter-class interactions which makes tenable the peasant's submission to authority and strengthens his sense of obligation in a series of disequal exchange relationships.

DIRECTIONS FOR SOCIAL CHANGE

Before bringing this chapter to a close, however, it is important to emphasize once again that the social system in rural Brazil is in flux, particularly as commercialization increasingly penetrates the hinterland communities. To a considerable degree, patron-dependency is breaking down, not simply because absenteeism tends to substitute the "straw-boss" for traditional authority, but also because there is real difficulty in maintaining and supporting a fixed following on the land. A set of economic processes are leading to the displacement of masses of peasants, while a set of panaceas elaborated by the government fail to fulfill their promise. While "rational" economic decisions regarding land use and production induce landowners to substitute wage labor (or no labor) for the "traditional" dependency relationships, they are simultaneously losing their control over the flow of spoils and information into the municípios.

The extension of government controls over municipal offices and expenditures after 1964 has substantially reduced the store of patronage that for the better part of this century allowed rural elites to compete for a following, thereby impairing the patron's ability to meet his former dependent's new demands. At the same time, newspapers, radio broadcasts, in some cases television, and the actual presence of urban organizers bring alternative messages into the countryside, thus broadening the peasants' horizons and further circumscribing the patron's sphere of influence. The politicization of the rural masses that accompanied these developments in the 1950s and 1960s resulted in their direct participation in the political process, hastening the transformation from dependency to clientship.

The occurence of these changes should not, however, give the impression of fundamental transformations in the basic structure of Brazilian rural society. For the time being, at least, social mobility is extremely limited and subject to the same structural constraints imposed by a dominant hierarchy. There has been some differentiation in the occupational structure in rural communities, as commercialization and rural industrialization have opened up some new opportunities, but these have been taken mostly by commercial elites and few real benefits have accrued to the peasantry.

Educational opportunity, too, has been strictly limited, except as some token advances over the past several decades has somewhat enlarged the pool of literate individuals. Illiteracy still runs well over 50 percent in Brazil and up to 100 percent in some rural areas. Rural primary schools often are taught by semiliterates, who, with no pedagogic materials, can provide little more than knowledge of the alphabet through repetitious copying of the ABC's and some rudimentary mathematics. Many towns and villages are entirely without schools, and even those wealthier communities that boast both primary and secondary schools suffer an enormous gap between increased enrollments and the availability of trained teachers. The only means to a better education is through a *vaga*, a place in a school in the municipal seat where a child can reside with a relative or a god-parent or, perhaps, in a boarding school run by a priest where education is concentrated on the trades. Such an education usually is followed by permanent migration to urban areas, where employment opportunities are not so restricted (L. Forman 1970).

The point I wish to make here is simple. Since the opportunity structure in rural Brazil is opening very slowly in relation to demand, the most significant transformation now apparent in the rural social system appears to be the change from patron-dependency to patron-clientship, which follows from the increased competition both among the rural masses for these limited opportunities and among the patrons for clients.

There is, then, in rural Brazil the possibility of some ascent within the social system for a limited few who, given their relation to a patron, are able to take advantage of the available opportunities. This process gives rise to an emergent intermediate strata of new elites and local bigwigs who remain for the moment in rather ambiguous positions in the social structure, alienated from peasantry and upper class alike. Some are able to reach positions of power which enable them to challenge the authority of the traditional elites (Gross 1970). Others suffer the fate of the president of the fishermen's guild in Coqueiral, who, in his desire to emulate the planter class, decided to accept the offer of a small farm from the sugar mill owners, who preferred to advance him the purchase price and contract with him for the milling of his cane, rather than extend the size of their own landholdings. Referring again to *The Raft Fishermen,*

Although he enjoys a relatively high degree of mobility, the president of the fisherman's guild is a man who is not accepted by either the lower or upper class. He is despised by the fishermen for his constant harassment of them, and he is used but not accepted by the upper class. Although he has one of the better houses in the village and a standard of living considerably higher than the norm, Sr. Nilo is subject to the same social and recreational restrictions as the poorest of fishermen. He is not invited to the homes of the upper-class townsmen in Guaiamú, nor do the planters from the valley visit him in his home during their vacations in Coqueiral. At the same time, Sr. Nilo refuses to participate in the social life of the village. He does not watch the Sunday soccer matches or attend the performances of folk songs and dances which are popular with the fishermen. He is able to maintain his children in the county seat, but rather than have them walk the seven kilometers each way to the better school in Guaiamú, they are forced to live in an old, virtually unfurnished house, which formerly belonged to his in-laws. Sr. Nilo owns property, but he is in debt. He has a position, but at the expense of the fishermen. He derides them for laziness; yet, he himself is idle. The size of his operation requires that he spend only one day a week at his farm, except during the sugar harvest, and most of his time is spent loafing in the village (Forman 1970:27–28).

This then is one price of social mobility. Patron-dependency opens the way for individuals who find themselves butting up against a ceiling placed on the limits of their achievement. They can either settle back in the torment of the world they have made for themselves or struggle openly to conquer the one that remains closed to them. In either case, their very appearance promises to hasten the course of social change.

Chapter four—
The Nature of Integration 2:
The Economic Dimensions of
the Agrarian Crisis and
the Panaceas of Development

Students of peasant society recognize the importance of the market economy for understanding decision-making processes within the household and the nature of articulation between the peasant sector and the national society.[1] In this chapter, I intend to describe market behavior in Northeast Brazil and to relate such behavior to changes in the agricultural economy in general. The ultimate goal is to understand how peasants are integrated into the national economy as commodity producers and consumers of manufactured goods. By concentrating on the internal marketing system for food staples in Northeast Brazil, I hope to point out the paradox which exists between the critical role the peasant plays in the domestic economy and the tenuousness of his position in the schema of national development. At the end of the chapter, I will discuss some of the government's development plans which have been offered as panaceas to a restive peasantry.

The integration of the Brazilian peasant into the national economy over time has been a function of the market sector. The demand for his labor, his own production decisions, and his patterns of consumption are all affected by the operation of complex internal and external marketing systems.[2] The peasant's involvement in these marketing systems is hardly new, as the preceding chapters have made clear, but it has increased markedly and decisively in recent decades, particularly as regards the movement of foodcrops on the domestic market. The Brazilian peasant is not an "economic zero," who buys little and sells little (Oberg 1965:1418), but an integral part of national patterns of food production, distribution, and consumption. He is deeply involved in regional and national marketing systems and reacts to changes in these systems.

Indeed, it can be said that peasant society in Brazil is a concomitant of the internal market mechanism and that the transformation of the "peasant" as a category, into the "modern farmer" whose calculations are geared to reinvestment of capital for profit maximization rather than simply for family consumption will undoubtedly result from changes therein. Obviously, such changes do not necessarily have positive results for the flesh and blood individuals who actually comprise such categories. In point of fact, development in the internal marketing sector in Brazil is often accompanied by the displacement of peasants and local middlemen from the increasingly commercialized rural economy.

As is the case throughout the major part of the Brazilian countryside, the peasant in Northeast Brazil operates within a capitalist society where land, labor, and product all have a market. He is highly valued as a commodity producer and laborer in an agrarian-structured society which exploits commercial export crops, predominantly sugar, on large-scale plantations. Extensive cattle ranches and innumerable smallholdings exist along with the export-oriented commercial enterprises, the small-scale producers supplying foodstuffs and labor to the dominant export-centered sector of the economy. In this brief description, it would seem as though little has changed since the colonial period; yet, in our field research in contemporary Northeast Brazil, we encountered an economy in transition in which a highly rationalized internal marketing system is profoundly affecting production, leading to an insufficient supply of food staples to burgeoning urban centers and to widespread discontent in the countryside.

The Brazilian Northeast is well known for its economic and social problems.[3] This area of approximately 800,000 square miles and 25 million inhabitants is roughly divided into three major ecological zones. Sugar is grown and partially processed along the coast, in a number of low humid valleys, for export on the international market and to the large market in southern Brazil. These coastal lowlands, or the zona da mata, are subdivided into large sugar plantations, attended by the problem of the proletarianization of rural labor (Hutchinson 1957). However, this area is also interspersed with a large number of renters and smallholders, some producing sugar cane to supply to the mills, but the majority selling mixed food crops grown on marginal lands not suited to sugar cane production.

To the west, along the rutted clay roads that traverse the Brazilian Northeast from the coast to the dry hinterland, is a transitional zone, the agreste, which is a mixed-farming area of food crops, fruits, and tobacco. Produce is sold locally and exported to other regions in Brazil. The agreste is comprised primarily of minifundia. As in the coastal lowlands, these peasant homesteads are organized in a variety of tenure systems, including: ownership, renting, sharecropping, and squatting. They are exploited by paleotechnology and long fallowing.

The sertão, or backlands, is probably one of the best-known areas of Brazil, popularized through Euclides da Cunha's novel, *Rebellion in the Backlands,* and brought to the consciousness of the world by the reports of the political and religious excesses of its starved peasants. It is primarily an area of cattle raising. The large cattle ranches are worked by cowboys who, until recently, herded cattle for a one-quarter share of the stock, but are today wage workers. While the former system enabled some cowboys to establish small ranches, the present system also leads to proletarianization. Some smallholders produce foodstuffs for sale on the internal market in settlements around the many *açudes,* or dams, built to counter the devastating effects of the periodic droughts.

In the summer of 1967, anthropologist Joyce Riegelhaupt and I undertook extensive research on the role of the peasant in the production and distribution of food staples—corn, beans, rice, and manioc flour—in the state of Alagoas, a microcosm of the region and, perhaps, the most underdeveloped of the traditional sugar-producing states of Northeast Brazil.[4] We began our research in two marketplaces in the município of Guaiamú, an area comprised of large sugar plantations and a mixed-farming zone of smallholdings. Our research soon indicated that the simultaneous study of several marketplaces at different levels of socioeconomic integration was necessary to an understanding of the regional marketing system, and we subsequently extended the research into the agreste and sertão through field surveys which covered some ten marketplaces in a three-state area.[5] In addition, we visited a variety of agricultural holdings and collected data on the extent of participation in the marketing process. No agriculturalist was found who did not participate to some degree as a commodity producer for the market.

In following the movement of goods and personnel, it became evident that we were not dealing with an agrarian society in which the traditional model of a marketing system was fully applicable. Food staples did not necessarily move upward through a hierarchy of marketplaces. There were clearly distinguishable levels of market activity, each with its concomitant functions, but these marketplaces did not in themselves constitute the internal marketing system of the region.

In the pages that follow, I will examine the nature of the relationship between the marketing and production systems for food staples by constructing a typology of marketplaces and relating these to marketing patterns in general. That is, by concentrating on the sociology of the marketing system—rather than merely on the ethnography of the marketplace—I hope to clarify the role of the peasant in a dynamic national economy. In addition, the analysis of the peasant marketplace within the rationalizing marketing system also raises several subsidiary problems which I shall discuss, including the functional importance of intermediaries at different levels of the marketing system, the nature of the food supply to rural and urban areas, the effects of consumer demands, and the nature of competition of varying cash crops for land and labor. In describing the regional marketing system, both the role of the peasantry in Brazilian agriculture and apparent trends in land tenure and land usage are clarified. Detailed knowledge of the relationship between peasant producers, middlemen, and consumers and their interactions in the marketing system adds to an understanding of the system of stratification in this traditional agrarian society and underscores the social structural, as well as the economic and ecological, implications for future agricultural development in Northeast Brazil.

The beginning of an internal marketing system in Northeast Brazil was characterized by the presence of feiras, or marketplaces, which supplied foodstuffs to the growing populations on the expanding plantations and in the coastal cities. The travel literature is replete with accounts of the movement of produce through market middlemen (Almeida Prado, 1941:442–43; Koster 1816:79, 82, 214 passim; Gardiner 1849:97–98). While most of this literature refers to the early nineteenth century, I believe that further historical research will document the prior existence of a network of rural marketplaces in Brazil. We know that warehouses existed in urban areas during the colonial period, and we can assume that the difficulties of transport and communications between coastal cities and widely scattered hinterland suppliers necessitated a multiplicity of marketplaces.

The history of the município of Guaiamú, traced in chapter 2 in order to exemplify the emergence of a peasantry in Northeast Brazil, provides us with some more specific data on the development of the network of marketplaces in that particular region. In the sixteenth and seventeenth centuries, the município supplied foodstuffs and other locally produced commodities, such as cattle, salt, and straw handicrafts, to the sugar plantations and the provincial capital of Pernambuco. By the beginning of the seventeenth century, an "agricultural highway" had been constructed along the coast connecting the rich fertile valleys that lay between Olinda and the São Francisco

River. Produce was transferred by a multiplicity of middlemen who bought and sold in a string of *feiras livres,* or free fairs, still located today in the municipal seats, that grew up along that road as the loci of commercial and political activity.

The rapidly expanding sugarcane fields of the province began to spread southward into the humid valleys of Alagoas in the late seventeenth century. Sugarcane was first planted in the valley of Guaiamú in the eighteenth century and quickly began to gobble up the lands in the region. Portuguese decrees protected the vast forest preserves so that hardwood resources could be fully utilized in the construction of ships for imperial expansion, but sugar soon began to infringe on the small peasant holdings, which were limited to the tablelands surrounding the valley. Peasants began to turn their fields from the production of manioc and other foodstuffs to the planting of sugarcane for the several engenhos, or animal-driven mills, that came to dominate the valley throughout the nineteenth century. A central sugar mill, or usina, was built in the municîpio of Guaiamú in 1927, and ownership was transferred to a corporation in 1939. The new owners continued to concentrate the usina's landholdings in the municipality, a trend which started in the last century.

Between 1959 and 1965 the mill's share of municipal lands stabilized at approximately 15,000 hectares, consolidating previously independent, noncontiguous plantations.[6] Further concentration is limited by salt marshes and tidelands to the east, by the mill owners' own cattle ranches to the west, by quotas which cut into potential production, and by the owners' preference to facilitate through loans the purchase of some land by "independent" suppliers who are then bound to them by debt relationships. During the same period, the number of wage laborers at the mill increased from a maximum of 125 in the harvest season (Andrade, 1959:75) to over 300, and the number of field hands working for the mill increased to over 800. A *feira de usina,* or mill fair, was established at this time.

An important variable in the growth of rural markets is precisely the nature of such competition among major farm crops for land and labor. Thus, when sugar became "king" in the valley of Guaiamú during the first quarter of this century, there was a decrease in the amount of land available for food production. The expansion and growth of the sugar economy in Guaiamú seriously curtailed food production, and the município soon changed from a hinterland breadbasket to a food importer (Andrade, 1959:81–82), a situation which continues today. Until recently, land in the município was rented by absentee landowners to peasants who maintained effective control over their plots for long periods of time. Today, however, tenancy, is often of short duration. As described earlier, tenancy arrangements reflect the production needs of economically active plantations, which are themselves obligated to increase their production of sugar cane for the central mill. A peasant might clear the land and retain rights to it for one year only, at which time it reverts again to the owner, who then usually plants it in sugarcane. In such cases, the peasant is hardly willing, even when able, to make any long-term investments in the land. In addition, large tracts of land are utilized for cattle grazing or left as forested reserves, which diminishes even further the land available for food production in the county.

At the same time that land appears to be moving out of food production, the rapid urbanization and industrialization of this region makes urgent demands upon the rural sector for an increased food supply at lower cost. The years between 1940 and 1960 were marked by tremendous urban growth throughout the nation. Within the state of Alagoas, itself, the population in and around the capital city of Maceió grew from 90,523 in 1940 to 170,134 in 1960 (IBGE 1966:38). This disparity, between decreasing land areas available for food production and increasing non-food-producing rural and urban populations that need to be fed, is one of the principal dilemmas facing agricultural planners in Northeast Brazil.

Brazilian developers often explain the problem of food supply in terms of inadequate production and marketing facilities. Yet, the situation is best described as one in which an archaic production sector is enmeshed in a highly commercialized distributive sector. This does not mean that the traditional peasant marketing system no longer exists. Rather, we are confronted in Northeast Brazil with the phenomenon of an on-going, increasingly viable system of peasant marketplaces, which are, along with the peasant who participate in them, well on their way to extinction in a "modernizing" world. Before discussing these changes in the marketing system, however, I will describe the traditional marketplace network.

The traditional marketplace, or feira, is a periodic market of itinerant sellers housed in nonpermanent structures (*barracas*) and convening in a designated place at a set time. A feira distributes primary goods and services among rural people who participate in it both as buyers and sellers. It also serves to distribute finished and semifinished consumer products in areas where the lack of liquid capital makes keeping of large stocks impossible. In other words, a feira moves goods in a money-poor economy.

At this point I wish to distinguish the feira from other rural commercial establishments, which also exist for the distribution of goods in the Brazilain countryside but differ somewhat in form, function, and the nature of peasant participation. A feira is to be contrasted with:

1. A market, or *mercado*, which is a permanent daily outlet for goods and services. Large numbers of sellers gather in one location in order to supply a predominantly urban group of consumers. In some large urban centers, the permanent *mercado* has grown up on the site of former feiras. On some days, the market is greatly enlarged by the addition of temporary stalls in the surrounding streets. In Portuguese, this market also is referred to as a *feira*, and market days are called *dias de feira*.

2. Warehouses, or *armazens*, which are privately owned or state-operated wholesalers' facilities for the storage of goods, principally food staples. These goods are ultimately distributed in part through feiras.

3. The general store, or *mercearia*, which refers to a permanent retail outlet and fixed capital goods (i.e., building, equip-

ment, and stock). *Mercearias* are usually located in cities and larger county seats, where there is a steady consumer market.

4. A shop, or *venda*, which is a rural, small-scale retail outlet.

Vendas operate primarily on credit, often buying their own goods at the weekly feira. A variant of the *venda* is the "company store," sometimes located in mill towns and plantation neighborhoods.

All of these marketing outlets are to be found throughout the Brazilian Northeast and—with the exception of the *armazen*— within the município of Guiamú.

THE MARKETPLACE

There are three types of marketplaces in Northeast Brazil: the local marketplace or rural buyers' fair *(feira de consumo)*, the distribution fair *(feira de distribuicão)*, and the urban consumers' fair *(feira de abastecimento)*. These types exist simultaneously, but there is not a steady flow of goods or personnel from one to the other; neither is the internal marketing system of Northeast Brazil by any means limited to these arenas of exchange.

THE LOCAL MARKETPLACE

The *feira de consumo* is a rural marketplace in which goods and services are distributed in areas of poor access among rural populations with limited capital. Each feira is a cyclical market which meets once a week, the day depending largely upon the primary economic activity of the area it serves. For example, fairs in the coastal lowlands usually are scheduled on Saturdays and Sundays in order to take advantage of Friday paydays at the sugar mills. In the sertão, cattle fairs may be scheduled any day of the week, in alternation with regular commodity fairs, so that in a given region an entire week may be taken up with one fair or another. Historically, the *feira de consumo* was characterized by a multiplicity of peasants selling their produce in a central marketplace. Today, distribution within the feiras is carried on by a variety of itinerant traders, called *feirantes* or *cambistas*, peasant retailers and local shopkeepers who sell non-bulk food-stuffs, garden produce, perishables, and manufactured goods. People come to the marketplace both to buy and to sell, and often buyers and sellers are indistinguishable.

The município of Guaiamú has three *feiras de consumo,* which serve the needs of some 4,540 townsmen and 18,044 rural dwellers. A *feira livre* takes place at dawn every Saturday on public fairgrounds in the county seat. There, over a hundred sellers of food staples, meats, and notions are housed in a per-manent shed surrounded by at least another two-hundred fifty sellers of perishables and manufactured goods, who display their wares in stalls and on the ground. A few women sell cooked food to the participants. A *feira de usina,* or mill fair, is located on privately owned lands in the nucleated settlement of mill workers. This fair attracts more than 350 sellers of food-stuffs, manufactured goods, and services. The sellers, the vast majority of whom do not attend the Guaiamú free fair, begin ar-riving at the usina late Saturday afternoon. The fair fades away by 8 A.M. Sunday. A third fair, somewhat smaller than the other two, services a nearby agricultural colony on Saturday after-noons.

While the form and function of the free fair and the mill fair are essentially the same, there are some distinguishing charac-teristics. The fact that the majority of residents on sugar mill lands are wage earners encourages a larger stock of manufac-tured goods and, thus, a higher degree of capitalization, at the mill fair. Since the mill owners provide half-hectare plots to field hands for subsistence agriculture, smaller quantities of perishable goods are sold there. For the most part, women deal in fruits and vegetables, while men handle dry goods, food sta-ples, and manufactured products. Consequently, greater numbers of men are found selling at the mill fair than at the free fair. In general, the mill fair takes on a highly commercialized, bazaar-type atmosphere, which is not characteristic of the poorer and slower *feira livre.*

A good deal more socializing also takes place at the *feira livre* than at the mill fair. In the county seat, buyers and sellers gather in festive moods for their weekly early morning meetings, often walking two or three hours in the pre-dawn darkness. It is at the marketplace that peasants exchange ideas and define their place in the world, apart from the restrictive influences of the local setting. Despite the rapid spread of the transistor radio in the past ten years, the fair remains the place where the peasant listens to the troubador spin his tales of culture heroes and newsworthy events. Here, too, he is exposed to the material encumbrances of the Catholic Church, encouraging him to replace his rock and shell amulets with golden chains and plaster saints.

At the sugar mill, plantation workers are hauled on flat cars by company tractors to and from the fairgrounds so that they can make their necessary purchases. The mills do not appear to dominate economically over the fairs, even in cases where their reputations are marred by the image of the company store. Instead, mill owners prefer to have a fair operate on their premises, where behavior can be watched, and they can be certain a full crew will be available for work on Monday.

There are three categories of sellers in these local marketplaces: 1) a few peasants retail their own produce at the fair, immediately spending their cash income for their own consumer needs; 2) an increasing number of peasants sell their own produce and market goods bought from others in transactions which still seem geared to their domestic consumption needs; and 3) a large number of middlemen resell products purchased elsewhere. The second category represents a growing body of peasants who enter the marketplace as middlemen in order to supplement their cash incomes in an increasingly commercialized rural world.

The fairs are arranged in orderly fashion with specific areas assigned to sellers who specialize in primary or finished goods. A man will deal in either wet or dry goods, but not in both. Since manufactured goods (textiles, leather goods, hardware and utensils, etc.) require a greater expenditure of funds, entrepreneurs dealing in such items are rarely drawn from among the peasantry, whose "place" in the commercial system is thereby reaffirmed. Men generally specialize in bulk and processed goods. They occupy the principal areas of the fairgrounds, with their large sacks of corn, beans, and rice arranged neatly within the protective confines of a large permanent shed.

Many who come to sell in Guaiamú travel long distances by truck and mule across the several ecological zones, trading goods en route in those areas where they bring the highest prices because of scarcity. Some return to hinterland fairs carrying quantities of salted fish and coconuts, the specialized food products of the coastal zone. Additionally, a large section of the outdoor area of the marketplace is occupied by semipermanent stalls, or *barracas,* in which local intermediaries sell dry goods. Butchers are located separately from the main part of the fair, where they are carefully scrutinized by local tax agents for the higher *impostos* they must pay. While some women work with their husbands at *barracas,* the majority of market women are involved in the more marginal, less capitalized operations, such as the sale of green vegetables, fruits, fresh fish, and small quantities of salted fish. The dependence of women on the sale of garden produce for incremental earnings can be likened to the Haitian pattern described by Mintz (1959, 1960a, 1960b), in which the lack of alternative employment makes marginal laborers amenable to hard work for minimal rewards.

Virtually all retail sales are for cash. Peasant producers are ill-prepared to set prices and depend upon price information obtained in face-to-face contact at the fair. Monopolistic controls are exercised on certain bulk products, such as rice and beans, through speculative buying and storing up of large quantities in warehouses. In addition, there are federal and locally fixed prices on certain commodities. Meat prices, for example, are regulated nationally, while the price of fish is set locally by the mayor and the president of the fisherman's guild. Often, information about federal price ceilings are adjusted to the needs of leading citizens of the local community; for example, during our research in Guaiamú, a new law repealing the paid registration of all vendors and lifting the price ceiling on meat was not com-

municated to middlemen by local authorities, whose own income and consumption patterns would have been affected by
the changes.

Very little haggling takes place at the feiras, and there is generally little competition between sellers with regard to price.
There is, of course, price variation within established limits,
and the process of price-setting often depends upon the position of the seller in relation to the means of production. Thus,
some vendors are able to sell for a lesser margin of profit than
others because they have produced the goods themselves. For
example, a female trader and a hired vendor, working for a
wage, both sold lemons at five for $100 cruzeiros, while a man a
short distance away was able to sell lemons at ten for $100
cruzeiros because, as he noted, he was "selling the fruits of his
own trees." Another vendor noted that he prefers to sell his
own produce because his "only capital outlay is his own
labor." However, he had his own produce to sell for only two
months of the year, and after selling off his own harvest he was
forced to obtain most of his goods from a warehouse.

Likewise, very little hawking is done at the fairs. Vendors
usually wait for their regular clients to come along and buy. A
good deal of social visiting accompanies these transactions. No
special prices are given for the aged, infirm, or for kinsmen, although beggers are often given some small quantity of produce.
Buyer-seller relationships are often strengthened by considerable generosity in weights and measures. Still, very few retail
buyers will be afforded credit at the time of purchase.

A sense of competition is present but never exaggerated. Financial ruin of a competitor is not something to be achieved.
Many vendors share weighing scales with their neighbor or sell
each other's produce when they themselves sell out, with no
share being paid. One vendor at the *feira livre* wanted to expand his operation to include the *feira de usina,* but waited
until a colleague desisted before giving it a try, simply because
he did not want "to enter into competition with his friend."

Food staples enter the marketplace in several ways. While
some produce is grown by peasants and carried to the feira for

direct sale, the bulk is handled by middlemen who may acquire it for resale either at the farm or from other dealers at local marketplaces. However, the major source of supply is now the large hinterland warehouses where goods are stored and sold wholesale. Regardless of the source, all buying for immediate resale in the local marketplace is done on credit, with payment expected immediately after cash transactions are completed at the fair. Default on payment is not usual, although there are cases reported. Reactions to failure of payment is individual. One man, for example, said he would never again give merchandise on consignment because several people sold his goods without paying him for them. In another instance, however, a fish hawker who fell into debt because of heavy losses incurred by overbuying was accepted back by his regular suppliers as soon as he became solvent again.

There are no binding contractual arrangements between buyers and sellers in wholesale transactions. These verbal agreements can be entered into or broken at any time. The strength of a wholesale buying relationship is directly correlated with the perishability of the product. Thus, most of the buying of beans is on a first-to-arrive-at-the-farm basis, while fish is handled on a semibinding relationship between fisherman and fishhawker.

Most vendors carry their goods to the fair on muleback or by truck, although some of the more marginal vendors come on foot, often balancing their merchandise in wooden trays on their heads. Transportation costs are calculated into the prices of goods so that a profit can be made, but there does not seem to be any fixed percentage mark-up above expenditures. Vendors usually stay with kinsmen or sleep by their market stalls under heavy tarpaulins, and no calculation of their own maintenance costs enters into the pricing of goods.

Another characteristic of the peasant marketplace is the lack of storable inventory. The rapid turnover of small quantities of goods based on cash transactions militates against the accumulation and concentration of capital, especially since the higher cost of manufactured goods relative to foodstuffs drains capital upward and outward from the local marketplace. Profits are difficult to calculate, but it can be said that earnings in the peasant marketplace are extremely low, owing in part to the small quantities of goods being moved and the low buying power of the people. Large entrepreneurial profits are also difficult to obtain in the arenas of peasant exchange, where the producer can still compete as his own middleman.

Furthermore, bureaucratic controls cut sharply into earnings. Taxes are paid to local, state, and federal authorities, and entry into the marketplace as a seller requires licensing. The mayor appoints tax collectors who regulate all market behavior. License fees and taxes are paid in advance to the mayor's office. Rent for floor space, prorated according to the quality and type of merchandise being sold, is paid on the spot to tax agents. License fees are not so high as to be prohibitive, but together with taxes, they discourage many people from entering the system and serve to prevent many peasants from marketing their own produce. Fishermen in the município of Guaiamú are explicitly prohibited by the mayor's office from selling directly to the consumer "so as not to make two profits." Taxes are high, especially for goods which bring the highest margin of profit, such as meat and manufactured items.

While such a graduated system of taxation has its advantages for the very poor, it also reduces the possibility of capital formation at the levels of entrepreneurship where it might otherwise be possible. Commercialization at the local level clearly suffers from this excessive taxation, as a troubador sings in the following verse from "The Lament of the Brazilians over Taxes and Fees":

> *O pobre negociante*
> *Que tem pouca transacão . . .*
> *Paga imposto e paga renda*
> *E direito do chão*

> The pitiful vendor
> Makes hardly a cent . . .
> All he earns goes for taxes,
> For fees and for rent.

Overall, difficulties of transportation and communication account for the persistence of the peasant marketplace. Lack of access roads to the multiple smallholdings in the Brazilian interior fosters the need for peasant middlemen. Goods produced on small peasant farms, connected to rural towns by paths so narrow that they sometimes are not even suited to animal-drawn vehicles, continue to enter the local marketplace. Nonetheless, as we shall see below, inproved transportation and storage facilities increasingly allow commercial elites, acting both as wholesalers and retailers, to penetrate and dominate rural economic life.

THE DISTRIBUTION FAIR

Two or three *feiras de consumo* usually form part of a marketplace network. The complete network includes a "distribution fair" to which most middlemen must go for their merchandise. The *feira livre* and *feira de usina* in the county of Guaiamú form just such a network with the larger distribution fair in the city of Arapiraca, some four hours by jeep along unpaved roads. However, a marketplace network exists only insofar as it is worked by middlemen. The same personnel need not frequent all of the fairs in a cycle, and some traders may choose to alternate between different marketplaces.[7] Thus, while all middlemen in the area of Guaiamú must go to Arapiraca on Mondays to make their purchases, as well as to the Sunday mill fair, they may choose between several local *feiras livres*, which all take place on Saturdays.

The marketplace network, then, is a matter of individual preference and not a fixed cycle of economic trading activities. The feiras an individual chooses to attend depends on their proximity to one another and nearness to his home, since the vast majority of sellers in the local marketplaces engage in other activities on nonmarket days, either as agriculturalists working their own lands or as shopkeepers in local *mercearias* and *vendas*.

The *feiras de distribuicão* are usually located in hub cities in the transitional mixed-farming areas between the humid coastal lowlands and the drier cattle-raising sertão. These fairs are the key links in the distribution network, since various products are collected from different ecological zones and redistributed for sale in rural peasant marketplaces and in urban consumers' fairs. The principal distinguishing characteristic of distribution fairs is the buying and selling of goods in bulk for further distribution by wholesalers. These wholesalers are rapidly coming to dominate the marketing system in Northeast Brazil.

In effect, we find two spheres of activity in the distribution fairs, one reinforcing the past and one representing the future. At first glance, we are confronted with a multiplicity of peasant middlemen in a vastly enlarged *feira de consumo*. Thousands of sellers fill the streets of the city, offering a bewildering display of foodstuffs from stalls and individual sacks on the ground. Not only do these sellers feed the resident population of the hub cities where distribution fairs are located, but they carry back goods for resale to local rural populations which are too scattered and without the buying power to attract a single large-scale operator.[8] Many of the food staples were purchased only the day before from wholesalers, whose warehouses are located behind the marketplace. It is within these warehouses that perhaps the most important marketing activities take place. Urban retailers, for example, also depend on distribution-fair wholesalers for their supply of food staples for the city, although they are rarely in evidence on the day of the fair.

THE URBAN CONSUMERS' FAIR

The third type of marketplace, the *feira de abastecimento,* meets on specific days of the week as part of a large daily market. As an appendage to the permanent *mercado,* this feira is comprised almost entirely of retailers who serve large urban populations.[9] On Fair days foodstuffs fill the streets surrounding the permanent market site. Large numbers of small middlemen join the permanent *mercado* vendors in selling a wide variety of products to the urban housewife and her maid. Very few peasants sell their own produce in these urban centers, probably because the large port cities of Northeast Brazil are surrounded by fertile sugar lands where almost every available piece of cultivable land is utilized for the production of commercial export crops.

It is precisely because of the specialized export function of Brazilian coastal cities and the concomitant dearth of locally produced foodstuffs that hub cities and their *feiras de distribuicão* developed in the transitional agricultural zones, settled primarily by small peasant producers. These "second cities" are truly the backbone of Brazil. It is from them that goods are supplied to the coastal capitals, either in bulk by wholesalers or in small quantities by middlemen. It is also through them that the products of a rapidly industrializing nation filter back to the local marketplace.

THE MARKETING SYSTEM

Rural marketplaces in Northeast Brazil do not in themselves constitute the internal marketing system of this region. As we traveled the market "circuit" and spoke with peasants and middlemen about the movement of produce, it became apparent that we were not dealing with an agrarian society in which the traditional model of a marketing system was fully applicable. Such a model posits a hierarchy of marketplaces, through which goods move both horizontally and vertically, eventually arriving at urban concentrations through the continual change of hands among a variety of middlemen (Mellor, 1966:341; Chayanov, 1966:258; Dewey, 1962). Although the price of goods increases with each transaction, the margin of profit accrues in the transfer of goods from place to place, and earnings for the primary producer remain relatively small.

Goods and sellers in Northeast Brazil do not necessarily move through a hierarchy of marketplaces. There are clearly distinguishable levels of market activity, but the marketplaces are not laid out in a "nested" arrangement, where goods move in step-like fashion from lower to higher levels of market integration as they approach urban centers. In effect, these marketplaces are operating within the context of a rationalizing marketing system. Traditionally, the peasant producer entered the system through the local marketplace, which was the starting point in the upward flow of primary produce. With increased urban demands on the food supply and with the opening up of transportation and communications facilities, the function of the feira has been altered. Now, food staples have begun to follow the model of commercial export crops, in a funnel-like movement from producer to consumer through large warehouses. Wholesalers go to the farm to buy produce in bulk. In this way, crops bypass the traditional peasant marketplace, which comes to serve primarily as a mechanism for the horizontal movement of foodstuffs and as the terminal point in the downward flow of manufactured goods. In other words, the peasant marketplace has become a buyers' rather than a sellers' market.

The foregoing ethnography of the different types of marketplaces in Northeast Brazil points up the dichotomy between the traditional market network and the developing marketing system. Because of the urban demands for more food at lower cost, the marketing system tends to do away with the multiplicity of middlemen and to reduce, rather than increase, the number of effective entrepreneurs. Nevertheless, within the interlocking network of rural marketplaces, the proliferation of middlemen is a necessary ecological and social adjustment to small and widely scattered centers of production and consumption and to the scarcity of transportation and storage facilities. This important point, made by Bauer for West Africa (1954), also is relevant in the Brazilian context. The large number of middlemen in Brazilian feiras provides the greatest possible spread and distribution of goods on the local level. These middlemen function as distributors of small quantities of goods among money-poor peasants; they do not compete with large wholesalers. Peasants recognize the utility of large numbers of middlemen. A single individual with minimal capital is unable to handle large quantities of goods and therefore, can incur neither substantial risk nor loss. Middlemen dealing in perishables, which demand rapid movement, exemplify this practice.

The important question to be asked is not why such middlemen persist, but what is their sociological significance in an economic situation which can only be described as extremely marginal? It must be pointed out that alternative employment opportunities in rural Brazil are virtually nonexistent. At the same time, the improving transportation and communication facilities bring to the hinterland quantities of manufactured goods that quickly become consumer needs. The appearance of manufactured goods in the remotest weekly marketplaces causes rises in expectation which are not easily met. The worker and the peasant are constantly being exposed to a wide variety of consumer commodities, from clothing to plastic flowers. Thus, many peasants are forced into the marketplace, as the only means by which they can acquire money to meet their families' new demands. They no longer return to the farm after selling off their own crop, but begin to buy and sell the produce of others. As one peasant put it: "Nobody wants to work; everyone wants to be in business!"

Apparent minimal earnings are not an indication of the nonexistence of entrepreneurial talent on the local level. Indeed, the peasant middleman is a highly effective operator, taking full advantage of the marketplace situation. For example, one man came weekly to the feira, selling from a single sack of beans purchased at a *feira de distribuição* for $25,000 cruzeiros. Over a two-week period he managed to sell the beans for $30,000 cruzeiros, an increment of 20 percent or $5,000 cruzeiros, which equals 2.5 days' wage labor. When asked about the efficiency of his small-scale operation, the man said that he had neither the capital to buy nor clients to whom he could sell in larger quantities. At the same time, he indicated that despite the harsh effects of inflation, taxes, and fees, his expenditures of time and energy were worth the additional income, which he needed to satisfy the pressing consumer demands of his large family.

Nevertheless, there is virtually no possibility for such a middleman to become an effective entrepreneur in a rationalized marketing system. As we have indicated, socioeconomic impediments in the form of the sometimes arbitrary imposition of taxes and fees, the lack of acess to strategic resources like information, credit, patron, or family connections, and a consumer audience with limited buying power restricts the vertical mobility of these small, independent middlemen.

Small-scale vendors do not group together in cooperative endeavors in order to operate in economies of scale as do the *baliks* in Java (Dewey, 1962:88–89 passim). The marketplace in Northeast Brazil is an arena of individualistic behavior, where other forms of self-protection prevail. Thus, middlemen attempt to diversify their capital in the form of their own labor. One man sells corn and beans at the market and manioc flour from his house. He also works as a trucker, but not a jobber, of wood and rice. He does not serve as a middleman for these products because his certainty of their freight income serves as a buffer which permits his speculative buying of other primary produce. There is, however, one known instance of middlemen in the município of Guaiamú grouping together in a marketing cooperative to sell fish. This endeavor failed because, lacking adequate refrigeration and transportation facilities, the cooperative was unable to move large quantities of fresh fish as a single unit to the urban consumer market.

Entrepreneurs operating in economies of scale do appear, along with a proportional decrease in the number of intermediaries in the ever-shrinking chain between peasant producers and consumer market, but they come from a rural commercial class which is in a strategic position to control "the flow of capital goods in exchanges between groups" (Firth, 1963:22). The multiple middlemen, who move minimal units of goods as highly functional components of the peasant marketplace network, are replaced by wholesalers who have the capabilities of moving produce in bulk. Few peasant middlemen have the capital necessary to maintain large stocks of goods in warehouses for months at a time and to pay cash for produce at its source. Indeed, it is from these wholesalers that local middlemen are themselves forced to buy during nonharvest seasons or when their own produce is in short supply.

The wholesalers also funnel food staples to the city from the countryside. The trend is clear. In the state of Alagoas from

1954 to 1955 alone, the number of wholesale warehouses increased from 89 to 125, and for the first time two refrigeration
facilities were constructed (Anuário Estatístico, 1966:230). With
the appearance of these warehouses crops began to bypass the
traditional peasant marketplace, thus reducing the number of
transactions in the movement of food staples to the cities. While
we were unable to gather statistical evidence in support of this
statement, given the time and resources available to us, a study
undertaken by the Latin American Market Planning Center at
Michigan State University in conjunction with the Agency for
the Development of the Northeast (SUDENE) amply documents this trend.[10] In a comparative study of two bean-produc-
ing regions of the same urban food shed, they describe the effects of the changing marketing system:

The market structure is changing slowly as competitive pressures force
the smaller, less efficient firms out of business. This appears to be taking place more rapidly in the Irece (Bahia) than in the Al-Pe (Alagoas)
area (LAMP 1968 Chapter 9-A, page 35). The Al-Pe channel has more
different types of buyers who handle smaller market shares and perform more specialised services. Irece, on the other hand, has fewer
types of buyers handling larger market shares . . . An average of 3.4
transactions is involved in the movement of beans from producers in
the Al-Pe area through the large urban wholesalers. This compares
with less than three transactions for beans moving from the Irece area
in Bahia . . . The Irece channel appears to have eliminated the need
for many small assemblers who still survive in the Al-Pe channel (pp.
12–13).

According to the LAMP study, this same process is occurring in
the rural marketing system for rice in the São Francisco River
region of the state of Alagoas (1968, ch. 9-B).

Prices for processed and bulked food staples are fixed by
wholesalers, who are able to store large quantities against the
time when supply is short. They withhold goods from the market and control prices both on- and off-season. Wholesalers
often buy from peasants and middlemen whom they intercept
on their way to the marketplaces. This type of buying, called
por atacado, brings a lower price to the peasant producer, but
enables him to avoid the risks inherent in marketplace sales.

Because of increased transportation facilities wholesalers now can go directly to the source to buy produce for cash.

The peasant prefers to sell to wholesalers for a lower price in cash than to sell to local marketplace middlemen on credit. The wholesalers coming into the countryside make the peasant aware of market conditions. As one peasant noted, "The warehouses set the prices!" Local marketplace middlemen also derive their price information from the speculative activities of wholesalers. For example, one vendor adjusted his own prices upward when he was informed that four trucks were buying up beans on the road to the marketplace. In a sense, the wholesalers set both the purchase price to suppliers and the sale price for retailers.

A characteristic problem of peasant societies is that they are communications poor. Where lines of communication do exist they are unidirectional coming down to the peasant from the elite sectors of society. If a patron-dependent relationship has not been established, this communication flow takes place through indirect links. Oftentimes these links are the intermediaries in the marketing system. Since wholesalers have storage facilities and better information about the size of crops and commodity supplies, they are in far better position than the peasant or the local middlemen to take advantage of buying and selling opportunities.

The penetration of wholesalers into the countryside has far-reaching effects, way beyond mere price setting and commodity control. It reaches into the very heart of the system of land tenure and land usage. As urban demands increase and access roads are built into the hinterland, wholesalers extend their commercial operations. The LAMP study confirms our research findings that wholesalers find it advantageous to deal directly with large producers rather than to engage in numerous transactions with small peasants (1968: chs. 9A–B). In effect, food crops become commercial crops, and those producers who can provide bulk shipments are placed in a favored economic position.

Interestingly, this process of commercialization of food staples reinforces the sharecropping arrangements characteristic of export-crop production in Brazil. Throughout this chapter I have been discussing those peasants who have the right to independently sell their own produce. I have not dealt with the large numbers of sharecroppers whose produce has liens upon it through a variety of contractual arrangements. The routes by which sharecroppers' goods enter the marketing system is well-known. As discussed in chapter 3, even his own share of the crop is turned over to the landlord at a predetermined price, often far below the going market price. In this way large landowners—often absentee—serve as central collecting agents for wholesalers. Goods bulked in this fashion do not enter the local marketplace directly.

The relationship between the large landowner and the wholesaler is beyond the scope of this book. However, it should be pointed out that, as in the case of commercial export crop production, wholesalers furnish credit in exchange for exclusive rights to food crops and, consequently, exercise an important influence over the production sector of the rural economy.

There is a greater concentration of capital in the higher levels of the marketing system where transportation and storage facilities and ready cash are required. This is indicative of development in the agrarian sector (Belshaw 1965:82). Such development is occurring largely because of the urban demands for agricultural produce which have stimulated a process of rationalization of the internal marketing system in Northeast Brazil. The resultant commercialization in agriculture has serious consequences for production and land tenure. Peasant farms are viable and competitive as commodity producers given the marketplace network as a means of distributing minimal quantities of goods. However, atomistic peasant producers and middlemen are in themselves incapable of meeting increased urban needs. Commercial elites, attracted to the marketing system by high middlemen profits, are better able to insure a steady and continuous supply of food staples if they can buy in bulk at the source. Larger productive units can more efficiently fulfill this need if increased profit margins make capital investment advantageous.

When the marketing system begins to involve fewer intermediaries and higher rates of capitalization, it appears that consolidation of farms occurs.

Given the structure of Brazilian agrarian society, I believe that the influx of capital into the countryside through modern marketing procedures will result in further concentration of landholdings and the increased proletarianization of the rural masses. In addition to attracting commercial elites to the marketing system, high food prices also drive up the value of the land. The peasant is neither able to compete for new land nor make capital investments for improvements in the land he already owns. Despite the fact that the peasant has always been the principal producer of food staples, he finds today that his mode of production is not adequate to meet current demands. In sharp contrast to the large landowner, the Brazilian peasant has extremely limited access to sources of credit.[11] In a highly competitive rural economy, the government leaves him largely to his own devices.

The data from Northeast Brazil suggests that there is a point at which capitalization in the distributive sector of a rural economy requires like commitments of capital in the production sector, leading to the displacement or transformation of a peasantry. Such a change need not be beneficial to the society as a whole. Despite increased commercialization in Brazilian agriculture, a crisis in food supply persists. In part this can be explained by the competition between food staples and export crops for land and capital investments. The beneficiaries of an increased food market are the intermediaries and not the producers. Thus, newly concentrated landholdings may be utilized for increased production by wage labor of commercial export crops supported by government incentives (CIDA, 1966:106–7 passim). In other instances, land is acquired as a speculative hedge against inflation and utilized for the extensive grazing of cattle (*ibid.*, 24).

While the stated aims of the Brazilian government are to stimulate the development of a "middle-class" agriculture, by grouping small properties into cooperatives and modernizing and democratizing medium and large plantations (Cantanhede, 1967:8), land speculation and concentration of landholdings continues throughout Northeast Brazil. Commercialization in agriculture outpaces government planning: peasants are being evicted from their lands thus "abandoning subsistence agriculture which supplies foodstuffs to the market places . . ." (*Jornal do Comercio*, 8/13/67:13).

From this body of data which describes the traditional system of peasant marketplaces in Northeast Brazil and the changes which are currently occurring in the distributive sector of the rural economy, I can now attempt to present schematically a series of stages that will demonstrate the integrative effects which a rationalizing market system has had on the Brazilian peasantry over time. It should be remembered that these forms of peasant-marketing integration in the supply of food staples may exist simultaneously but represent a continuum of development. Together with Joyce Riegelhaupt, I have delineated five stages in the process of rationalization of the regional marketing system in Northeast Brazil (see Table 6).

Stage 1. The peasant retails his own goods in the local marketplace. This is an ideal stage, representing near-perfect competition (Belshaw, 1965:57, 77), which is unlikely to have existed in Brazil. Indeed, the early travel literature reports the buying of bulk goods by wholesalers and strict controls over the marketing of certain produce.

Stage 2. The incipient upward flow of goods through peasants who sell to middlemen. This occurs primarily at the local marketplace, but also at distribution fairs. Most sales to middlemen are done on credit, the producer being paid immediately after the cash resale has been transacted.

Up to this point both stages are characterized by labor intensive operations in both production and distribution.

Stage 3. Middlemen go to the source to buy in larger quantities and sell either in the marketplace or, occasionally, to wholesalers. Again, the initial transaction usually is made on

Table 6. Stages in the Marketing System

Participants	Predominant Types of Markets	Marketing Inputs	Production Inputs
Stage 1. pp-co	Local marketplace	Labor-intensive	Labor-intensive
Stage 2. pp-mm-co	Local marketplace and distribution fair	Labor-intensive	Labor-intensive
Stage 3. pp-mm-W-co	Distribution fair with increased growth in local marketplace	Increased capitalization through wholesaling	Labor-intensive
Stage 4. pp-W-co	Distribution fair and urban consumers' market	Increased capitalization on all levels of distribution	Labor-intensive
Stage 5. alternatives: (a) P-W-co	Urban consumers' market	Capital-intensive	Capital-intensive
(b) pp-Wmm-co	Marketing cooperatives for urban areas	Capital-intensive	Capital-intensive
(c) Ppp-W-co	Urban consumers' market	Capital-intensive	Capital-intensive through voluntary cooperation

pp = peasant producer
co = consumer
mm = middlemen
W = wholesalers
P = large-scale producers

credit, while subsequent sales are for cash. At this stage the economic system is labor-intensive in agriculture and industry, although there is increased capitalization in the marketing of goods, particularly manufactured items. The cost of both primary produce and finished goods is high. The growth of the local marketplace is stimulated by the appearance of manufactured goods and increasing horizontal exchanges.

The marketing system in the county of Guaiamú and in the state of Alagoas is now transitional between this stage and the stage below.

Stage 4. Wholesalers begin to bypass the middlemen and go directly to the peasant producer. Since they pay cash, the peasant producer is willing to sell on a first-come first-served basis, often at a lower price. This stage is marked by development of the rural infrastructure, although a lack of information prevails at the local level. A high degree of capitalization is required in the distributive sector. Prices for the entire system are controlled at this level by the wholesalers. The stage has many of the characteristics which Chayanov describes as a "sweatshop system" of agriculture (1966:257).

Between Stages 4 and 5 a transition occurs, in which market demands require adjustments in the agrarian structure. This leads to a number of possible alternatives.

Stage 5. (*a*) The prevailing tendency in Northeast Brazil is for wholesalers, operating in highly capitalized economies of scale, to want to deal directly with large-scale producers, who assure a steady and continuous supply of food staples at a central delivery point. Purchases are made on credit to privately owned, large-scale farms. (*b*) Another form of supplying urban areas with quantities of foodstuffs grown on small individual plots is through marketing cooperatives. However, these are rare in Northeast Brazil. (*c*) Peasants group themselves into cooperatives for the production and sale of goods to wholesalers. A number of experimental "cooperatives" which furnish technological and educational assistance to their members are now found in Northeast Brazil.

It is this "vertical concentration" of small farms through cooperatives that Chayanov thought would enable the Russian peasant labor farm to compete successfully on the market (1966:266).[12] It is important to note that cooperatives are viable only at this level. I feel that cooperatives are best viewed as a concomitant of this stage of development, rather than as a catalyst to development per se, a suggestion I will pursue further in the next section when I take up the general topic of cooperatives.

I believe that Northeast Brazil now finds itself in the critical transition between Stages 4 and 5, and it is precisely this state of affairs which is largely responsible for the tensions that exist in the rural society. I am not suggesting that the rationalization of the marketing system presupposes a particular system of production, nor will I speculate on the comparative benefits of the apparent alternatives.[13] I certainly cannot predict here the type of land-tenure system which will develop in any one nation. Such a prediction would involve a complex set of ecological, demographic, social structural, economic, and political considerations (Moore, 1966; Warriner, 1965). After all, agricultural development is a two-part process: the marketing system will lead to a restructuring of the production system when the latter is unable to meet consumer demands. In the Brazilian case, this restructuring will result in the consolidation and concentration of landholdings, reinvestment in commercial crop production, as in cattle raising, the displacement of peasants from their land, and the proletarianization of rural labor.

PANACEAS OF DEVELOPMENT

The Brazilian government has taken a number of steps, short of outright agrarian reform, to "alleviate" the peasant problem, and it seems appropriate at this point to discuss, however cursorily, some of the alternatives presented to peasants who find themselves funneled out of the traditional agrarian system in increasing numbers. A discussion of the movements of social protest and the politics of confrontation that enliven Brazilian agrarian history will be deferred to chapters 5 and 6 in favor of a more specific focus on the "developmental" panaceas that now appear to be in the forefront of government planning (*Brasil-Plano Decenal . . . 1967*).

I am not suggesting that these alternatives are viable or that the real solution to Brazil's agrarian crisis will not of necessity be an essentially *political* one. Indeed, the proposals that are being put forth at the highest levels of government are responses to political pressures which reflect, in every respect, the prevailing "developmental" ideology of the Brazilian ruling class.[14] They have been precipitated more by a recognition of the retarding effects on national development of a lagging agricultural sector and by the need to ensure a supply of foodstuffs to a demanding urban electorate, than by any real concern for the desperate plight of the peasantry.

A reliance on industrialization and rural-urban migration as a "natural" solution to the agrarian crisis only shifts the locus of social tension from the countryside to the city, while heightening the crisis in food supply. Colonization and resettlement schemes, rural industrialization, and various attempts to come to grips with mounting rural worker discontent through ad hoc legislation on work contracts and fringe benefits are piecemeal measures and not a comprehensive program to ameliorate the worsening condition of the rural masses. At best they represent the vague hopes of a government committed to the inviolability of private property and to the idea of development at any cost.

By failing to come to grips with the fundamental problem of an inequitable agrarian structure and by fostering increased commercialization in agriculture through inputs into the marketing sector, the Brazilian government only aggravates an already extremely serious problem. By encouraging the development of commercial agriculture on large farms while at the same time attempting to stabilize existing small farms through a system of "cooperatives" with little funding and few guarantees, they generate a situation of potential conflict. By moving excess populations en masse to undeveloped agricultural frontiers, which are already the locus of exaggerated land speculation, they recreate the fundamental dilemma of Brazilian agrarian society.

RURAL-URBAN MIGRATION

Brazilians have always demonstrated a high degree of geographic mobility. Internal migration is part of an extended historical process through which a massive labor force has moved freely across the nation from the slave plantations and drought-ridden hinterland of the Northeast to the gold mines of Minas Gerais in the eighteenth century, to the coffee fields of Rio de Janeiro and São Paulo in the nineteenth century, to the Amazon rubber trails in the late nineteenth century and, in the early twentieth century, to the cacao plantations in southern Bahia state. However, the two current trends in migration have as their most immediate precursor, the vast movement of people in the 1930s and 1940s from the Northeast to the coffee and cotton fields of São Paulo and Paraná states and to the burgeoning industrial triangle that frames the cities of São Paulo, Rio de Janeiro, and Belo Horizonte (Diegues Junior 1959a:111–12).

These current migratory streams are of several kinds. On the one hand, there is a sizable rural migration from farm to farm, within and between the diverse geographic regions. Some of this intra- and inter- regional rural movement is seasonal and not unlike migrant farm labor elsewhere. However, the bulk of it represents a permanent resettlement of rural populations along Brazil's booming southern frontier, where they enter into the coffee economy as dependent colonos on ever-expanding estates. Each of these different trends in migration—temporary rural-urban, permanent rural-urban, seasonal, permanent rural resettlement, and even the specific case of the exodus of drought victims from the Northeast—necessitates a complete

study in its own right if we are to be able to isolate the total
range of factors which enter into a peasant's decision to migrate
or to remain on the land in each case.

For the moment, I would like to look at the better-known
phenomenon of rural-urban migration, since it is sometimes
suggested that industrialization and urban growth could be a
"natural" solution to the problem posed by the dislocation of
masses of peasants and rural workers. Although it was always
an historical phenomenon that accompanied the manumission
of slaves in the seventeenth and eighteenth centuries, rural-urban migration to Brazil's coastal cities has grown to significant
proportions, estimated at approximately 6.3 million people between 1950 and 1960, or roughly one-sixth of the total rural population in 1960. The movement of these people into the shanty
towns and squatter slums of the major Brazilian cities has had a
tremendous effect on general demographic patterns, and while
Brazil remained an essentially rural nation in the 1960s, the
population balance was rapidly shifting into the cities.

Population grew explosively, by 37 percent, in the decade
after 1950. Yet, the rural growth rate of 17 percent lagged far
behind the 70 percent estimated for some urban centers during
the same period (CIDA 1966:46–47). Paraná was the only state
in which the rural population kept pace with urban growth, and
that too is attributable to the migration of rural workers to the
expanding coffee fields along the state's western frontier. The
enormous growth rate of virtually all Brazilian cities is explained by rural-urban migration rather than natural rates of
growth. For example, migration to Rio de Janeiro and São Paulo
from other parts of Brazil accounted for more than 68 percent
and 60 percent respectively of the population increases in those
cities between 1940 and 1950 (Smith 1963:155). However, since
all Brazilian cities, whether industrial, commercial, or administrative in character, grew at essentially the same rate (Schmitter
1971:35), it is unlikely that industrialization alone can explain
the massive exodus from rural areas.

While many of the migrants to Brazil's southern states are

from the hard-pressed Northeast, the major source of migratory labor is the developed central-south region itself.[15] Camargo argues that industrialization in the Rio de Janeiro–São Paulo–Belo Horizonte triangle stimulated interregional migration, from the Northeast to new rural areas in the south, by draining off local rural populations into industry and requiring their replacement. He suggests that it is higher industrial salaries, as compared to wage opportunities in agriculture, that attracts migrants to these cities (1960:115).

While there can be no doubt that the city represents a hope and a promise to the peasant, it is obvious that the tremendous regional mobility of rural Brazilians reflects the general agrarian crisis now facing the nation. Chief among the constellation of socioeconomic factors affecting rural-urban migration are the highly unfavorable work contracts and the dislocation of peasants in the face of land concentration (Souza Barros 1953:36). However, it is also likely that rural-urban migrants are attracted away from more advantageous land-tenure arrangements by employment, educational, and recreational opportunities in the cities.

Rural Brazilians place a high value on *movimento,* or action, and they know that it is to be found in the coastal cities. In addition to limited occupational opportunities, rural towns and villages do not offer sufficient educational facilities. Many rural villages have no schools at all, and there is a serious lack of good teachers even in those that boast a tiny schoolhouse. Men who manage to obtain the rudiments of education in rural Brazil are likely to move away in search of more secure and profitable jobs, and those who have gone off to seek further education in the cities are unlikely to return to the village, which they come to look upon as *atrasado,* or backward. Entertainment, even in the large interior towns in rural Brazil, is limited to the local movie house, Sunday soccer matches, or an occasional dance at the local club. Most rural towns and villages, which are without electricity, cannot even boast these diversions, and entertainment is often limited to folk games, serenades, and "footing" around the main square. There is, then, a compelling attraction in the city's promise of excitement in addition to work or school.

Throughout Brazil, the migrants have been collectively designated as *pau de arara,* or parrot's perch, an apt if somewhat denigrating description of the passengers traveling down the hot, bumpy roads, crowded into open trucks where they stand clutching the railing for balance. Each day, many make the trip on buses and trains, or even on foot, sometimes leading a heavily laden mule or balancing their meager possessions on their heads. A still larger number of these *retirantes,* as the escaping victims of the periodic droughts in the Northeast are known, travel on the paddle-wheel steamers that make the long, twenty-day journey through the backlands up the São Francisco River from the Bahian sertão to Pirapora, Minas Gerais, from where there are bus connections to São Paulo. On this trip, the migrants suffer devastating heat and dryness, sleeping on top of cargo on the lower deck or in hammocks strung one above the other on flatboats towed behind. Yet, the deprivations of the journey are minimized by the hope of a future, when none was left behind.

The flow of traffic into the cities goes on at an incredible rate. The ultimate destinations are São Paulo, Rio de Janeiro, and Brasilia, where the promise of jobs in industry, the building trades, and as domestic servants, lures men and women with little training and few skills from across the nation. However, the migrants also come from the interior to all of the state capitals and to other cities that are sprouting along the heavily traveled new highways. Migration formerly occurred in step fashion, with individuals gradually making their way from rural villages to municipal seats, then on to the state capitals and the great cities of the central-south. Now, however, many migrants go directly to metropolitan areas where they take up residence with relatives who often have prearranged jobs for them.

The majority of migrants actually travel with their families and remain permanently at their destinations. Once exposed to the adventure and promise of the city, few want to return home.

Only 27 percent of the migrants to the south in 1952 returned to the Northeast, and this percentage is usually lower (Diegues Junior 1959a:119). It is interesting to note that the largest number of returnees came from São Paulo, one indication perhaps that the promises of that fast-growing industrial center often go unfulfilled.

Those who choose to see the agrarian crisis in Brazil as stemming from overcrowding on the land, rather than as a structural problem of limited access to plentiful land resources, hope that rural-urban migration will drain off excess population from rural areas while, at the same time, supplying labor to turn the wheels of the burgeoning industrial economy. To date, however, the rapid growth of Brazil's cities has only added to the particular difficulties of unemployment, housing, crime, health and sanitation, public services, and the long extant problem of maintaining an adequate supply of foodstuffs and other primary produce to the urban and industrial sector of the economy. Mechanized industry is simply not absorbing the greater number of migrants into its labor force (Schmitter 1971:27). Then, too, the demand is for skilled labor in the industrial complexes of Brazil, and the great bulk of rural migrants are ill-equipped to do more than manual or domestic labor. While the salaries they command are often far higher than their previous earnings, they are still inadequate to meet the skyrocketing cost of living in urban areas.

Living conditions in Brazilian cities are exceedingly difficult. Upper- and middle-class demands for housing have created a building boom, accompanied by excessive land speculation and extremely high rents, forcing young people and the lower-middle classes, who operate on limited budgets in an inflationary economy, to distant suburbs from which they must commute many hours a day. The recent immigrants live anywhere and nowhere. The slums and squatter settlements that they come to occupy are in many ways worse than their previous homes in rural areas. In Rio de Janeiro, despite untiring government attempts to clear them away, the infamous favelas cling precariously on the mountainsides, tapping power lines for electricity but lacking in water and sanitation facilities. In São Paulo they hug the marginal areas of the city, where transportation is inadequate and commuting to the industrial parks difficult and costly. In Salvador, Recife, Belém, and Manaus they are built on makeshift piles and walkways above the tidelands, which are sometimes reclaimed by the repeated dumping of garbage. They surround Brasilia, wooden shacks standing in pitiful contrast to the monumental architecture of that futuristic city.[16] In other places, laborers often sleep on the construction sites where they work. A carnival song describes the plight of urchins, called "sand captains," in Salvador. It goes, "I have nowhere to live. Therefore, I live in the sand!"

Industrialization and rural-urban migration, then, need not go hand in hand, and offer a rather troublesome alternative to the agrarian crisis. Within a short time, and certainly with the passing of a generation, that initial sense of excitement and of upward mobility which the peasant might have felt in his encounter with the city has passed. The feeling of elation that came with the acquisition of a radio, a wristwatch, or any other commodity that serves as a mark of status and an indicator of the good life turns rather quickly into the economic and social frustration of the slum dweller. The job he hoped for he cannot obtain, and the security of the peasant household dissolves somewhat rapidly in an urban setting where each individual must learn to fend for himself. His poverty, his manner, and his style of dress soon make the migrant feel out of step with the *movimento* of the city, and the much talked-about *cachaça, fütebol*, and samba are hardly palliatives to the urban worker once he has been exposed to a better way of life. Despite the fact that the federal government subsidizes education, the shanty towns and squatter settlements, like the rural village, lack school facilities, and the possibility of a secondary education means little when time is money that cannot be spent on schooling.

As Charles Wagley notes, the second generation of migrants to the cities is not as likely to be complacent in face of the deprivations of the city (1963:121). It is no wonder, in fact, that the focus of revolutionary attentions has shifted to the cities and that the government's major concern in the 1970s has become the urban-based insurgent movement. For some, at least, the trouble in the cities is attributable to rural-urban migration, and many would like to see it slowed down or stopped entirely (Smith 1963:156). The government has begun to try to fix rural populations on the land, either through rural industrialization, colonization and resettlement schemes, or—more deliberately—by organizing work gangs on roads and dams in the Northeast, for instance, as they did by the hundreds of thousands during the drought of 1970–71.

RURAL INDUSTRIALIZATION

Rural industrialization has gained widespread support in Brazil as an alternate means of developing the hinterland, stabilizing rural populatons, and upgrading the quality of rural life. As a panacea for modernization in the rural sector, it has been in the forefront of development planning for the Northeast and has been widely encouraged by USAID and a number of university-sponsored development projects in Brazil. Following the example of the original Asimow project, through which the University of California undertook the development of a variety of cottage industries in the northeastern state of Ceará, several light industries were set up in the 1960s throughout the Northeast by RITA (Rural Industrial Technical Assistance), under the joint sponsorship of the Brazilian state governments and American universities. Unfortunately, although all of these endeavors are said to be experimental in nature, there have been few attempts to date, to accompany them with related anthropological or sociological research. Yet, it would seem to be highly appropriate to evaluate the projects underway from the perspective of the social sciences, as well as to undertake studies in the many factory towns that already exist throughout Brazil, as Juares Brandão Lopes has admirably done in a recent study (1967). Textile mills, fruit-canning plants, ceramic and glass factories, and the like have dominated many a rural Brazilian community in this century and the last, and the careful study of these extant factory towns would undoubtedly provide us with important data on income distribution, social stratification and social mobility, political participation, etc., in these communities.

Implicit in the idea of rural industrialization is the notion that a preindustrial peasantry can be transformed into a participating member of an industrializing society. Yet, the evidence we now have would seem to indicate that despite increased social differentiation and differential evaluation of occupational statuses in the lower strata of these factory towns, they are not very different in social organization from the traditional agrarian-structured communities in the same areas. Similarly, the establishment of new industries in rural Brazilian towns does not necessarily redistribute income in rural areas to any great extent, but serves largely to strengthen the hand of existent commercial elites who are in favorable positions to take advantage of the new opportunities as they arise.

Even when new entrepreneurial talent is evidenced, as in the sisal-growing economy of the Northeast, traditional patterns of stratification predominate and few benefits appear to filter down to the lower strata of rural society (Gross 1970), as was discussed in the last chapter. On the contrary, all too often the local peasantry is transformed into an impoverished rural industrial proletariat. In one specific case, the owners of a textile mill at Penedo, on the São Francisco River, turned their considerable political capital into investment capital by arranging to receive substantial financial and technological assistance from USAID for the purchase and operation of new machinery. The net result was that they laid off a large number of their own employees and so outstripped the production of a rival textile mill across the river that it was forced out of business, causing a very serious problem of unemployment in the region.

COLONIZATION AND RESETTLEMENT

Colonization and resettlement schemes have been devised in Brazil since the colonial period, when they were advanced in order to supplant slave with free labor on plantations or to ensure production of necessary foodstuffs to growing urban centers. The earliest colonization projects involved the planned immigration of Europeans and Japanese to the coffee plantations of Rio de Janeiro, São Paulo, and Paraná states, or to mixed-farming agricultural colonies primarily in the southern states of Rio Grande do Sul and Santa Catarina.[17] However, in 1945, after innumerable difficulties with concentrations of German settlers, the Vargas regime issued a decree on colonization which stipulated that at least 30 percent of the land in any colony had to be ceded to Brazilians (Diegues Junior 1959a:137). In 1953, Vargas approved the National Colonization Plan (*O Plano Nacional de Colonização*), which was later modified to include a variety of resettlement projects by which native Brazilian populations could be removed under the auspices of a private company to frontier areas or to large estates appropriated for the purpose in the states of Paraná, Alagoas, Guanabara, and São Paulo. Since the present government is advancing plans for the colonization and development of the Amazon Valley as a solution to the current agrarian problems in Brazil, it might be useful to examine briefly some of these earlier resettlement schemes.

THE MARANHÃO PLAN

The so-called Maranhão Plan, elaborated in the early 1960s, envisioned the resettling of 5,000 people per year over a five-year period in lands held in the public domain in the Pindaré-mirim region of the state of Maranhão. The actual settlement project was to be undertaken by "young" families, comprised of four working-age members, who would agree initially to work, for a wage, on the construction of roads, wells, houses, and other necessary facilities, before settling down on plots of land to which they would receive a "title" as renter. Although no school-age children were to be included in the project, in order to avoid, for the time, the costs and logistic problems of education, the plan was elaborated around the family as a basic economic and social unit.

A number of working families were to be grouped together in circular villages with individual plots of land radiating out, in a pie-shaped manner, from each home. Each family was to receive 50 hectares of land, along with some initial financing and technical assistance, in return for planting only 5 hectares each year, and rotating their plots every eight years. No wage labor was to be utilized apart from occasional seasonal workers at harvest time, in order to reduce disequalities and thereby "maintain the social equilibrium of the community." A cooperative was to undertake all operations of production, maintenance, and marketing. Some local industries were envisioned once the colony was well-established. The cost for the initial three-year period was estimated at $10.300 million cruzeiros or slightly more than $2 million U.S. dollars at that time (III *Plano Diretor*, 1966–68:128ff).

The Maranhão Plan was widely criticized in Brazil on a number of counts. It was undertaken in an extremely remote area, far from consumer markets and without roads for transporting produce. The planners, from the Agency for the Development of the Northeast (SUDENE), showed a grievous lack of concern for the social, educational, and health needs of the colonizers. By concentrating on a mere 2 percent of the population of the Northeast's least densely populated areas, the agreste and the sertão, the project was said to be "pulverizing" resources that otherwise might be applied more generally to the problems of the region. Certainly, the Maranhão Plan was not coming to grips with the basic structural problems of Brazilian agrarian society. In fact, before the project of resettlement even could get underway, an estimated 50,000 to 60,000 squatters took possession of the colony's lands. The project's planners disclosed that they thought this was a "blessing in disguise," since it resolved the logistic problem and cut the cost of moving settlers there; but, in effect, the Maranhão Plan ended up as a salvage operation, attempting to limit the flow of squatters into the area in the hope of saving one of the last forest reserves in the Northeast.

PINDORAMA

The Pindorama colony, in the Northeast state of Alagoas, was founded in 1956 by the Companhia de Progresso Rural under the directorship of Rene Bertholet, a Swiss who came to Brazil in 1949 to supervise the resettlement of German refugees at the agricultural colony of Guarapava, in the state of Paraná. The ex-

periment at Guarapava had been initiated by Caritas and the
Swiss Social Democrat Labor Movement and financed fully by
the Swiss government, to which Bertholet attributed the colony's success. The progress made at Guarapava led the Brazilian government to invite Bertholet to elaborate Vargas' National
Colonization Plan of 1953, which he claims to have done under
the guiding principle that "to avoid the trouble of bureaucracy,
all projects of colonization should be privately operated" (personal interview, 10/5/67). He was also asked to found another
immigrant colony in southern Brazil, but declined in the belief
that the attentions of the Brazilian government should be
directed to their own peasants in the Northeast, where the need
for experiments in agrarian reform was acute. With a colleague
from Caritas, Bertholet founded the Companhia de Progresso
Rural and acquired government permission to start two internal-
colonization programs, one at Pindorama and the other in the
state of Minas Gerais.

With minimal financing through a Brazilian government
agency, the Superintendencia de Moeda a Credito (SUMOC),
and the sale of some stock (agios), the Pindorama colony was established on an extensive forested plateau that stretched for
33,834 hectares along a humid valley, largely owned by a family
of sugar planters and local political power-holders. Although
the rich valley bottom lands were entirely planted in sugarcane,
Bertholet believed that with fertilization and irrigation the tablelands could be made to yield productive farm crops. The
original colony, comprised of 70 settler families, soon ran into
financial difficulties and, in 1959, Bertholet withdrew from the
Companhia de Progresso Rural and moved to Pindorama to become resident manager of the faltering venture in cooperativism.

By 1967, 520 colonist families were each settled on 25-hec-
tare plots scattered in small communities throughout the table-
land, where they cultivated the maracujá fruit as their principal
activity. An additional 80 families lived at the central town of
Pindorama, where they provided the fruit-canning plants, the
administrative offices, the school and health posts, electricity

and machine shop, ceramic kilns, and lumber mills with 130 workers. Another 100–150 families lived in the area awaiting the assignment of plots of lands, which Bertholet estimated could be made available to at least 600 more settler families.

All of the colonists at Pindorama came from the Northeast states of Alagoas, Pernambuco, and Sergipe. The only requirements for receipt of a plot of land were that the family be landless, homeless, possessed of a birth certificate, and "well acquainted with agriculture." Families received an initial loan to finance the land purchase, the construction of a temporary thatched-roof house of wattle-and-daub, and the planting of a small crop of maracujá and certain subsistence crops, like manioc and corn, some of which could be sold at the local marketplace that now operates at Pindorama. After an eighteen-month trial period, if the colonist seemed well-integrated into the life of the colony, another loan was granted for the construction of a permanent house and the extension of his fields. In return, the colonist promised to continue to grow a stipulated quota of maracujá, which was processed into a juice concentrate at one of the colony's two processing plants. The second plant processed a fruit called *rosela*, which is made into jelly.

The growth of the maracujá industry is striking. The land area on which the fruit is planted increased from 50 hectares in 1959 to 620 hectares in 1962 (Correa 1963:481). By 1967, the colony was producing 1,200 tons of fruit a year and bottling over 25,000 cases, which were marketed in all of Brazil's major cities through the colony's own marketing apparatus. In addition, coconuts, rosela, rice, and mangoes were being produced in sufficient quantities to be sold abroad. The colony also boasted a herd of over 200 high-bred cattle. Foodstuffs are grown for home consumption with some small surplus being sold at the local Sunday market. The lack of an extensive local market for food crops evidently led to the industrialization of maracujá and rosela as the mainstay of the colony (Bernades 1967:75).

Pindorama does stand out as a remarkable achievement in sharp contrast to the extreme poverty and misery of neighboring villages, but it does so only through continued massive outside assistance. Each of its several nucleated villages has its own water system, chapel, and primary school. There are, in fact, a total of fifteen schools and thirty teachers in the colony, as well as a trade school sponsored and financed by the German government. Technical aid in the form of five engineer-agronomists were also provided by the German government. In addition, the American Peace Corps, Dutch and German overseas volunteers, and Papal Volunteers have at one time or another served the colony with well over fifty people, mainly technicians, nurses, and teachers. The colony boasts a permanent doctor and dentist, both of whom are supported by German funds. When I visited Pindorama in 1967, both German and Brazilian flags flew over all of the public buildings in the colony.

In an interview I conducted with Rene Bertholet on that occasion, he confessed to being overly hopeful in his belief that the colony could be viable without the massive financial support of the Brazilian or foreign governments and that the Northeast Brazilian peasant could easily become an independent farmer. As formerly landless agricultural workers, the Pindorama colonists were unaccustomed to making autonomous decisions about production. They came to depend fully on the dictates of the colony's administration, which was developing along obvious bureaucratic lines. The colonists, like the other peasants in the area, expected the same noblesse oblige that they received from former patrons, particularly from former landlords who, in fact, still owned sugar plantations in the valley and vied with Bertholet—often violently—for political hegemony in the county, a subject which will be discussed in some detail in chapter 5. However, perhaps the most significant admission about the success of this agrarian experiment came in the form of Bertholet's request to the Institutó de Acucar e Alcool (The Sugar and Alcohol Institute) for permission to turn large areas of land over to the production of sugarcane and the construction of a sugar mill at Pindorama, a request which was denied, largely at the insistence of the neighboring sugar mill owners.

ITAGUAÍ

Benno Galjart (1965, 1967) has recently provided us with a generally pessimistic view of the function of colonization and resettlement projects in the scheme of agricultural development in Brazil. Galjart describes in detail the Nucleo Colonial de Santa Cruz, an agricultural colony of some 12,000 hectares located only about 70 kilometers southwest of the city of Rio de Janeiro. The project began in 1930 when 270 farms were established at Santa Cruz, part of a large, rather neglected estate previously owned by Jesuits and reclaimed for the purpose of establishing an agricultural colony which would provide foodstuffs for the growing population of Rio de Janeiro. An additional 800 farms were established after World War II at Piranema, a section of the same estate lying to the south of a river of the same name that divides the colony into two distinct halves. This latter project clearly has suffered from lack of contact with the urban center, owing to faulty communication that resulted from the loss of a bridge in 1954, which has never been replaced.

Each of the settlers at Itaguaí was given a farm of approximately 10 hectares at an advantageous price, with small installment payments scheduled over a ten-year period. Cash crops were grown primarily for the Rio de Janeiro market. Large tracts of land were given over to pasture. Technical assistance, while haphazard and unorganized, was available, and the settlers readily accepted all forms of innovations. As Galjart stresses, "The ease with which innovations are adopted and dropped again, and the ease with which one crop is substituted for another suggests that the settlers have little trouble in accepting change. There seems to be little mental resistance to technological innovations" (1967:47).

Still, the project can hardly be considered a success, particularly if success is measured by the stability of the settlers and improvements in their own standard of living. To be sure, the colony has increased the supply of foodstuffs to Rio de Janeiro, but this very integration might well be leading to its demise. As an immediate threat to the colony's stability, there has been a tremendous turnover of farmers, manifest by considerable farm-to-farm mobility and the selling off of lands. At least 60 percent of the farms have changed hands in the forty years of the colony's existence and many of these more than once (Galjart 1965:52). About 40 percent of the landowners have become absentee (*ibid.*, 53), and 62.4 percent use sharecroppers and wage laborers for their farming activities (*ibid.*, 60).

Galjart attributes the selling off of farms to dissatisfaction with the individual results obtained to date and with pessimism about the colony's future prospects. The lack of financial resources is not seen as a major problem in itself, although obtaining available credit involves farmers in bureaucratic red tape that many prefer to forego. Rather, the colony appears to suffer primarily from ecological and economic factors which affect both productivity and profit. Lack of drainage and subsequent flooding is a constant problem. The incidence of plant disease and plague also has been high, and insecticides have produced poor results (*ibid.*, 57–58). In addition, prices paid to the colonists for their produce generally have been quite low, largely because market middlemen take excessive profits, exercising particular control over the settlers at Piranema, who lack direct access to the weekly markets in Rio de Janeiro.

It is not surprising, given our previous discussion of the effects of a rationalized marketing system on land tenure and usage, that consolidation of farms and concentration of landholdings is a serious problem in the Itaguaí colony. The intrusion of outside land speculators is occurring mainly in the Piranema section, where land is cheaper because of poor drainage (*ibid.*, 49–50) and where market middlemen have greater control over the disposition of crops (*ibid.*, 55). In its discussion of the Itaguaí colonization project, the CIDA study describes the "hemming in" of the colony by extensive cattle ranches, which do not allow for the expansion of farms, causing excessive subdivision of existing units and subsequent overcrowding on the land. And Galjart, too, notes that although the aim of the colony is "to provide the poorest with the means of progress . . . the study has proved that poor peasants are unlikely to build up a modern, efficient and profitable family farm from scratch" (*ibid.*, 139). In fact, many have been forced to engage in wage labor as a supplement to their own farming enterprises.

Unfortunately, Galjart does not inquire into the feedback effects of marketing on the system of land tenure in this region of tremendous urban growth and industrialization, where commercialization in agriculture increases at a heightened pace. Rather, he prefers to seek an explanation on another level, namely that "the process of modernization must comprehend a change of ethos in Brazil" (*ibid.*, 30), and sums up by stating: "For the great majority of the settlers the project has made little difference; they have remained at a low level of living and agricultural development. Part of the reason for this stagnation lies, as asserted, in the persistence of traditional value patterns in farming and social relations" (*ibid.*, 138).

On the one hand, a "Grand Tradition" of Brazilian agriculture in which a preference is shown for large landholdings, cash-crop production, and monoculture is viewed as inimical to the success of colonization schemes, although it has been pointed out elsewhere that a better explanation for the high turnover in farms and the concentration of landholdings might be found in a discussion of the optimal size of farming units there (Warriner 1969:302). On the other hand, the inability of the settlers to cooperate for the good of the community is held to account for the lack of sustained economic growth, although it occasionally furthers the success of specific individuals. Itaguaí, like most colonization projects, is intricately tied to a cooperative program. An extended discussion of rural "ethos" and cooperative behavior will follow in the next section. For the moment, suffice it to say that there is sufficient ecological and economic material available within Galjart's study to account for the lack of success at Itaguaí and, perhaps, to explain the persistence of the so-called "traditional values" themselves.

Explanations in terms of ethos or culture too often lead to invidious comparisons of ethnic groups in order to account for the differential success between foreign and native-Brazilian colonization programs. Yet, the cultural differences between foreign and native Brazilian settlers should not be overemphasized. The CIDA study makes an important point regarding Japanese and Brazilian settlers in Itaguaí:

The idea that 'cultural differences' explain the differences in the success of the two groups of settlers is perhaps exaggerated or incomplete. No one can deny that the upbringing and experience of the Japanese prepare them for intensive land use and a close cooperation for production and marketing; while Brazilian farm people had centuries of lessons in extensive farming under autocratic traditions in rural communities and have been contrivers or victims of political influence. But it is also clear that the conditions under which Japanese and Brazilian settlers were admitted to the project, and under which the project had been allowed to develop, were so different that they too explain in part the divergencies between the two groups (1966:539).

The Japanese at Itaguaí boast efficient organizational support and close social and business relationships. They were aided by their own government representatives in Brazil and were afforded considerable freedom by the Brazilian government, which released them from the social and political constraints that characterize most colonization schemes. They had their own credit and marketing institutions and were not effected by outside political influences that came to play in the project (*ibid.*, 540). Then, too, they joined together to present a united front against an alien society into which they had moved, a fact that might partially account for the differential success in foreign colonization schemes (Warriner 1969:313). In describing the success of the well-known Japanese colonization project and giant cooperative, COTIA, in the state of São Paulo, Doreen Warriner writes: "Why should there not be a COTIA for all Brazilian farmers? The answer is obvious. The Japanese government looks after its own people; the Brazilian government does not, because the big landowners can look after themselves" (*ibid.*, 316).

It should be fairly obvious from the foregoing accounts that a number of extremely serious problems confront the strategists of development who see a solution to the agrarian crisis in colonization and resettlement schemes. In most cases to date, lack of previous study of ecological and economic conditions has led to failure (Diegues Jr. 1959a:198), although lack of effective government planning, as in the Maranhão Plan, appears to be equally responsible.

The geographer Nilo Bernardes describes a settlement project at Igaci which failed miserably despite its strategic location only 70 kilometers from Maceió, the capital of the state of Alagoas, along a paved road. In the forty years of the colony's existence, no settler has yet received title to his land. In consequence, no improvements have been made, and there is a tendency to sell one's house and crop (and, in effect, the untitled property) at the first opportunity. According to Bernardes, the size of landholdings fell far short of that amount necessary to provide an adequate system of land rotation: 75 hectares in his estimation, with a median of only 25 hectares among the most prosperous farmers in the colony (Bernardes 1967:67). Until 1956, the colonists were required to give several days in *cambão* to the state agricultural post, although they received none of the promised technical assistance in return.

The colony also suffered from the usual financing problems. The cost of colonization is enormous and all too often the return on investment in food crops is hardly enough to warrant systematic inputs. Such was the case with the Pindorama colony, which soon succumbed to commercial farming and tried in vain to stabilize its income through the establishment of a sugar mill. Bernardes suggests that the well-situated colony of Pilar, also in the state of Alagoas, was also faced with this dilemma (*ibid.*, 73).

The competition for land and labor, then, spreads rapidly into colonization lands and threatens settlers, just as it does the majority of Brazilian peasants. The general trend toward consolidation of landholdings now being felt throughout Brazil also affects the colonists. Internally, there is a tendency toward concentration of landholdings by wealthier colonists. Externally, there is the constant threat of encroachment on colony lands. Even the best land resources in the Amazon basin, which the Brazilian government is now developing for resettlement projects, is undergoing speculative buying by large landowners and industrial entrepreneurs. The construction of the Transamazonian Highway and the resettlement of large numbers of peasants from Northeast Brazil on deforested lands are unlikely to provide long-term solutions to Brazil's agrarian crisis. Immediately, such steps might satisfy the reform-mongering of a few government officials and resolve some of the problems of a small proportion of the nation's population. However, what is needed in Brazil is a full-scale agrarian reform, not simply in terms of land redistribution, technical assistance, and credit financing, but a total restructuring of the agrarian society so that even the stop-gap measures of colonization and resettlement can be guaranteed.

COOPERATIVES

Cooperativism has become a byword of Brazilian development schemes. It is assumed that cooperatives can and do play a vital role in economic development as vehicles for organizing scarce and limited productive resources, for distributing credit and technological assistance among small, independent units, for ensuring equity and local control in the marketing of produce, and as institutions which encourage the democratic participation of a broad membership. Yet, in my earlier discussion of peasant economic integration I suggested that cooperatives should perhaps best be viewed, not as catalysts to development, but as concomitants of a certain stage of development in which independent farmers group together for the production and sale of their produce.[18]

I did not intend that remark as an economic statement alone; although it does assume a certain level of market integration, small-farm autonomy, and basic rural infrastructural development, on the one hand, while recognizing, on the other, that successful cooperativism might indeed encourage a degree of stabilization in agriculture that is itself a precondition to further economic growth. Notwithstanding, I believe that the successful operation of a system of cooperatives requires a degree of democratization in the structure of landholdings and the distribution of agricultural wealth, as well as a system of government guarantees that ensures the rights and privileges of all members of the social system against the infringements of the dominant socioeconomic strata of the rural society. In other words, I am questioning whether a system of cooperatives can exist and flourish in rural Brazil at all without succumbing to the continual pressures of an agrarian system which encourages the growth and prosperity of large, commercial agricultural units at the expense of small, independent peasant farms. I will pursue this discussion in the context of material already presented in the preceding section on colonization and resettlement.

In his study of Itaguaí, the government-sponsored land settlement project near Rio de Janeiro, Benno Galjart offers us another explanation of obstacles to development in the guise of "amoral familism" (Banfield 1958) and the "image of limited good" (Foster 1965). Galjart argues that one of the chief obstacles to development in Brazil is the inability of peasants, or farmers, to cooperate for the general good of the community, owing to a traditional rural ethos that is "inimical to the emergence of cooperative attitudes and joint action by social equals" (1968:85). The "traditional ethos" is described as the "patronic syndrome," characterized by:

1. The assumption that any real improvement in one's own socioeconomic situation depends not so much on one's own efforts as on favors granted by secular or supernatural powers, or on a stroke of luck.
2. The disposition to seek to establish patronage relations with people who are, or in the future may be, able to do one a good turn.
3. The absence of feelings of solidarity toward people with whom one is not related by kinship, friendship or patronage. This absence is associated with a disbelief in the presence of such feelings in others. (*Ibid.*, 86–87)

Galjart seeks to make his point by attributing the failure of three cooperatives in Itaguaí to a lack of community solidarity and to the pattern of political patronage that he sees as pervading the entire fabric of Brazilian society. One of the principal failings he notes is the lack of incorruptible leaders. His solution: ". . . in the absence of charismatic leaders, the next best [sic] is to institutionalize patronage" (*ibid.*, 113).

Even if we were to accept Galjart's implicit assumption that a system of cooperatives could be the catalyst to further development at Itaguaí, there are a number of problems inherent in the particular kind of analysis that he undertakes. First among these is that he offers us no satisfactory causal explanations for the failure of cooperativism there. While his description of rural ethos in Brazil may well be adequate, such description does not constitute an explanation of the events that occurred there. Quite to the contrary, the evidence seems to indicate that outside interference contributed greatly to the demise of the Itaguaí cooperatives, and Galjart himself indicts the leaders of the cooperative movement for their "corruption."

The "patronic syndrome" which is held responsible for these ties to the outside is said to derive from historical circumstances, but we are not given a clear picture of the ecological, social structural, and economic dimensions of the wider system in which these particular patterns of behavior manifest themselves. For example, Galjart notes that an urban cooperative in Rio de Janeiro failed because it was unable to market all of its produce and incurred substantial losses, but he does not ask similar questions about the local cases. He prefers to speak of the lack of "joint action by social equals," without ever discussing the possibility of such action within the context of a stratified social system (or within the context of the stratified subsystem that he is studying at Itaguaí). Members of the cooperative seem to have been drawn from one particular segment of the settlement's population, but unfortunately there is no calculation of differential risks as opposed to benefits for small as opposed to large farmers. We are provided with little information about intergroup relations within the settlement, and nowhere are we given a measure of "community solidarity" for this subsystem of only some forty years time depth. Indeed, why we are to expect community solidarity at all remains something of a mystery.

To return to the main point of this chapter, however, not enough was said in Galjart's account of Itaguaí about the relationship between the marketing and production sectors of the rural economy. Although Galjart is fully aware that feedback exists and that the market influences most production decisions, he does not consider that increased market demands can have serious effects on the rate of farm turnover and the concentration of landholdings in the colony. Again, studies of the kind Galjart undertakes can be faulted for seeking ultimate explanations in terms of values and norms rather than in more fundamental causes, as, for example, when he discusses land tenure, production, and the allocation of resources in the settlement as part of the "Grand Tradition" of Brazilian agriculture—large landholdings, cash-crop production, and monoculture. I do not doubt that these exist as values in rural Brazil, just as I do not doubt that there is a "patronic syndrome," but I do ask for a better explanation of why these values and attitudes persist in an area of tremendous urban growth and industrialization marked by a high degree of commercialization in the rural sector. Only when we know the nature of the total socioeconomic system in which these norms and values operate will we be in a position to understand fully their persistence and their possible long-range effects on future agricultural development in Brazil.

In my own previous study of *The Raft Fishermen* I pointed out that there is both a long tradition of mutual aid among Brazilian peasants and a continuing need for cooperation, familial and interfamilial alike, if the peasant economic system is to be maintained (Forman 1970). As Johnson also recently describes, peasants seek to maximize security and minimize risk by extending socioeconomic ties both horizontally and vertically in a tight network of interpersonal relationships (1970).

The vertical ties of patron-dependency and the changes that they are undergoing in the increasingly commercialized rural economy were described at length in chapter 3, where it was pointed out that both individual competition and factionalism in local communities are often closely related to processes of social mobility and to social change. That is, potentially disruptive rivalries tend to manifest themselves in situations where local bigwigs attempt to shoulder aside their compeers in the competitive quest for new opportunities. For their part, the horizontal attachments that characterize social life in rural communities appear to garner some strength, at least temporarily, in the wake of increased socioeconomic pressures at the local level. That is, through the close cooperation of kinsmen and friends individual peasant units seek to insulate themselves as best they can from the negative effects of commercialization.

Such recent expressions of cooperation or reliance on others manifest themselves in the pooling of resources and in the sharing of earnings acquired through individual activities in diverse household occupations, more than in the traditional forms of mutual aid, such as the *mutirão*, or cooperative work party, which has been described in much of the literature on rural life (Caldeirão 1956; Freitas 1948; Galvão 1959). The *mutirão*, as a form of reciprocal labor, was often utilized for the completion of specific agricultural tasks such as clearing the land, planting, or harvesting, and it still finds occasional expression today in cooperative house-building endeavors among peasants who do not have the cash resources to hire carpenters and bricklayers. Invariably, these work parties are undertaken under conditions of considerable hardship, although the ritual friends, or compadres, kinsmen, and neighbors who participate by rhythmically kneading mud under dancing feet and daubing it onto wattle walls, are treated to food and drink throughout the day. The work effort is always accompanied by song and dance and usually terminates in considerable horseplay.

Traditionally, when the *mutirão* was the accepted means of accomplishing agricultural and other tasks in lieu of a paid labor force, the members of the work party expected that they would be able to call upon the labor of their hosts, and others present, at any time that their own needs required them to do so. Today, however, as would be expected in the increasingly commercialized agricultural economy, the *mutirão* has been replaced, for the most part, by wage labor; and there is no expectation of a direct, even if delayed, return of labor in kind. It has become a simple act of giving one's time and energies to those who have been made less fortunate in the throes of socioeconomic change.

The *mutirão* was an informal expression of mutual aid based on the reciprocal exchange of labor among a relatively egalitarian and homogeneous population, often comprised of kinsmen. The cooperative, on the other hand, incorporates the peasant into a formal institution that depends for its maintenance upon a stipulated set of contractual rights and obligations between members, a system of economic redistribution for the sale of commodities and the sharing of profits, and, most important, upon a hierarchy of relationships. It smacks of authority, bureaucracy, and strict socioeconomic controls, often becoming the object of manipulation on the part of elites who seek to use it for their own aggrandizement. For example, in my study of *The Raft Fishermen,* I described the demise of the locally instituted savings and loan cooperative as a reflection of the broader sociopolitical system. Largely because they were illiterate and thus incapable of keeping necessary records and accounts, the peasant fishermen were forced to depend upon local elites, who, as representatives of one of the political parties vying for power at the village level, wanted to use the cooperative to their own advantage.

As in the case of Itaguaí, the failure of the cooperative in Coqueiral has to be seen in the broader integrative context that conditions the lives of peasants at the local level. Until this context is clearly apprehended and comprehensive measures are taken to deal with the agrarian crisis at its root, all of the so-called *panaceas of development*—rural-urban migration, rural industrialization, colonization and resettlement, cooperativism—become mere palliatives which, in the end, will also place additional pressures on the system and tend to heighten social discontent.

Chapter five–

The Nature of Integration 3: Rural Masses and the Brazilian Political Process

Democracy in Brazil was
always a lamentable misunderstanding.
BUARQUE DE HOLLANDA   1936:122

"Consequently, everything seems to assure the central authority, in the future, of a definitive triumph over the centrifugal forces of provincialism and of localism." So predicted Oliveira Vianna in 1933 in a revealing one-line epilogue to his fascinating social and political history of the Brazilian people, *A Evolução do Povo Brasileiro*. Written at a time when a fresh, liberalizing "revolution" held out the promise of a popular democracy to an emergent middle sector, this and subsequent works of the astute chronicler of the Brazilian masses (*o povo-massa*, as he called them) are all the more remarkable for the extraordinary footnote they provide to the unfolding of the Brazilian political process. For not only does Oliveira Vianna record with ingenuity and foresight the social structural and cultural components that impede the development of a democracy in Brazil, but his own interpretation of events echoes the fundamental liberal and elitist ambiguity that has haunted Brazilian political thinkers since the founding of the empire.

The question of elite versus mass is one of the fundamental obsessions of Brazilian political history, matched in intensity only by one other closely related theme, centralization versus local autonomy. I noted in chapter 2 that the economic and political units established in the colonial land-grant system (the sesmarias) provided at the outset for a smooth transition to local control by landowners rather than centralized control by Crown officials of the New World colony. Nonetheless, a problem was created for Brazil, which for centuries thenceforth has pitted centralists against localists in a protracted struggle for control over the administrative and legal apparatus of the municipality, the province, and the nation-state.

In the colonial and imperial periods, and even through the First Republic, this struggle represented no serious sectorial clash, just a polite game of politics to determine which group should govern: the elites at the center or those at the periphery.[1] Power oscillated back and forth, sometimes favoring the side of national unity, sometimes the proponents of extreme localism, but most of the time resting in the hands of provincial agrarian interests. With compromise and conciliation as the prevailing norms, agrarian and commercial elites closely followed a set of ground rules whereby politics was carefully preserved as their domain, to the exclusion of the masses of urban and rural workers alike. Occasionally, a few more participants were added to tilt the balance of power in favor of one set of elites or another. However, it was only after 1930, when urbanization gave rise to a highly vocal middle sector, that mass participation in politics actually became a concern in Brazil. Even then, the *significance*—as opposed to the extent—of that participation merits careful scrutiny.

Brazilian elites, whether agrarian or commercial, have always adopted a tutelary and paternalistic attitude toward the urban and rural masses that they have enlisted in *their* political struggles. Despite a series of liberal constitutions that sought to model Brazil along French, English, and American lines, participatory democracy has always been illusory. The cumulative inclusion of the masses in the political process in no way justifies the oft-made assumption that a democratization of the Brazilian political system was in the offing in the tumultuous de-

Rural Masses and Political Process 143

cade that ended with the military coup d'état in April 1964.[2]
Inclusion *and* exclusion more readily describe the process of
manipulation of the Brazilian masses by the real participants in
this basically anthoritarian political system. As we shall see, the
urban proletariat that Getulio Vargas molded into a political
mass was not intended to speak in its own behalf: the rural
worker could not.

Peasants and agricultural laborers in Brazil have long been
subject to the politics of dependence. As I stated in chapter 2, the recognition of property rights in slaves, as opposed to
jurisdictional rights over resident native populations, allowed
for an economic rather than a legal-political relationship between landowner and laborer, which set the pattern for the form
of social control that has since characterized Brazilian social
structure. In this system, political power was derived from ownership of land and, through property, the recruitment of dependents whose labor contracts implied additional services at the
landowner's behest. A social and cultural dimension was superimposed upon these basically economic relationships, providing a cover for the asymmetry of the economic exchanges. Submissiveness, obligation, and a profound sense of loyalty were
the peasant's contributions to the dyadic arrangements, which
had peculiarly little political content.

Until quite recently, in fact, these interactional relationships
between patrons and their dependents (and the cultural system
that reinforces them) served to impede meaningful political action among Brazilian peasants, a phenomenon which I will ana-
lyze at some length in the next chapter. For the moment, I wish
to examine the history of the struggles among elites for political
power that contributed so markedly to the process by which the
peasants began to find their own voice. These *altos e poderosos
senhores,* "high and mighty men," (Sodré 1967:211)—the patriarchs of the colonial period, the ennobled coffee bourgeoisie of
the empire, the ruling oligarchs of the Old Republic, and the
agro-industrialists of the New Republic—have wielded power
over the rural masses, either in the form of local autonomy or as
control over the legally constituted authority in their respective

municipalities. The nature of their power struggle at any given time, has defined the nature of peasant political participation, as well.

Obviously, there are continuities in the way peasants have been linked to the national polity throughout Brazilian history. The politics of dependence and the ideologies that derive from and give meaning to such a system can be identified in the colonial, imperial, and republican periods, and even today, in what Schmitter has aptly dubbed the period of "portugalization" (1971b). Yet, it would be a serious mistake to simply collapse historical time and posit a set of "traditional" relationships— like patron-dependency—as a timeless baseline against which to measure change.[3]

These traditional relationships, which anthropologists to date have used as a descriptive category for a set of relatively neutral observations about hierarchical, dyadic interactions, have been borrowed by political scientists, as a base upon which to construct a new paradigm, which the latter believe will serve them as a powerful explanatory model for certain kinds of political systems and political change (Powell 1970; Scott 1972a). For example, in his analysis of the dynamics of political action in Southeast Asia, Scott has written:

> . . . when we leave the realm of class conflict or communalism, we are likely to find ourselves in the realm of informal power groups, leadership-centered cliques and factions, and a whole panoply of more or less instrumental ties that characterize much of the political process in Southeast Asia. The structure and dynamics of such seemingly *ad hoc* groupings can, I believe, be best understood from the perspective of patron-client relations. The basic pattern is an informal cluster consisting of a power figure who is in a position to give security, inducements, or both, and his personal followers who, in return for such benefits, contribute their loyalty and personal assistance to the patron's designs. Such vertical patterns of patron-client linkages represent an important structural principle of Southeast Asian politics . . . Although patron-client analysis provides a solid basis for comprehending the structure and dynamics of nonprimordial cleavages at the local level, its value is not limited to village studies (1972:92).

In my view more can be explained through an examination of the changing nature of the political system than through an analysis of the content of patron-client relationships per se, particularly when these are so loosely characterized. Briefly stated, I believe we have to focus on political process in broad historical perspective and not on the content of dyadic interactional relationships itself, although an examination of their content is necessary to understand the cultural or ideological dimension of these systems of relationships as they feed back upon political action, as we will see in the next chapter.[4] For, as I stated earlier, patron-dependent relationships acquire different form and serve quite different functions in each historical epoch as the constellation of social, economic, and political elements that nurture them are themselves transformed. As one example, patron-dependency only becomes patron-clientship when the peasant is presented with a choice among potential benefactors who offer him differential returns for services rendered (de Kadt 1970:23). In the Brazilian case, as we shall see, this change becomes generalized only in the republican period when electoral politics begins to infuse the political system with a relative degree of competition.[5] What is required for an understanding of that set of events is an examination of differentiation in the elite sectors of the social system and the changing constitutional basis for the Brazilian polity at different times. Patron-clientship is an interesting structural and cultural phenomenon, but it can neither generate a political system nor, *by itself*, even adequately begin to describe one. To my mind, the system of distribution within the social system is far more critical than the content of the specific exchanges that are generated therein. Patron-dependency, patron-clientship, brokerage—these forms of exchange simply represent the mode of dispersal within a political system at a specific point in time.

The changes in rural politics that began to take place in Brazil during the Second Republic, particularly the appearance of populism, have to be viewed not simply as a breakdown in "traditional forms of social alignment" at the local level, but as an *incremental* process in a national political system in which agrarian control over state and national government, notably the executive branches, began to be seriously threatened by the appearance of powerful new sectors. In the colonial and imperial periods, Brazil was characterized by a peculiar sort of class homogeneity among rural elites. Conflict of interest remained minimal among agrarian enterprises until the actual locus of power began to shift from the sugar economy in the Northeast to coffee in the South late in the imperial period. The fall of coffee prices on the world market in 1929 caused further power transitions, from the hands of the coffee barons into those of a new, self-interested, and self-conscious industrial elite in the early decades of this century. In turn a process of mobilization and redefinition of political action was set in motion, leading to the mass political movements, which transfigured the social and political systems at both local and national levels.[6] These I will describe later in the chapter.

Attention must be focused not on the sets of dyadic relationships that characterize the politics of dependence but instead on the making of the oligarchy, on the importance of the governorships as loci of rural power, on the expansion of the electoral system, and on the proliferation of spoils in exchange for votes at the local level. The analysis of political action must be placed in the perspective of a dynamic set of historical processes. Throughout, I will be seeking to answer one basic question: What is the impact of different kinds of political systems— for example, limited parliamentary representative regimes versus bureaucratic nonrepresentative regimes—on political action and behavior at the local level? The underlying assumption is that politics on the local level in Brazil is both a reflection of and a response to social, economic, and political changes at the national and international levels. It is the interaction between the local and national levels that interests me here. Even to the anthropologist, village "nonpolitics" (Riegelhaupt 1972) seem trivial when compared to the enormity of the national political crisis in contemporary Brazil.[7]

Given the realities of the Brazilian polity (or polities) over the centuries, perhaps the best common denominator for our inquiry is the município, the local administrative center and its surrounding hinterland.[8] For it is actually over the disposition of resources among commercial (later industrial) [9] and agrarian elites that the battle between the forces of centralism and localism has been fought, and it is over control of these resources, once dispersed, that local political struggles take place. As the locus for many of these sets of events throughout Brazilian history, the município mirrors the structure of power in the Brazilian polity. For example, during the colonial period, politics at the municipal level contained a crucial element of decision-making that affected the well-being of local powerholders, and the municipal councils thus became the focus of considerable conflict. Under the empire, on the other hand, the role of municipal government became increasingly administrative, and elites allowed themselves to be co-opted into the imperial ranks, where the reins of power were firmly held. By the time of the First Republic, "municipal autonomy" had become an empty phrase that reflected little more than the unbridled authority of local bosses in the administration of resources derived from the state and later from successive federal governments. Municipal dependence had become the order of the day.

But to return to our initial discussion of the interrelationship between the dominant themes of localism versus centralization and elite versus mass, this shift in the locus of power had the effect of incorporating the rural masses in the electoral process. Whereas in the colonial and imperial periods there had been a mobilization of armed retainers in the struggle for supremacy among rural elites, the advent of the Republic witnessed the rise of voter mobilization, initially in the pursuit of oligarchic favor, and later in a determined effort to elect political partisans to office, and also as an antidote to the urban and industrial social forces that began to threaten even the local hegemony of the landholding class.

The exclusion of the urban and commercial vote throughout the colonial period gave way at the end of the empire to the "liberal" onslaught of a growing urban middle sector that turned its back on the rural populace, substituting, for the previous income and property requirement for suffrage, one based on literacy. Given the nature of the social and economic system in rural Brazil and, particularly, the state of education, the expansion of voter suffrage within this framework would inevitably work in favor of the urban sector, unless rural patrons could fatten electoral lists with increased numbers of clients. From the point of view of these agrarian elites, the ensuing mobilization of voters was merely a new configuration of an old political-dependent pattern in which the ballot replaced the bullet. Nonetheless, the heightened political activity that resulted from the competition among rival factions, acting in the name of a multiplicity of state-based and personally controlled political parties, contributed in no small measure to the process of breakdown of the old patrimonial order.

Encouraged by the appeal of populist leaders and unable to satisfy their needs through either local interpersonal relationships or the party structure, peasants and rural workers began to increase the tempo and volume of their demands, expressing them through urban-based rural syndicates and peasant leagues (Forman 1971). It is this process of "massification"—not democratization—of the political process that led, in large part, to the military coup d'état (the "redemptive" revolution) of 1964, the demise of the electoral system at the state and national levels, and the resultant reintegration of rural society under a new kind of oligarchic regime, one that would administer the rule of an authoritarian central government to the far reaches of the nation.

While it is still too early to know, it is possible that the military government might well have beheaded the agrarian hydra that has plagued Brazilian politics for the past half-millennium. Appearances to the contrary, the government has not restored the hegemony of the rural landed class, now reincarnated as a corporate establishment, in which agrarian enterprise and commercial entrepreneurship have become one. Rather, through a series of federal decrees, the military government has demonstrated its intent to play a more decisive role in the affairs of the municipality and to intervene with all its well-placed judicial and political powers whenever local interests threaten the proper administration of its programs.

Moreover, by continuing to allow the rural masses to elect the prefects who administer these programs, the government is in some sense making itself, at least theoretically, responsive to the rural electorate. Perhaps it inadvertently is laying the groundwork for the peasants' direct participation in national political life for the very first time. For their part, the new breed of landowning elites has indicated that they would rather be rich than powerful. By agreeing to direct government intervention in local affairs, by exchanging their hegemony for the right to prosper in peace and harmony in the countryside, they may finally be acknowledging the possibility of a thoroughgoing transformation of political life in rural Brazil.

FROM MONARCHY TO REPUBLIC: THE MAKING OF THE OLIGARCHY

Brazilian political process has as its initial locus the *conselhos de município*, which were established as administrative centers within the original land-grant system, and these are in many ways the first key to understanding political development in Brazil. The narrative that follows is intended to elucidate their structure and function in relation to the dominant trends in the social system during the colonial and imperial periods.

Portuguese colonial society in Brazil was originally comprised of a rural upper class, consisting of the grantees of sesmarias and their families; a small "middle class," made up of Portuguese mercantilists, mainly New Christians, some administrative staff, and the clergy; and an enormous under class, filled with slaves and freemen, attached to the plantations through a variety of land-tenure arrangements (Riegelhaupt and Forman 1970). Throughout the colonial period, the rural masses, mercantilists, and service personnel in the fledgling municipal centers were systematically excluded from the governmental affairs of state. These prerogatives were left largely to local patriarchs who exercised their dominion through the municipal councils, established and made legitimate by the Portuguese Crown, and sometimes through direct petition to the king in Lisbon.

Despite the absolutist nature of the monarchy, the ecological realities of the colony in the distant tropics encouraged local autonomy. As one observer has written, ". . . the efficacy of the central system of government in colonial Brazil was minimal, and for all practical purposes the king's power stopped at the gates of the plantations" (de Kadt 1970:14). These landed estates, geared to the production of sugar for the European market, were—in large part because of their isolation—socially and politically self-contained. The authority that the Crown originally invested in the *capitão-mor*, as subject-head of an administrative "captaincy" which grouped together a number of sesmarias, and later in the governor-general, was quickly undermined by the power of the land grantees themselves. The sesmarias became seigniories, the personal fiefs of aristocratic potentates "which possessed all of the conditions of sovereign power" (Oliveira Vianna 1933:226).[10]

The basis of this discretionary power was located in the domestic relationships characteristic of the slave plantation, where, according to Gilberto Freyre, the three dominant symbols of Brazilian rural life—the sugar mill, the big house, and the chapel—were also to be found (1964:159).[11] The rural patriarch, grown rich on sugar, surpassed viceroys, bishops, and even the governor, in wealth and opulence. He was

. . . lord, master and virtually temporal god in his family and within the reach of the *engenho's* attraction. He was father, husband, master of women and sons, primary overseer of tenants and slaves, and absolute leader for a diverse retinue of followers. (*Ibid.*, 161)

Within the confines of his estates and those of his kindred, which were often kept within the patriarchate through cousin marriage, the *pater familias* was sovereign. There was, in fact, no public challenge to his authority. Judicial, legislative, and political power all came under patriarchal control. The seignior was the ruler of his domain, and he devised the rules under which it was to be governed. Even justice, often arbitrary, was based on his private standards. The Brazilian historian, Sergio

Buarque de Hollanda, accurately documents the spirit of the times, when he describes a family council convened to consider a charge of adultery against a daughter-in-law, who was summarily sentenced to death (1936:88).

It was not long before the private power of the planters became public, however, extending itself to the municipal councils.[12] Senators, judges, councilmen, attorneys, treasurers, notaries, and clerks of the court were among the many officials empowered by the Crown to look after municipal affairs in the colony; but the only individuals who could vote for and serve in these posts were the so-called *homens bons*, or worthy men, enfranchised by their ownership of landed estates. Without a doubt, "The power of the councils was . . . that of the landowners" (Prado 1957:28). Through them, the seigniorial class imposed its control over salaries and the price of commodities, the flow and value of money, the payment of royal tribute, war and peace with the Indians, the building of villages, commerce, industry, and public administration in general. Additionally, they could suspend governors and *capitães-mor* and nominate their substitutes, as well as make arrests and clamp in irons any functionary or royal dignitary (*idem*).

In fact, not only did these municipal councils exercise full authority in their respective localities, often modifying Crown policy, but they also helped to mold that policy by reminding Lisbon ". . . of the power of the latifundiários and their interest in local government" (Queiroz 1969:15). This they accomplished by dispatching municipal representatives to Lisbon to argue cases directly before the king, as exemplified by two successful petitions in the seventeenth century which stayed the execution of decrees, sought by the Jesuits, that would have prohibited Indian slavery in the provinces of São Paulo and Maranhão. As Queiroz emphasizes in her study of local bossism in Brazil:

For these rural masters, the particular interest was inextricably wound up with municipal interest; the resolutions taken by the municipal council not only reflected a preoccupation with the common good, but also the preoccupation of the rural master to defend his private interests; there was no separation between the one and the other because the economic, political, and social reality of the colony was the rural property owner.(*Ibid.*, 15–16)

The fact that these municipal councils were, for the most part, mere extensions of private domains is reflected in the innumerable interfamilial struggles over their control that took place in the colonial period (Costa Pinto 1942–43). Although excluded from the electoral process, the rural masses were enlisted as "seigniorial henchman" in these often-virulent rivalries, as for example in the nearly a hundred years' feud between the powerful Camargo and Pires families in the province of São Paulo. The struggle began in 1654, when the municipal council of São Paulo, controlled by the Pires family, refused to seat the head of the Camargo family as Chief Justice. The ousted patriarch led his kinsmen and followers in an armed siege of the council, which was followed by open hostilities. The overwhelming power of these families in the face of "public" authority is brought sharply into focus by Oliveira Vianna:

Impotent before these *caudilhos,* who were incomparably more powerful than it, the public authority, in its turn, could neither contain nor repress them. It tried, instead, to conciliate them, acting as mediator. Finally, an accord was reached. In this accord, there is a clause which declares that, thenceforth, there should always be seated in the council members of both the Pires and Camargo families "in equal number," with, however, one "neutral" member. (1938:244)

The Portuguese Crown, for its part, was interested primarily in fiscal matters and was content to receive its one-fifth tithe and import and export duties, which were collected at ports of entry and exit. Sugar in the fields and in the mills was of little interest to the distant monarchy (Jaguaribe 1968:103), which saw no need to intervene in local affairs until its expansionist dream was finally fulfilled in the mid-seventeenth century with the discovery of gold. At that time, the Crown's laissez-faire policy quickly gave way to greater stringency in the governing of the colony, and the first concerted attempt at centralization began.

Royal functionaries tested their authority in the municipal

councils, particularly in those whose jurisdiction extended over gold-mining regions. A hierarchy of officialdom was established with Portuguese hegemony throughout, save for a few native-born Brazilians at the base of the expanded administrative bureaucracy. Intent on combating the power of the patriarchs, which now extended over vast territories, the Crown set up new administrative districts, entitling local potentates and thereby co-opting them into the king's service. Accordingly, by the nineteenth century,

. . . these *caudilhos*, who lived so violently and rebelliously, are already pacified, already revere authority, already deepen their veneration of the House of Braganza; great is their recognition by the King and his delegates. (Oliveira Vianna 1938:264)

In this way, too, the colonial administrative machinery began to spread beyond the coastline, accompanying the migrations of the population into the hinterland.

But the hegemony of the rural patriarchs was to be challenged on another front as well. In 1808, João VI fled the Napoleonic invasion of the Iberian peninsula and moved the Portuguese Court to Rio de Janeiro, where the declaration of an open-port policy and of freedom for native industry began to stimulate commerce and the development of a Portuguese commercial and urban bourgeoisie that would soon compete with native Brazilian agrarian interests for elected offices in the coastal municipal councils (Prado 1957:39). Although this planter class wished to model itself on the flamboyant nobility and their urbane and cultured life-style, educating their sons in the capitals of Europe and at Coimbra, it also came to realize that Portugal itself was not particularly necessary to the prosperity of the colony.

With the defeat of Napoleon and British assurances of Portugal's independence, the Portuguese began to clamor for the return of their king. With the encouragement of the native Brazilian elite, João VI sailed back to Lisbon in 1821, leaving the fledgling empire in the care of his son, Pedro I. In theory, Brazil had left behind her colonial past. Yet, the spirit of independence that created the empire on September 7, 1822, was hardly engendered by *significant* changes in the structure of Brazilian society. The economy was still geared to an export-agriculture based on slave labor, albeit with the domain of the seigniorial class now extended from the sugar plantations of the Northeast to the coffee fields of the central-south and then on to the great cattle estancias of the southernmost province.

A Portuguese mercantile class was continuing to grow rich in the coastal cities on a lively commerce in English manufactured goods. The native elite had long resented the presence of this foreign merchant class and their own secondary position to it at Court and in the colonial bureaucracy. Aware of the winds of change then blowing across Europe and inspired by the events of the American Revolution, they were eager to accept the de-Portugalization of their New World monarchy and offered their support to the succession of Pedro I in exchange for a set of titles that would add to their own local prestige and power. In the course of the next half-century, as we shall see, this rural aristocracy would take over the imperial bureaucracy, appropriating the governmental apparatus from the Portuguese and consolidating its own position within the centralizing regime.

The tendency toward centralization that began with the discovery of gold reached fruition in the imperial Constitution of 1824.

It was in fact a vigorously centralizing constitution. In the Emperor was concentrated a comprehensive authority called the Moderating Power. He had a suspensory veto over legislation and the right to dissolve or summon Parliament at will. He chose not only the senators but also the ministers, the bishops, and the provincial "presidents" or governors. He was given the power of pardon and of revising judicial sentences. Provision was made for the election of provincial councils, but they received little or no administrative or political authority. On the contrary, through his ministers the Emperor might exert a preponderant influence upon local government. Through them he could control the appointment of local judges and chiefs of police, annul municipal elections, suspend magistrates and the resolutions of the provincial councils. (Haring 1958:29)

As to the inclusion of the masses in the new political milieu, the constitution clearly reflected the ideology of Dom Pedro I who, in his enunciation of individual liberties, followed the liberal-democratic principles fashionable in his day, but carefully subordinated them to his own absolutist and elitist predilections.[13]

Notwithstanding its tacit agreement to accept the leadership of a powerful monarch, the seigniorial class had really not given up its much-prized place in Brazilian social and political life. While allowing itself to be co-opted by the nobility, this class zealously guarded its own rights and prepared to become guardians of the nation. The sentiment for regionalism and localism that characterized the colonial period was hardly dispelled during the autocratic reign of Pedro I, who abdicated under exacerbated xenophobic pressure in 1831, in favor of his native-born infant son, and returned to Lisbon to occupy the throne left vacant by the death of João VI.[14]

Several insurrections with republican overtones and strong undercurrents of native versus Portuguese antagonism, in the first decades of the nineteenth century, had demonstrated the landowners' discontent, and now they forced an experiment with republicanism in the opening days of the Regency (1831–40). For several years thereafter, the private power of local potentates reasserted itself as excessive municipalism undercut the authority of the State. For example, the promulgation of the Codigo de Processo in 1832 placed the police under the jurisdiction of a locally elected justice of the peace, thereby reducing the power of the emperor's appointed judge of law (Oliveira Vianna 1938:27). Furthermore, while the public prosecutor, municipal judge, and justice of orphans and widows were still nominated by the regent, they were selected from among a list of candidates supplied by the municipal council, which was elected locally by the seigniorial class. Thus, police, judicial, legislative, and municipal administrative services were once again firmly under the domination of local potentates. To give full credence to their newly recovered power, the election of officials to the recently formed National Guard was also delegated to the "worthy men" of the municípios, thus placing a military force under local command also.

While this period of extreme localism was to be short-lived, the power of the landowning class was nonetheless strengthened in the course of the Regency and the Second Empire. In 1834, an Additional Act created autonomous provincial assemblies and gradually elevated the police, judicial and administrative forces, and the National Guard, to provincial jurisdiction. The municipal administrators, police commissioners, and criminal magistrates were all combined into the unitary position of mayor, or intendant, to be appointed by the provincial president who, in turn, was appointed by the regent. The president and the provincial assembly assumed complete fiscal responsibility for the municipalities, although the regent retained a veto over all legislation. In effect, the intendants' role came to be one of executing provincial law and appointing municipal employees, ". . . two attributes in which local bossism encountered the principle font of its force and its prestige" (Oliveira Vianna 1938:274).

The seeds were sown for the system of exchange of votes for political spoils that would underwrite the statewide oligarchies of the First Republic, a subject I will probe in considerable detail below. For the moment, it was necessary for the seigniorial class to consolidate its hold over the government, which it accomplished by yielding up its educated sons—the so-called *bachareis*—to the administrative posts of the empire. In the long run, the sudden subordination of the municipal councils would make little difference because, with the steady extension of seigniorial hegemony over provincial and even national political institutions, centralization became the equivalent of subordinating rural elites to themselves (Queiroz 1969:39).

Thus, provincial power was carefully consolidated between 1834 and 1840, the year that marks the advent of the Second Empire with the ascension of fourteen-year-old Pedro II to the throne. In the shadow of the young Brazilian emperor's popularity, a Law of Interpretation returned control over the administrative bureaucracy and the police to his imperial majesty. Delegates and subdelegates, criminal magistrates, the municipal judge, all became imperial appointees. The central government also secured the right to annul local elections. In 1850, the National Guard came under imperial command through the issuance of commissions and ranks. The institution of "seigniorial henchmen," that had provided the balance of power in Brazilian backland politics for nearly four centuries, gave way to the rule of law. For the next three decades, a *pax imperial* would reign, backed by the authority and prestige of the emperor. During the Second Empire, the ballot would replace the bullet, as we shall see, but the structure of the Brazilian political system would remain very much the same. For in the socioeconomic realities of the slavocracy, coffee had become "king" and its barons, the ministers of the empire.

The political system in the Second Empire was organized around Conservative and Liberal parties, with provincial presidents as their leaders. At the apex of the system was the emperor and his ennobled advisers, drawn from the tenured members of the imperial Senate and the Council of State. The rest of the pyramid was filled out by members of the landholding class. Political power oscillated, but it was uniform. There was no real ideological split between the Conservatives, dominated by the coffee barons, and the Liberals, drawn from among the ranchers and planters in the frontier provinces of São Paulo and Minas Gerais; although ultimately, the former would be monarchical, and the latter, republican and the wellspring of the abolitionist movement. Dom Pedro II moderated between these parties. Alternating between them in his selection of the president of the Council of Ministers, he created a "politics of adherence," in which the opposition was satisfied to patiently wait its turn rather than try to hasten it at the point of a gun.

It was incumbent upon the minister to call an election, first for the municipal councils, then for the provincial assemblies, and finally for the national assembly. Naturally, he sought a sympathetic and partisan legislature. Toward this end, he was assisted by the provincial president, appointed by the emperor on advice of his counselors. In the words of Joaquim Nabuco, one of the outstanding statesmen of the day:

The moderating power can call who it wants to organize ministries; this person makes the election, because he has to make it: the election makes the majority. This is the representative system of the country.

The president (of the province) is an electoral instrument. It is through him that the chancellary of our dissembled absolutism is periodically elected. To mount, direct, perfect the electoral machine is his historic mission, his daily and nightly concern. (Cited in Oliveira Vianna 1955:306)

At the base of this political machine were the local landowners who came together to aggregate their vote totals, forming what Oliveira Vianna has called "electoral clans" (1955:298), each representing its province's party structure at the municipal level. Here, too, Liberal and Conservative elements alternated in the municipal posts that were the spoils of electoral "victory." It was preferable to wait one's turn, rather than compete in an election that would certainly be annulled if the opposition were to defeat the party in power. Yet, since municipal elections preceded provincial and general ones, parties had occasion to gauge the strength of their support, and in at least one case, a premature discussion of abolition led to the downfall of a minister when the election he convoked returned the opposition to the Chamber of Deputies that he had just dissolved (Queiroz 1969:51–52).

The seigniorial class had reserved to itself the true reigns of power, establishing what Sodré has aptly called the "hierarchy of manioc, the standard of political money in the new country" (1967:212). Candidates for elective office had to be owners or renters at long term of a landed estate or a mill. The electoral system was itself conducted in two stages. In stage one, an electoral college was selected by qualified voters, those who had annual earnings of at least the value of 150 alqueires (a dry measure corresponding to approximately 30 kilos) of manioc flour. In stage two, the electors, comprised of seigniors whose earning were above the value of 250 alqueires, chose members of the Chamber of Deputies and proposed three candidates with the highest vote totals to the emperor, who selected one among them for life tenure in the imperial Senate. Candidates for deputy had to earn more than the value of 500 alqueires, while senatorial candidates were required to exceed 1,000. Those who made their living as clerks in commerce and the

laboring classes, whether urban or rural, continued to be excluded from the electorate on the basis of their income (*ibid.*,
211–12; Jaguaribe 1968:127). The political process was fully
subordinated to agrarian interests.

While the important doctrines of the day—liberalism, parliamentarianism, constitutionalism, federalism, republicanism, democracy—were being debated in the imperial Senate, in newspapers, and in a plethora of political pamphlets (Bello 1966;
Cruz Costa 1964; Freyre 1970), the incorporation of the masses
into the political process was nowhere discussed. The abolition
of slavery was the burning issue of the time, but at its base an
elitist and tutelary ideology remained. Dom Pedro II himself
mediated between aristocratic and progressive ambivalence.[15]
He thought universal suffrage a calamity and that new electoral
laws "only could be perfectly well followed when political education was other than that of our people" (quoted in Sodré
1967:214).

An electoral reform in 1846 made metal money the basis of
voting rights, doubling the minimum values required, but extending suffrage nevertheless. Still, in 1876, there were only
24,637 voters out of a population of 10 million. The Saraiva Law
of 1881 provided for direct and "universal" suffrage for all
males over twenty-five years of age, but instituted a literacy
requirement that disenfranchised the mass of ex-slaves, who
were now wage earners, along with foot soldiers, beggars, and
adherents to religious orders that required the abnegation of individual liberty (Queiroz 1969: 80; Rodrigues n.d.:155).[16] At
the end of the imperial period, a senator could still be elected
for life with fewer than 500 votes (Sodré 1967:216).

Thus, while the Second Empire witnessed the centralization
of authority and the unification of the nation, political and economic power was secured by an agrarian elite that continued to
compete among itself for favors from the Crown.[17] The periphery had become the center, and it was precisely this consolidation of power in the hands of the agrarian aristocracy that
would come to threaten national hegemony. In the final days of
the empire, the Chamber of Deputies became dominated by a

liberal opposition to the absolutist authority of Pedro II. It also manifested a distinct preference for provincial autonomy. As I will describe below, the advent of the Republic would usher in an era of extreme federalism, in which the trade-off for votes between the provincial president and municipal intendants that began with the Additional Act of 1834, would develop into the most characteristic political institution of rural Brazil, *coronelismo*, exercised through state-wide control of the Republican Party.

FROM OLD TO NEW REPUBLIC: THE MAKING OF THE ELECTORATE

At the death knell of the empire, Brazil was undergoing the first stirrings of significant social and economic change. The abolition of slavery in 1888 caused the tottering sugar economy in the Northeast to suffer severe reversals. The rapid ascension of coffee had shifted the locus of power to the central-south where immigration and incipient industrialization were beginning to mould a new middle sector (Freyre 1963).[18] The empire was struggling with fiscal reform, necessitated by the heavy burden that the war with Paraguay had placed on the imperial treasury. This same war had swelled the ranks of the army with a new breed of young officers drawn from the urban middle class. Its pride quickened by victory, its ire aroused by an effete emperor's disdain and consequent neglect, the army became the whip of the republican movement and, on November 15, 1889, effected the coup d'état that sent Pedro II back to Lisbon.

There can be no doubt that republican influence in Brazil reflected the growth of this urban middle sector and their receptivity to a host of foreign ideas (Bello 1966; Cruz Costa 1964; Freyre 1970). The idea of republicanism, dormant in the last days of the Regency, began to flourish again during the reign of Dom Pedro II, as reports of political events in Europe fed the francophilism of the philosopher-statesmen of the Second Empire. Liberal manifestoes in 1869–70 called for the abolition of the Moderating Power, the Council of State, the National

Guard, and human bondage. They demanded direct elections and widespread suffrage, abolition of permanent tenure for senators, popular elections for provincial presidents, magistrates, and other local officials, an independent judiciary, complete religious liberty, and freedom of education and association (Haring 1958:96–97).

In 1870, the Republican Party was founded, providing a rallying point for partisans of electoral reform, decentralization of government, an elected senate, and the abolition of slavery. Nonetheless, these philosopher-statesmen would not legislate in favor of a new social and political order. Their debates, in fact, raged for nearly twenty years when, despite a paradoxical last-ditch attempt by a Liberal minister of the Council of State to stave off the inevitable by actually recommending extensive reforms to the imperial parliament, the First Republic was declared.

The highly disciplined army officers who founded the First Republic had also been nurtured on continental thought, but theirs was a meager diet, generously spiced with positivism (Cruz Costa 1964; Torres 1957). This Comtian sentiment, as Haring reminds us, was opposed to ". . . monarchy, hereditary rights, and aristocracy." Yet

its adepts showed little immediate concern for such considerations as democracy, equality, popular majorities, or the lot of the common man. Comte's ideal was a dictatorial republic, ruled by an elite. The watchwords of Positivist society were 'Order and Progress.' It was a philosophy that appeared as a godsend to the political and social oligarchies ruling everywhere in Latin America. (1958:140)

In point of fact, the military coup d'état that gave rise to the republic was undertaken not to substitute liberalism for authoritarian rule, but to give credence to that rule; not to replace paternalism with popular participation, but to give direction to that paternalism; not to make *order and progress,* but to provide "progress-within-order," as in Gilberto Freyre's telling transposition.

The petty bourgeois Jacobins of Brazil were radical only in their politico-juridical expectations. For them it was a question of establishing certain precepts—Republicanism or Federalism—which seemed to them to be providential in themselves, and, by invoking such precepts, to keep themselves in power for as long as possible. For the rest, the Republican middle class clung to the traditional attitude toward private property and the liberal economic doctrines. (Jaguaribe 1968:141–42)

thereby sealing an implicit pact with the rural oligarchy whose power would not be called into question again until the revolution of 1930.

It was not so much partisan debate that gave rise to the First Republic, as a set of disaffections that hastened the fall of the empire. The republican crescendo had not reached fever pitch in 1889, and the statemen who gave it voice seemed content to defer their cause until after the death of the ageing Emperor. The army preempted their glory and in doing so, presented the middle sector, which it had come to represent, with a seemingly illusory victory, as it would do once again in the revolution of 1964. The new order was quickly hailed by the conservative rural aristocracy, who were disgruntled over the abolition of slavery without indemnification. It also won the blessing of the Church, whose fury over the condemnation of two of its leading bishops to four-year terms in prison at hard labor, for their defiance of a government order to admit Freemasons to religious organizations, was not abated by the emperor's commutation of the corporeal aspect of the sentence. The seignioral class had embraced the Republic.

The authoritarian army rule in which the nation was conceived shortly gave way to a civilian government that dismantled the centralizing structures of the Second Empire. The republican Constitution of 1891 provided for extreme federalism, to the point of actually yielding up all Crown lands to the former provinces. If the United States of America had provided the model of a unified federated system to the authors of the Brazilian constitution, the United States of Brazil came off as a deliberately inexact version that suited the liberal economic policies of a landed elite desirous of fostering free trade and economic growth in essentially independent states. As one observer declared:

That Nation is understood as a balance or armistice between local power groups. The power of these groups, acknowledged by the Monarchy, is extended under the Republic to the point of the states openly contracting foreign loans, collecting export taxes, creating interstate fiscal barriers, and maintaining their own armed forces. The national political-governmental institutions are, not rarely, simply emanations of state power.(Vieira de Cunha 1936:16)

With constitutional guarantees for state control over tax revenues and their own militias, the power of the landowning class over national political life was, once again, assured. In fact, the continuities among the power elite, in personnel and personalities, suggest that little of consequence actually occurred when the new national banner, emblazoned with the motto "Order and Progress," was hoisted above the Emperor's palace. In a very real sense, the empire had anticipated the republic. Coffee was still "king," and its barons the very same ministers that Pedro II had choreographed in his peculiar "political ballet" (Freyre 1970:167).

. . . if the implantation of the republican regime was a victory of the middle class, rising against slavery,monarchy and aristocracy and aided in the struggle by deserters from the rural nobility, the political power that had been royal or aristocratic did not become popular except in theory, and the old economic power and the political power remained closely associated. (Azevedo 1950:106–7)

As for the masses, the founding of the republic had little bearing on their place within the sociopolitical system. Despite the first stirrings of light industry, there was still no urban proletariat agitating in its own interest, and the illiterate peasants and agricultural laborers remained totally subject to the authority of the landholding class. At best, the constitutional basis of republican Brazil assured that they would be included in ever greater numbers as pawns in the rural elite's new game of party politics.

At the apex of this federated system—and largely as an afterthought—the liberal constitutionalists provided for a president, to be elected by direct suffrage and an absolute majority of votes.[19] The vice-president, a bi-cameral legislature, the state governors and legislative assemblies, the municipal prefects, or

mayors, and town councilmen were also to be elected by direct
vote. However, the warmed-over elitism of the imperial statesmen also made constitutional the literacy requirement for voters
imposed by law in 1881. The essence of their position was the
same tutelary one of first educating the masses so that they
might participate fully and correctly in the "democratic" process, but they belied their own rhetoric by also excluding from
the Declaration of Rights, the right to a free primary education
that had been guaranteed, along with voting rights for illiterates, in the imperial Constitution of 1824 (Rodrigues n.d.:155).

The elimination of illiterates from the electorate had the effect of excluding all recently freed slaves from the political process (*ibid.*, 156) and may have been intended to reduce the size
of a dependent rural electorate. What it did, in fact, was concentrate political power in the hands of agrarian elites, especially
the coffee planters of the fast-growing central-south. At a time
when the bulk of the potential electorate still resided in the
more populated rural areas, the formation of the republic and a
representative regime gave a breath of life to the declining private power of the landowning class.

There can be no doubt that the political system of the First
Republic emerged as a compromise between several contend-
ing forces (Leal 1948), a compromise that would style national
and local political life until 1964. On the one hand, the need of
the military center to negotiate their authority with the traditional power domains in the countryside resulted in the federated system. On the other hand, the need to satisfy the demands
of the emergent middle sector gave rise to the "cartorial state,"
(as Jaguaribe calls it), which absorbed urban populations in a
rapidly expanding military and civilian bureaucracy, through a
system of clientage that echanged "superfluous jobs for votes"
(Jaguaribe 1969:395). At the outset, the extension of this "cartorial state" into the countryside provided the rural oligarchy
with a critical new resource in its struggle for power. It also
subordinated government to politics, creating an administrative
crisis in rural Brazil that would last throughout the republican
era and contribute, in some measure, to eventual politicization
in the countryside,[20] as we shall see below.

In effect, the political system of the First Republic became little more than a calculated trade-off, fully elaborated in the "politics of the governors," [21] in which the heads of state government and the president of the republic agreed to mutually respect each other's authority, in their respective domains. For the president, this meant congressional support for national policies necessary to the preservation of fiscal credibility abroad. For the governors, it meant a de facto return to provincial autonomy and a guarantee of federal patronage, including the right to appoint public functionaries at the state and municipal levels. The currency in this exchange was votes, and the electorate soon began to expand in relation to political demand.

In this system, the so-called "electoral clans"—those patriarchal groupings that emerged in the Second Empire—coalesced into state oligarchies, super-local and super-familial coalitions that were bound together through common affiliation with their state Republican Party, which was, for all practical purposes, the only party operating in the First Republic.[22] The party itself was little more than a congeries of local political elites united at the state level through the personalism of its leader, who himself most often aspired to the governorship.

There was little party coherence at the national level. In the prevailing agrarian economy, characterized by extreme regional diversity and a history of monocultural booms and busts, strong state rivalries were evoked. Yet, with few exceptions, the presidential succession tended to alternate in orderly fashion between the two most powerful states, São Paulo and Minas Gerais, where approximately half of the national electorate resided and could be enlisted in the coffee planters' quest for direct control of the policy-making office of the chief executive. Direct suffrage and absolute majorities became simple mechanisms to affirm the choice of the presidental successor, since the nominee of the party caucus, officially backed by the incumbent, was virtually assured of election through the complicity of key state governors.

In addition to providing electoral support for the president himself, the governors were expected to assure the chief executive of a congressional majority, by making certain that his official candidates were also elected. This was accomplished in a subsequent trade-off with the municipal chieftains, or coroneis, who controlled the rural electorate. In this set of transactions, the governor enlisted the coronel's support for official candidates at both the federal and state levels in exchange for carte blanche in the running of the município, including control over the granting of bureaucratic sinecures at the local level.

Thus, in the First Republic, ". . . the real protagonists of political life were state oligarchic groups, based locally on the power of the large landowners" (Lopes 1966:61). By indirectly controlling the municipal electorate, the state oligarchs exercised a direct influence over the Congress. Through the *politica de governadores,* they came to indirectly influence the executive branch as well (Oliveria Vianna 1933:307).

The key broker in this apical political exchange system was the coronel, the backland chieftain, whose place in the hierarchy was dependent upon his ability to deliver municipal votes to the state oligarchy.[23] During the empire, the coronel was actually the commander-in-chief of the municipal regiment of the National Guard, a position that enabled him and his followers to consolidate their power through direct control over the principal public force in the locality. With the advent of the republic, the title became honorific, and the "cartorial state" and the representative regime put another set of resources at the coronel's disposal.

The attributes of leadership were considerably enhanced by political bargaining, in which a dependent municipal electorate became the counter in a straightforward exchange of vote totals for political spoils. By expending municipal revenues on public works, such as roads, dams, electrification, bridges, schools, hospitals, and the like, the coronel built his reputation as a local benefactor, thereby ensuring himself a following. By nominating public functionaries and officials—often his own kinsmen— as schoolteachers, tax collectors, clerks, public prosecutors, judges, inspectors, public health officials, etc., he became a patron to well-placed personnel and thereby directly and indirectly extended his network of supporters. He also took into his debt the legitimate judicial and political authorities, who then became the high command of his "seigniorial henchmen," when the bullet was needed to reassert his authority against rivals who challenged his usurpation of state and federal patronage. Often, the state oligarchy would watch dispassionately as local rivals fought for the right to supervise the municipal electoral machinery, since it hardly mattered to them which of the local notables actually delivered the votes.[24]

Although he rarely held elective office himself, preferring to handpick candidates for municipal posts from among bureaucratic and commercial elites resident in the municipal "seat," the victorious coronel's control over the political machinery usually went unquestioned. An effective coronel engaged "lieutenants" who filled out the electoral lists by teaching potential voters how to sign their names (often skirting the literacy requirements), by attesting to the voting age of individuals who had no birth certificates, and by paying the costs of voter registration. Opportunities for fraud were rampant. On election day, the lieutenants rounded up voters—hence, the references to *votos de cabresto,* or "halter" votes—and transported them to the polls. If necessary, they saw to it that any opposition never got to the polls or that their ballots were never counted. More often than not, however, local elections were not seriously contested. The coronel, supported by the state oligarchy, could hardly lose at the ballot box.[25]

A minority opposition, eager for some share of the favors dispensed for electoral support of congressional candidates, occasionally might have tried to collect some votes to use in bargaining at election time. Nevertheless, they were competing for the privilege of adhering to the ruling oligarchy in the state, not to elect a rival slate to state office. The idea was to aggregate votes on electoral lists, not to win elections. Between elections, the "politics of adherence" reasserted itself. It would only give way to more continual opposition in the form of a fully developed factionalism at the end of the Vargas dictatorship when, in the Second Republic, the competition among a multiplicity of parties for hotly contested elections, particularly at the local level, made electoral victory—and not simply the aggregation of votes—the *sine qua non* for the receipt of political spoils.

The revolution of 1930 that brought Getulio Vargas to power and laid the basis for his syndicalist *Estado Novo* (New State) was built upon the very compromise between the "cartorial state" and *coronelismo* that characterized the First Republic (Jaguaribe 1968). However, by awarding the presidency to Vargas in the disputed election of 1930, the military was not simply recognizing the ascendancy of the cattle barons over the coffee planters in the wake of the collapse of the world market, even though on the surface one state oligarchy had seemingly replaced another.[26] Rather, they were acknowledging a more fundamental social change. A new configuration of elements was beginning to reshape Brazilian social structure (Wagley 1960) and would affect profoundly the nature of events in the Second Republic.

During the Vargas years, three new sectors burst in upon the Brazilian political scene: an articulate middle class that would demand electoral reform, "honest" politics, and a vastly enlarged state bureaucracy; a bourgeois industrialist group that would usher in an era of economic development based in an ideology of economic nationalism; and an urban proletariat that would coalesce into a new and critically important political mass. These three sectors would not only alter the balance of power in the nation, but establish new ground rules for a highly competitive political system that would seriously threaten established patron-dependent relationships in the countryside.

The years of the first Vargas presidency and his dictatorship were the "years of gestation" (Lopes 1971:86n), during which power was siphoned off from the states to the central government, the hegemony of the established rural oligarchs began to be systematically dismantled, and the urban mass began to find their voice. In fifteen short years, between 1930 and 1945, and most particularly after 1937, Vargas consolidated executive power within the federal government by establishing an elaborate system of federal ministries and administrative agencies subject ultimately to presidential authority. He also extended federal control over local areas by appointing his cohorts as interventors in many states and their outlying municípios.

By carefully manipulating federal patronage, Vargas brought down the entrenched oligarchs in state after state. In some places, within the sphere of influence of urban centers, they were replaced by a clique of bureaucrats from the nearby cities.[27] However, for the most part, one set of landlords simply took the place of another. "Traditional authority" in the countryside remained very much intact. The rural masses simply became dependent on another set of landed elites, one that comprised the new political "ins." [28] In the aftermath of the Great Depression, "king" coffee had been deposed, but the rural masses remained subject to the dictates of the landowning class.

Thus, the Estado Novo retained many of the features of the republican regime without the inconvenience of open elections. It also "set in motion a process of spontaneous change which could later be accelerated and oriented more deliberately" (Jaguaribe 1969:397) when the electoral system was reintroduced. Industrialization in Brazil got its first real boost during World War I and began to "take off" in the 1940s when World War II sharply limited the importation of manufactured goods from abroad.[29] As a consequence, the locus of power began to shift from the countryside to the nation's cities, particularly to the industrial triangle that was forming in the Southeast around Rio de Janeiro, São Paulo, and Minas Gerais, where mass migrations of rural workers added to the growth of a large, unattached electorate.

From 1945 to 1960, the national electorate grew from over 7 million, or 16.1 percent of the total population, to over 15 million, or 23.4 percent (Wells et al., 1962). However, there was a progressively higher proportion of the total population voting in the developed Southeast as opposed to the less-developed Northeast, a rise that correlates closely with an increase in literacy and urbanization.[30] In the four presidential elections that took place between 1945 and 1960, between 50 and 60 percent of the votes were cast in the southeastern states and Vargas' own home state of Rio Grande do Sul.

The importance of this new urban sector was not lost on Vargas (or his successors), who openly courted political support among industrial workers by using the apparatus of the state to provide them with substantial social legislation, while at the same time restraining them through a hierarchically organized system of trade unions under government auspices.[31] If the ideology of the Vargas era appeared to be a break with the elitist political philosophy of the Old Republic, it was equally tutelary in its authoritarian, paternalistic, and corporativist outlook (Wiarda 1969). The people only came together as ". . . a mass to be manipulated by leaders emerging from the dominant groups as a tool for the acquisition and preservation of power" (Lopes 1966:63). Nonetheless, as we have just seen, the large number of urban workers that Vargas had incorporated into the syndicalist state would provide an important legacy for post-dictatorial politics in the Second Republic. Along with the proliferation of political parties and ad hoc coalitions at the state level, they would provide the basic support for populist leaders, who would also come to compete for the rural vote.

Vargas himself had begun to anticipate a return to electoral politics shortly before the military—newly liberalized by their small role in the defeat of fascism in Europe—acted to end the Estado Novo by another coup d'état in 1945. A new electoral law in 1932 had met the demands of the urban middle sector by providing for honest elections through federally controlled boards under a strengthened judiciary, extended suffrage to include women and eighteen-year-olds, a secret ballot, a mandatory vote, and proportional representation. Still, the literacy requirement remained.[32] While it did not impede the enfranchisement of a rapidly growing urban populace with access to the rudiments of education, this requirement did limit the size of the rural vote, thereby ensuring that the "executive committee of the coffee planters and exporters" (Jaguaribe 1969:398) would not reassert their control over the presidency and the governorships. It did not, however, prevent the landholding class from extending their dominion over an enlarged rural electorate, thereby ensuring them of continued control over the federal Congress, state legislatures, and their own municipal bailiwicks. In fact, it has been argued that in states where the demographic balance weighed heavily in favor of rural zones, the system of proportional representation disproportionately valorized the rural vote in congressional elections.

The Constitution of 1946 both legitimized the Second Republic and laid the basis for a multiple-tiered political system, so full of inherent conflict that within two decades it would be dissolved. On the one hand, the constitution strengthened the office of the president, giving him wide powers to enact legislation by decree and providing for his direct election by popular vote, thereby making him responsive to the demands of the newly emerged urban mass. On the other hand, it guaranteed continued rural domination of Congress by providing for equal representation of all states in the Senate and proportional representation in the Chamber of Deputies, where seats were allocated on the basis of the total party vote in each state (Soares 1964:165–66). While candidates for executive offices increasingly appealed to an independent electorate [33] to whom they promised basic reforms, the Congress remained a composite of conservative and parochial interests, creating a governmental impasse between the executive and legislative branches (Furtado 1965).[34]

Thus, the constitution itself was an improbable accommodation between an outmoded structure and a new constituency that could not be easily satisfied. The impasse was duplicated at the state level as well. By stipulating direct elections through popular suffrage for governors, state legislative assemblies, mayors, and municipal councils, the constitution encouraged a proliferation of party politics and a highly competitive political system at the local level that was equally unresponsive to the needs of the electorate.[35] As we shall see, the party structure was little more than a vote-getting mechanism, which operated primarily at election time. The parties were responsive to the needs of the political leadership that they were organized to serve, but they were quite unable to meet the demands of the electorate they helped to create.

Vargas' unionization and labor welfare policies served as the rallying point for the most important of the new party organizations, the Partido Trabalhista Brasileiro (PTB), the Brazilian Labor Party, which united urban workers and union chiefs under the leadership of its new patron. His policy of conciliation toward middle-class bureaucrats, landowners, and industrialists wedded these seemingly incompatible elements to his cause through the Partido Social Democrata (PSD), the Social Democratic Party. An anti-Vargas coalition, comprised of liberal middle-class elements disaffected by the Estado Novo dictatorship and those rural oligarchs who had been ousted while the regime consolidated its position, later established the União Democrata Nacional (UDN), the National Democratic Union. The Brazilian Communist Party (PCB) made a brief appearance on the scene until it was forced underground in 1947. The only other major party to be formed was the Partido Social Progressista (PSP), the populist Social Progressive Party, with its main base in São Paulo. Still, the party structure multiplied, coalesced, and transfigured, until in the 1962 election, a total of thirteen parties competed nationally for congressional seats (Soares 1964:165).

In many ways, these "personalistic and clientelistic parties" (Schmitter 1971a:387) were multiple emanations of the former Republican Party of the Old Republic. They were, in essence, state-wide organizations with no overarching ideology and no national platforms (Ianni 1965:37ff.). Like the old Republican Party, they embodied a congeries of local interests that varied from region to region, only now several parties participated in elections in each of the states, and usually two in each município. For example, in the agrarian-based northeastern state of Alagoas, the UDN came to be the party of the sugar planters, who developed highly mechanized industrial mills under the tutelage of Estado Novo interventors; while the PSP was comprised of cattle ranchers and tobacco farmers, who appealed directly to the small urban vote and struck up bargains with some "independent" sugar planters along the coast.

There was no longer a single Republican Party that served as a smooth-running electoral machine for an entrenched oligarchy. Rather PTB, PSD, UDN, PSP, and several minor parties, which were organized so that additional aspirants could have the vehicles necessary to run for public office openly, competed for political power. No doubt deals were made, and there was no lack of "unholy alliances," like the PSD/PTB ticket that won the 1947 gubernatorial election for the brother of Vargas' former minister of war, or the PSD/UDN coalition that backed his labor minister's son-in-law in a bloody campaign for the governorship in 1950 in which both opposition candidates were assassinated.[36] Still, the final decision was made by the "people" on election day,[37] and even in this backland state—notorious for its *politica de cangaço*, shoot-'em-up, gangster-style politics—the growth of an independent electorate began to make itself known at the polls.

Muniz Falcão, a former labor deputy (PTB) under Vargas, established a coalition that was to become the state PSP, defeating the candidates of both the UDN and PTB in the gubernatorial elections of 1954. A new force had emerged in state politics that was decisive in both the legislative elections of 1958 and the gubernatorial elections of 1960 in which an independent with a reputation as an honest reformer swept into the statehouse on the coattails of Janio Quadros. Nevertheless, each of these successive governments immediately set out to secure and extend its following in the state by offering innumerable bureaucratic sinecures and other forms of patronage, in what was now standard republican procedure. It has been estimated that Muniz Falcão appointed some 4,000 employees in the last days of his administration. Major Luís Cavalcante, the successful gubernatorial candidate in 1960, was adhered to by a UDN constituency that quickly filled out his administrative bureaucracy, placing it in a strategic position to capitalize on the USAID funds that poured into the state under the Alliance for Progress in 1961.

Every município in the state received funds for school construction, small-scale industrialization, electrification, and other projects, which filtered down through the UDN machinery, assuring them of a substantial victory in the legislative elections of 1962. The power that was taken from the sugar planters by Vargas in 1930 was returned to them in the form of foreign aid. Moreover, little of this aid reached the people for whom it was intended. The clientelist politics that pervaded the Second Republic was based on relationships between two individuals, the elector and the candidate (Weffort 1965:166) or, more often, the candidate's broker, who distributed all revenues as spoils in exchange for votes.

At the municipal level, it was politics as usual, except that now two competing factions serving the interest of rival local notables—sometimes new commercial elites opposing the landowning "native sons"—organized along party lines as well. Political parties became the instruments of bitter factional struggles for access to municipal resources. The Constitution of 1946, despite its centralizing tendencies, made control over municipal offices particularly attractive by specifying a degree of local "autonomy" that allowed prefects to organize their own administrative and public services, raise and expend their own income, collect certain taxes and licensing fees exclusively for their own use, and utilize at will a proportion of state and federal revenues that were returned to the municipal treasury. It also guaranteed that the system of state patronage so highly developed in the Old Republic would grow apace, since municipal officeholders were provided with insufficient funds to supply any kind of regular local services (Donald 1959:21).[38] Political prestige and a political following were still entirely dependent on kickbacks from state and federal officials. At the same time, control over the granting of municipal status, and thus over the dispensation of revenues, was awarded to the states. Since the cleaving off of each new administrative district also established a new political bailiwick, local leaders were eager to "deal" with state officials over the question of municipal independence.[39] "The bargain on which the Estado Novo

had been founded—patronage in return for the promise of support—served as a buttress to the political parties of the Second
Republic, votes exchanged for political posts" (Jaguaribe
1964:144).

For all practical purposes, ". . . the principal result of the political transformation for the interior municípios was that their
political structures ceased to be monolithic" (Lopes 1971:189).
The simple aggregation of vote totals on electoral lists was no
longer a guarantee of support from the state oligarchy, as it had
been in the Old Republic. There was no longer an entrenched
super-patron in the statehouse to whom the coronel-in-power
could adhere. It was now necessary for local political competi-
tors to procure votes that would win municipal elections as well
as contribute to their party's victory in the state, since the government in power would not likely honor its obligations to a
município whose political chieftains were members of the opposition party. In this system, the same fraudulent techniques
for voter registration used in the Old Republic were revived,
only now *cabos eleitorais,* [40] or ward heelers, were employed to
organize as many voters as they could in the município. Illiterates were taught to sign their names; minors were issued false
birth certificates; fees were paid; and registrants were offered
"moral support" during their appearances before the electoral
boards.

In this way, rural powerseekers expanded their electoral following,[41] although additional mechanisms were now required
to control the votes that were created. Coercion was added to a
long list of subtler measures used to enlist electoral support.
The secret ballot was rendered inoperative at closely super-
vised polling places by printing separate ballots for each
party—often in conspicuously different colors—or by providing
separate urns so that peasants could be watched while they de-
posited their "secret" vote. When envelopes were handed out
as safeguards, they were previously stuffed with marked ballots
in order to automatically nullify opposition votes. In this highly
competitive local arena, the politics of adherence began to
break down as party politics were becoming institutionalized.

These points can be illustrated with data from my own field research. In Guaiamú, Alagoas, the município in which I undertook my study, the *política de cangaço* that characterized the interfamilial struggles for power among the slaveholding sugar elites in the Old Republic gave way to relative peace and prosperity under the Estado Novo. A central sugar mill, or usina, was erected in the main valley in 1927 and converted to a highly mechanized, corporately owned agro-industry in 1939. The new owners, a former textile manufacturer and his two sons, immediately began to concentrate their landholdings in the county, gobbling up the formerly independent cane producers and becoming the largest single landowners with some 15,000 hectares in 1965. At that time, the mill employed 300 workers and 800 field hands, making it the largest employer in the município, with direct control over a significant proportion of the district's, 3,115 electors. This family-run enterprise, with its big house, chapel, and mill, in many ways typifies the plight of the modern factory-in-the-field, mediating between the expectations of the peasants and agricultural workers, who are still partially in tune with these symbols of former times, and the managers' own businesslike demeanor.

I have already described how the mill owners, or usineiros, dominate political life in Guaiamú, utilizing its administrative and legislative structures for their own economic ends. As the principal taxpayers, responsible for the greater part of municipal income, their influence over public life is assured. Still, they themselves select candidates for municipal offices from among the bureaucrats and commercial elites resident in the county seat, financing their campaigns through the UDN, the majority party in Guaiamú. As owners of the third largest and fastest growing mill in Alagoas, with sizable investments and a main office in the state capital, they wield considerable influence over state politics as well. The mill owner has been invited on several occasions to run for governor but always declines, protesting that "politics is not my field." He is consulted, however, on all matters pertaining to UDN in the state, and in the congressional elections of 1962 he saw to it that a former employee was slated high enough on the party's list to win a seat in the federal Chamber of Deputies.[42]

Despite their wealth and power, the usineiros' sovereignty in Guaiamú did not go unchallenged. Their principal rival was Sr. L., an elderly coronel and owner of a sizable sugar plantation, who had been the uncontested powerholder in the region during the Old Republic. Since 1945, Sr. L. was a member of PSP and represented its interests in the município. In one sense, he was somewhat of a glorified *cabo eleitoral* for the state party organization. In another, he was an old-style politico, both loved and feared by the local populace. His principal following consisted of 400 henchmen and their families, fugitives from justice, who had taken refuge on his plantation. There they benefited from the immunity he enjoyed as a state assemblyman, and he did not hesitate to use them to complement his more conventional (for the time) political activities.

Until 1956, Sr. L.'s family had owned an enormous tract of land, some 34,000 hectares, most of it located in a neighboring county, with substantial portions extending into the município of Guaiamú. The land was sold to a colonization project under the directorship of a Swiss Social Laborite who had been invited to Brazil by Vargas to organize agricultural cooperatives. Although the administrators of the colony chose to remain aloof from municipal politics in Guaiamú, preferring to adhere to the policies of the sugar mill, they were subject to repeated armed assaults by Sr. L.'s henchmen, who sought to win back with bullets the domain that their patron could not dominate through the ballot box.[43]

While the mill owners remained above the fray, operating through *cabos eleitorais* who represented UDN in outlying villages in a direct line of command from party regulars holding most of the administrative posts and bureaucratic sinecures in the municipal seat, Sr. L. himself participated fully in the political struggle. He made speeches, promised favors and, perhaps most important, became godfather to innumerable children and co-parent to a vast network of loyal supporters. His personal prestige and following was far greater than that of the *cabos eleitorais*, who were themselves indebted in one way or another to the usineiros for patronage received, but who could not translate their own loyalties into a faithful following.

Feverish campaign activities took place throughout the município: the registration of voters, the distribution of propaganda, and the round-up of votes on election day. Villagers were organized into UDN and PSP factions, whose leaders fought bitterly for electoral victory and the subsequent spoils.[44] Whole villages were divided along party lines, and factionalism came to pervade every aspect of village life. In Coqueiral, the community in which I lived during 1964–65, UDN and PSP adherents acted separately in economic, religious, and social activities. UDNistas fished with UDNistas, and PSPistas worshiped in a chapel constructed by their village leader. (The church was opened only when the priest came to town, and he was an UDNista, closely associated with the usineiros and political bosses in the county seat.) The UDN *cabo eleitoral* was director of the local branch of the fishermen's guild, established up and down the coastline during Vargas' syndicalist state. The PSP leader was secretary of a fishermen's cooperative savings and loan association whose membership was derived from those who refused to pay their taxes and dues to the guild, arguing that they never received any of the benefits.[45]

Most of the infighting was over benefits. There were few issues, lots of promises, and some payoffs in each political campaign. For example, the village obtained a health post for its participation in the 1950 election and a diesel engine for electricity after the election of 1962. The benefits from each were dispensed along party lines. Injections and electricity were given out freely to *partidários*, while the sinecures connected with each were "kept in the family." The UDNista president of the fishermen's guild distributed a variety of political plums among his three brothers, sister, nephew, niece, and uncle (Forman 1970:38ff.). Such nepotism hardly won him favor among the impoverished villagers, who were further alienated by his dastardly use of the municipal police to keep the opposition in line. In contrast with the distance that separated the villagers from the sugar mill owners, it was this local bigwig's arrogant misuse of power that began to turn the local electorate against the party in power. Rather than an alien populist appeal, it was their trust and faith in the paternalistic leadership of the traditional elites in the person of Sr. L. that won them over to the PSP.

Slowly but surely, the Social Progressive Party made inroads among the electorate, principally in the elections in which Muniz Falcão himself participated. In the last statewide election in 1965, UDN carried the município of Guaiamú and the village of Coqueiral by a small margin, but there is evidence that members of the fishermen's guild voted overwhelmingly for the PSP candidate, despite vast sums spent by the usina for the purchase of votes ($1 apiece in Brazilian currency at that time) and sides of beef used for pre-election feasts.[46]

The outright purchase of votes in the elections of the 1950s and 1960s is one among several indicators that the increased competition for political support was no longer played out in the idiom of patron-dependent relationships.[47] *Cabos eleitorais* and political bosses also cajoled and coerced voters in a desperate attempt to control the rural electorate. On one occasion, I witnessed the following encounter in the offices of the sugar mill, when a worker was summoned to discuss an overseer's report that his wife was backing the PSP candidate:

Q: "Who are you voting for, Zé?"
A: "Why, for your candidate, Sir!"
Q: "And your wife?"
A: "Uh . . . that's more difficult, Sir. Sr. L. is her compadre."

Zé was fired the following day and ordered to leave the plantation town and environs.

The voter disaffection that this kind of decidedly nonpaternalistic behavior engendered was reflected everywhere in the high degree of voter abstention aimed at circumventing the mandatory electoral rule. For example, only 56 percent of the registered voters in Alagoas turned out for the election of 1954, which, along with subsequent events, suggests a voter boycott of the sugar planters. In 1958, after an interventor replaced the populist PSP governor, Muniz Falcão, in the wake of the assassination of the UDN speaker in the state assembly, a record 92.3 percent of the voters came out to demonstrate their will, increasing PSP's assemblymen from 3 to 14 at the expense of the UDN representatives.

But these defections do not occur overnight. At the outset, the willfulness on the part of the rural labor force was confined to an independence in voting behavior, ". . . an absence of submission to the chiefs" (Blondel 1957:101). This change began when competition from newcomer commercial elites and the extension of the "cartorial state" provided peasants and agricultural workers with an alternate model to the monopoly power of the coronel.[48] Dependency became clientship as peasants and rural workers came to be offered a choice between patrons (de Kadt 1970:23). Later, the activities of political brokers began to convince them that the vestiges of paternalism were no longer viable. The end result of this phenomenon is well described in a study of labor relations in agro-industries in rural Brazil:

The bonds of obligation and loyalty are broken. A cumulative and circular process implants itself and behavior and relations increasingly diverge from patrimonial patterns. The process is irreversible and its result is a gradual dissolution of the patrimonial ties. (Lopes 1971:192)

Yet, on closer examination, it appears that if the patrimonial order was breaking down, it was because the patrimony no longer existed.

Concurrently, a process of politicization had also been set in motion. As the objects of competitive vote-seeking at the local level, peasants and agricultural workers were offered a variety of promises and payoffs which, at the very least, taught them the cash value of their vote. Moreover, presidential and gubernatorial candidates began to appeal directly to the electorate, promising them basic reforms for problems that no longer seemed unique and individual. The rhetoric of their national media campaigns quickened the rural masses' demands for some of the answers that the government claimed to possess.

They also began to place some blame. For example, villagers in Coqueiral metathetically decried the *brogueses* (bourgeoisie) who reaped all of the benefits of development in the município. By the time the military staged their preemptive "revolution" of 1964, every rural worker was convinced that SUDENE, the Agency for the Development of the Northeast, whose agricultural experimentation stations and industrialization projects dotted the countryside, would resolve in the long run the agrarian crisis that beset the nation, and each and every one of them sought his own share.

It soon became apparent, however, that the relationship between the client and the candidate's broker was not geared to respond to the kinds of demands that the peasant was now making on the system. The party structure was equally unresponsive. Since local government officials served largely in an administrative capacity—except when they were expending resources to reelect their benefactors—they, too, could not be used to channel peasants' grievances upward to the real powerholders. Increasingly, the rural masses began to turn to outside leaders who were capable of articulating their demands and applying pressures on the social system as a significant national lobby.

FROM NEW REPUBLIC TO "REDEMPTIVE" REVOLUTION: THE MASSIFICATION OF THE POLITY

In a recent paper, I attempted to explain the conditions that gave rise to mass political participation in rural Brazil and to describe the forms which that participation took (Forman 1971). It was my opinion, then as now, that urbanization, industrialization, and subsequent commercialization in agriculture created demands for increased production and consumption in rural areas that ultimately led to a breakdown in ongoing forms of land tenure and land use and to widespread discontent. The years between 1946 and 1964 were marked by tremendous urban growth in Brazil and followed by rapid industrialization. Population shifts brought great pressures to bear not only in

urban areas but also in the countryside.[49] Increased demands
for agricultural produce and a rationalization of the internal
marketing system contributed to a sudden valorization of agricultural land and the subsequent displacement of masses of
peasants. Rural-urban migration and the remittance of new
ideas contributed to the making of a peasant consciousness or,
at the very least, to a recognition that their defined set of needs
could not best be expressed through "traditional" channels.

At the same time, the accoutrements of a rationalized internal
marketing system—i.e., vastly improved transportation and
communications facilities—opened up rural areas to urban
organizers, who recruited peasants and agricultural workers en
masse into rapidly proliferating peasant leagues and rural syndicates in the 1950s and early 1960s.[50] State federations of rural
unions held meetings across the country, and the First National
Congress of Farmers and Agricultural Workers met in Belo
Horizonte in 1961.[51] Because of the intense interest in the organization of rural workers, the Ministry of Labor—once the fly in
the ointment of unionization—published a pamphlet in 1962
containing instructions for union organization (Brazil, Ministry
of Labor, 1962).[52] In addition, the Agency for Agrarian Reform
(SUPRA) was created in 1962 especially to work with the growing peasant movement. By 1963, 500 unions with over half a
million members were grouped under a National Confederation
of Rural Workers (*Desenvolvimento e Conjuntura* 1964a:
33–34).[53]

In reality, there was not one peasant movement in Brazil but
several, which were differentiated in terms of the rural socioeconomic types comprising their membership and by the leadership through which they voiced their demands. The National
Confederation of Rural Workers was made up of such diverse
groups as the Church-sponsored rural unions, the peasant
leagues, the radical Catholic Agrarian Front of Paraná and Rio
Grande do Sul, the Union of Agricultural Laborers and Rural
Workers of São Paulo, and the Federation of Associations of Agriculturalists and Rural Workers in the state of Ceará. In addition, from 1960 to 1963, peasant associations sprang up in the
states of Goias, Bahia, Santa Catarina, and Minas Gerais.

For the purpose of the present analysis I will focus on two principal groupings, the peasant leagues of Francisco Julião and the Church-run rural syndicates. The former, led by politicians and student organizers, worked primarily with smallholders, tenant farmers, and sharecroppers, voicing demands for widespread agrarian reform based on the redistribution of agricultural landholdings. The latter, sponsored by dissident members of the Catholic Church hierarchy, including two well-known bishops and several outspoken priests, concentrated on extending labor legislation, salary increases, and fringe benefits to rural wage laborers. In addition, there were other radical Catholic and independent peasant associations which appealed primarily to salaried workers, but which adopted a more militant reformist stand, advocating specific changes in the land tenure system.[54]

The goals which each of these movements espoused were different, not simply because the ideologies of their leadership differed, but also because the needs of their memberships reflected the differential effects which commercialization in agriculture and the rationalization of the internal marketing system was having on the variety of rural types in the Brazilian countryside. At the same time, the style and pattern of the movements, particularly the relationship between popular leaders and rural masses, manifests a clear affinity to the general design of Brazilian political "culture" as described at the outset of this chapter. As we shall see, rather than a break with the past, the peasant league and rural syndicalist movements of the 1950s and 1960s represent an almost predictable episode in the continuing political history of Brazil.

THE PEASANT LEAGUES OF FRANCISCO JULIÃO

Francisco Julião, lawyer, politician, and proclaimed leader of the Peasant Leagues in Northeast Brazil, was aware that different land-tenure systems and productive arrangements produced different peasant subtypes who could be expected to react differently to appeals for political mobilization. He divided the rural population into proletariat, or rural salaried workers; the semi-proletariat, or workers in temporary labor service arrangements on the land; and peasants, or those who have some sort of effective control over the land they farm, either as sharecroppers, renters, squatters, or small property owners (1962:11). It was these peasants, he believed, who presented the best conditions for waging a protracted struggle against the latifundia (*ibid*, 58), and he appealed to them to join together in the building of an effective agrarian society.[55]

As it came to pass, the ranks of the peasant leagues were to be filled by smallholders who were unable to compete with the expanding latifundia. Generally, the leagues spread most quickly in the agreste, the transitional mixed-farming zone of small landholdings, which was under constant threat of incursions by the sugar estates in the coastal lowlands and the ranches in the cattle-raising sertão (Furtado 1965:148–49). There is every reason to believe that it was a desire to transform a subdivided plantation into an expansive cattle-raising operation that led to the eviction of the peasants from the now-famous Fazenda Galileia, in the município of Vitória de Sto. Antão, in the state of Pernambuco (Callado 1960:35; Harding 1964:47).[56] Julião's legal defense of these peasants and the subsequent expropriation of the plantation and its distribution among the sharecroppers was, in effect, the first act in the ten-year drama of the Brazilian peasant leagues.[57] Furthermore, the first league founded in Sapé, in the state of Paraiba in 1959, resulted in part from the eviction of its leader from his land. João Pedro Teixeira was put off the land he occupied without indemnification after the owner sold it to one of the commercial elites from the city, who wanted to use it for speculative purposes (Carneiro, cited in CIDA 1966:338).[58] More to the point, however, the vast majority of agricultural workers in Sapé farmed their own small plot (CIDA 1966:319–20), but had to compete for land with the large sugar mill located in the county. Thus, as this case would seem to indicate, even when the peasant leagues operated within the sugarcane zone itself, they were apparently appealing to the large numbers of peasant farmers who inhabit these areas and not specifically to the limited numbers of agricultural wage earners at the mills.

In discussing the foundations of the movement, an optimistic Brazilian journalist wrote that "The [peasant] league begins in the market place, goes to the notary, and takes over the world" (Borges 1962:255). Actually, the traditional marketplace did play a role as the physical locus of the encounter in the recruitment of peasants in Northeast Brazil. However, the quote might better read "The peasant league comes to the market place . . ." for it was there at the weekly feiras that the leagues' urban organizers found a ready audience amoung the usually dispersed peasantry. It was to the marketplace that they came to tell the story of Galileia and of Francisco Julião and to offer legal advice and medical assistance to the peasants gathered there. It was in the marketplace that the peasant traditionally listened to the troubador spin his tales and sing his songs of culture heroes and newsworthy events. And it was through the troubador that Julião carried his "Letter of Liberation of the Peasant" to the countryside. In point of fact, the peasant political movement in Brazil, as elsewhere, has clearly been led from the outside.[59] Julião quite explicitly called for the organization of a highly centralized peasant movement with a base in urban areas, where it could be insulated from the landholding class (1962:46–47). At the same time he preferred to organize the leagues into rural societies rather than unions subject to the bureaucratic rigors of the unionization law.[60]

When I visited the peasant league headquarters in Recife in 1962, I was impressed by the lack of any formal bureaucratic structure. Housed in rather modest facilities donated to the leagues by the Brazilian Socialist Party, which Julião represented in the federal Chamber of Deputies, the headquarters were open to students and peasants, who intermingled freely, discussing their needs, the movement, and Francisco Julião, their leader. During several days of conversations which I had with the young student organizers of the leagues, I was struck by their lack of any clearly defined ideological position. While telling me of their projected plans, their individual differences became apparent. The only goals they seemed to share was to make the peasant "aware of social justice and of his rights."

Openly critical of the failure to build an organization that could make the peasant leagues a cohesive unit on the national level, they believed that they had to pique the social consciousness of the nation before they could begin to structure and define the movement. They questioned Julião's leadership abilities and admitted that his image had been largely inflated by the foreign and domestic press, but still clung to him loyally as their charismatic and devoted standard-bearer. More important than this personalistic aspect of the movement, however, is that its tutelary and paternalistic tone placed it from the outset within the elitist political tradition of the Brazilian system.

There has been a great deal written about Julião's personal convictions. The descriptions vary from caustic criticism to highly romanticized sketches (Callado 1960, 1967; Horowitz 1964). While he undoubtedly clamored for radical and even revolutionary change, it is questionable whether Julião ever intended to undermine the system of which he was so much a part. He did demand an effective agrarian reform. However, while he advocated land invasions and the *threat* of violence, he strongly urged prior use of the judicial process. Perhaps the League's motto—"within the law or by force"—best sums up his own view of the possible strategy of a movement which clearly had radical potential but which lacked radical leadership.[61] It must be remembered that Julião was himself the son of a large plantation owner, and there is some question whether a peasant league meeting actually ever took place within the município in which his family's property is located, even though it was the area of greatest agitation in the state.

All indications are that Julião was appealing to an audience which was radical by the very nature of its demands for changes in the agrarian structure, but which he intended to use largely as his own power base in the established system of order (Leeds 1964:196). He undoubtedly understood the plight of the peasantry and had their interest in mind. Nonetheless, he explicitly stated that one of the basic reasons for working with peasants, rather than with the rural proletariat, was because sharecroppers, renters, and smallowners greatly outnumbered rival wage laborers (1962:67). Indeed, the peasants were to be very telling in his success at the polls.[62] In point of fact, Julião was then taken to task by a spokesman of the Communist Party for neglecting the peasants and concentrating his political energies in the cities (Borges 1962:259). There is further evidence which suggests that he was also intent on obtaining leadership of the peasant leagues as a whole,[63] at a time when his ambitions obviously had surpassed his base of support in his native state of Pernambuco. While a number of autonomous peasant associations in Northeast Brazil never did accept him as their leader, there can be little doubt of the populist nature of his appeal to the rural masses.

The relationship between the peasant leagues and the Communist Party is very telling in this regard. Although the peasant leagues were founded with the help of the communists (Callado 1967; Price 1964:45), it is important to point out that Julião and the Brazilian Communist Party had very serious differences.[64] In part, these resulted from the latter's interest in the rural salaried worker and their strong belief that agitation for agrarian reform should be subordinated to efforts to extend labor legislation to rural areas.[65] Indeed, the major concern of the PCB, since it founded the first peasant league in the Northeast in 1945–46, has been with minimal demands for legal aid, schools, medicines, and burial funds (Borges 1962:253), rather than with appeals for radical agrarian reform.[66]

Furthermore, the communists were evidently suspicious of the autonomy of the leagues and of Julião's independence. They distrusted his use of the peasant movement for what they believed to be personal aggrandizement and feared his emergence as a charismatic leader (Borges 1962:259). They insisted that the success of the movement depended not on individual leadership but on organization and legalization, and they sought to register the leagues as unions. Again, it must be emphasized that the Communist Party was organizing not among the peasants but among the rural proletariat. This fact placed them primarily in competition with the Catholic Church rather than with Julião.[67] Their argument with Julião was essentially that his appeal for political support elicited radical demands from the peasantry, which could be detrimental to the party. They were concerned that radical action might upset the slow gains made possible through legislation by provoking an extreme reaction from the landed elites,[68] a fear which, as we shall see, was to prove very real.

THE RURAL SYNDICATES

The tutelary aspect of the rural syndicalist movement is even more transparent. The Catholic Church had been hard at work since early 1960, trying to extend its influence among workers in agricultural enterprises throughout Brazil. Church-sponsored rural unions were founded in a number of states, but they were particularly strong in Rio Grande de Norte, Pernambuco, and São Paulo states, and to a lesser extent in the states of Paraná, Rio Grande do Sul, Santa Catarina, and Minas Gerais. Like the other peasant movements, the Church-sponsored unions were highly centralized organizations with leadership coming from the ranks of more enlightened members of the clergy.[69]

It has been said that the Church-sponsored rural syndicates in Brazil developed as a response to the peasant leagues, and it is probably true that the clergy was attempting to counterbalance a secular political force in the countryside. Yet, it is important to emphasize that until recently the syndicates operated almost exclusively among the rural proletariat. Inspired by the papal encyclical "Mater et Magistra," the Church defined its role in the peasant movement as primarily reformist and conciliatory, stressing improvements in living conditions for the salaried worker, cooperation with the federal government, and the inapplicability of the concept of the class struggle in the Brazilian context.[70] Their primary concern has been with the promotion of labor legislation for the rural salaried worker.[71]

Padre Antonio Melo, an outspoken parish priest from Cabo, Pernambuco, has criticized the Catholic Church for its conciliatory role in the peasant movement. When I interviewed him in August 1967, Padre Melo accused the Church of disguising its real motives in organizing rural unions, noting that its historic ties with agrarian elites made it an unlikely advocate of real agrarian reform. He criticized the clergy for working primarily with trained union leaders rather than with the peasants themselves and suggested that a strong grass-roots organization would be necessary to press for real reforms.[72]

Speaking out strongly against the use of violence, Padre Melo advocated the strike as the most effective weapon for change. The young priest noted that he led a successful strike in the sugarcane zone of Pernambuco in 1963, which culminated in a collective work contract and an 80 percent salary increase for 200,000 rural workers. Still, while the strike can be an effective weapon in the hands of the rural proletariat, it should be clear that such advances depend on a variety of factors which are again outside of the workers' sphere of influence. For example, Furtado leaves no doubt that the success of this particular strike coincided with decreased opposition on the part of the landlords because of a concomitant rise in international prices for sugar from 1962–63 (1965:138). Those landlords who did not want to pay the increased wage merely ignored the provisions of the agreement, laid workers off or, in some cases, closed down their operations.

In addition to the strike, Padre Melo believes that pressure can be placed on sugar mill owners by correcting the balance of supply and demand in the labor market. He suggests withdrawing large pools of labor by resettling rural workers in colonization projects and on half-hectare plots around rural towns and cities. In this way, he believes, the sugar mills will be required to make technological improvements in their operations, leading to increased profits and to a willingness to increase salaries. At the same time, he maintains that garden plots encircling populated areas will greatly alleviate the problem of urban food supply. Thus, while Padre Melo certainly works for changes within the prevailing system, he distinguishes himself from a more conservative Church organization in his pressing of demands for land for the peasant and rural worker, albeit in the very same paternalistic fashion.

INCREASED RADICALIZATION AND OFFICIAL REACTION

What had really begun to change, then, in these two decades of political agitation was not so much the attitudes and motives of the popular leaders, but the conditions of the peasantry itself. The distinction between rich, middle, and poor peasants, each having different access to adequate land and the means of production is well known to all of us.[73] The rich peasant is the commodity producer who farms commercially, utilizing hired labor. It is the poor peasant, bereft of land, who is forced to sell his labor on the market. The middle peasant is in the most precarious position, however, because his land is adequate for subsistence only in the best years, and he is under constant pressure from above to also sell his labor. Eric Wolf suggests that it is precisely this "middle peasant" who suffers the greatest strains from the pressures of the marketing system. Hence, it is this stratum of peasant society, led by middlemen in the system, which is most likely to participate in peasant revolutions (Wolf 1967:8–9).[74]

I would contend further that it is this sector of Brazilian agrarian society that gave a radical impetus to the peasant movement as a whole. It was not the salaried worker who made radical demands for changes in the social system but the tenant farmer and sharecropper threatened with the loss of their land.[75] The salaried worker is primarily concerned with his share of increased production and the benefits of an increased wage. His demands, theoretically, can be met by legislation and do not pose a threat to the system per se. The peasant, on the other hand, knows that he is an unlikely competitor in the new market arena. He is being displaced by a rationalized system of production and distribution and, in Brazil, he sought fundamental changes in the prevailing agrarian structure. His demands for adjustments in the land tenure system were radical by their very nature and were bound to provoke a far more extreme reaction on the part of agrarian elites.

From this fundamental fact, separate rural movements with

different ideologies developed in Brazil. Yet, these divergent organizations did manifest solidarity on a number of occasions. The general trend was toward an increased radicalization, and radical Catholic groups were in the vanguard in pressing demands for a true agrarian reform. This trend has been attributed to communist infiltration of the movement (Price 1964:54–55). However, I would like to suggest another alternative: that the demands of the peasant, aligned with the rural worker, had become the dominant ones in the rural movement. Thus, while only a few priests had supported the extreme demands of the Declaration of the First National Congress of Peasants and Rural Workers in Belo Horizonte in 1961 (I Congresso 1962; Vera 1962:94–95), by 1963 the once conciliatory group led by priests in Rio Grande do Norte was also calling for basic agrarian reform.[76]

The development of the peasant movement in the state of Paraná emphasizes this point. The First Congress of Rural Workers of Paraná met in 1960 in apparent harmony with government officials and local political and economic elites. The tone of the meeting was substantially nationalistic, while at the same time decidedly reformist and nonrevolutionary (Silva 1961:61). By 1961, however, peasant leaders were denouncing armed attacks on agricultural workers by the landlords' private police. The Second Congress, held in Maringá in 1961, had a very different tone, with the calling for radical agrarian reform and the liquidation of the landowners as a class (Vera 1961:63–64). It is important to note the effects of the expanding coffee economy on the character of these meetings. The late 1950s was a period of general prosperity in the state of Paraná. There was rapid expansion of the agricultural frontier, and salaries there were actually higher than the legal minimum, a fact which attracted large numbers of agricultural workers to the region (CIDA 1966:234). Yet, there is evidence that here, too, land speculation and frequent consolidations by resale were displacing smallholders in a general trend toward land concentration (Wagley 1963:91–92; Frank 1967:198, 231). I suggest that it was the plight of this peasantry rather than the demands of the rural proletariat that led to violence and the increased radicalization of the rural movement in Paraná.

In my view, government and landlord receptivity to the demands of the rural proletariat emboldened the peasant movement as a whole. Pulled to the Left and pushed by the Right, President João (Jango) Goulart sought popular support for his shaky presidency. He asked Congress to enfranchise illiterates and encouraged rural syndicates and peasant leagues as a means of solidifying his own political base.[77] At the same time, he was unwilling to let these movements get out-of-hand, as the enactment of the Rural Labor Statute of 1963 amply demonstrates. Thus, while the statute may have attempted to emphasize previously ignored provisions of rural labor legislation (Price 1964:12), it also sought to reestablish government control over the burgeoning rural movements.[78] The courting of rural labor, like the extension of suffrage, was an exercise in the methods of co-optation that Goulart had learned so well during his apprenticeship as Getulio Vargas' minister of labor (Schmitter 1971a:211).

The Rural Labor Statute was directed quite clearly to the demands of the rural proletariat rather than to the problems of true agrarian reform (Caio Prado 1963:6). The hierarchical structure of the union organization (see note 60) and the legalities required to acquire recognition placed the peasant movement under extreme bureaucratic controls, precisely what Julião had tried so hard to avoid. Furthermore, the arbitrary division of rural types into two broad categories of workers and employers failed to come to grips with the sociological realities of the Brazilian countryside (Price 1964:16; Freitas Marcondes 1963:56; Caio Prado 1963:3). For example, small property holders were lumped together with salaried workers, renters, and squatters, while the inclusion of the sharecropper as an independent worker militated against his negotiating with his landlord as an employee. Under the statute, the unions were constituted to deal with the economic activities of the laboring class, and political activity was strictly forbidden, *at least in theory*. The

strike as a weapon was made illegal. Instead, arbitration councils were established to redress grievances in rural areas.

Despite this apparent attempt to appease both sides in the
conflict, Goulart failed to satisfy either the landowning or the
rural laboring classes. The landowners entrenched at each new
concession to the masses, while the peasants and their leaders
took apparent receptivity in the presidential palace as a signal
to press for more radical reforms. Unable to get Congress to act
on pending legislation, including enfranchisement of illiterates,
Goulart finally used his presidential decree powers, a step that
all previous presidents had hesitated to take. At a massive rally
on March 13, 1964, he posed an unacceptable threat to private
property by calling for the nationalization of all privately owned
oil refineries and issuing his now-infamous SUPRA decree,
which provided for the expropriation of all underutilized properties of over 1,200 acres located within six miles of major road-
ways, and lands of over 70 acres which were within six miles of
federal dams, irrigation, or drainage projects.

Since no constitutional amendment had been passed to provide for payment in bonds for expropriated lands, and there was
not money in the federal treasury for such expenditures, the
application of the decree would have meant the outright seizure
of the property of the landholding class. The lines of battle had
been clumsily drawn. After two decades of conciliation, the
chief executive had finally managed to alienate both the industrial bourgeoisie and the agrarian elite, which already was re-
sponding with increased violence to peasant agitation in the
countryside. In addition, organized demonstrations and strikes
among students and urban workers, mass mobilization, and runaway inflation filled the vulnerable middle class with overriding fears of "communism and corruption," leading once again to
their strong support of the military coup d'état that seized
power on April 1, 1964.

Landowner opposition to the peasant movement has long
been a fact of life. The strong agrarian interests represented in
Congress successfully resisted rural reform for many years. The
Consolidation of Labor Laws, which provided for rural unioni-

zation, had also legitimized the Rural Brazilian Confederation of Landowners, which was organized for collective action on its own behalf. Its early opposition to Goulart's plan for rural reorganization had helped to oust him as Vargas's minister of labor in 1954 (Wilkie 1964:6). In an obvious attempt to reassert its flagging control over labor resources, it again vigorously protested the rural labor movement in 1963.[79] In short, the landed elite publicly lobbied for the status quo in rural Brazil, defending their time-honored right to hegemony in their own domains.

Back in the countryside, the flagrant use of private power again became the vogue. The threat of land invasions and assaults on local markets by starvation-driven peasants had placed the landholding class on constant alert. Private and sometimes public police forces carried out reprisals against the peasants in every region of the country. In the northeastern state of Paraiba the dreaded Syndicate of Death stood ready to execute the patrão's most dire requests. In the state of Alagoas, resident landowners banded together to defend themselves against any encroachment by the peasant leagues. They proudly showed the arsenals they kept in their plantation houses to "stem the tide of communism" in Brazil. Their fears were reinforced by exaggerated press reports, and they began to react with violence at the slightest provocation. The peasant league meeting I attended in Pernambuco in 1962 and described at the beginning of this book ended with an armed assault on the humble gathering in the town square. The meeting had been called to peacefully protest the destruction of a tenant's manioc crop by a landowner who was trying to evict her from her plot. It ended when the local parish priest, from the sanctity of his church, directed the townspeople in a violent counter-demonstration which left at least one peasant wounded and a twelve-year-old boy dead from a bullet in his head. Subsequent reprisals significantly increased this toll.

The military coup d'état which ousted João Goulart from the presidency on April 1, 1964, carried its purge down to the local level of the peasant political movement. The peasant leagues and independent associations were disbanded and many of their leaders were arrested. Francisco Julião spent several months in a military prison before making his way into exile in Mexico. The Church-sponsored rural unions were allowed to continue, but with government interventors in leadership roles (SORPE 1967).[80] The political plowhands had been removed and the team muzzled and bridled. Nevertheless, it was clear to all that the peasant movement could not be made to disappear simply by legislating against its leaders.

The direction that the peasant movement now takes will obviously depend on the responsiveness of the present military regime and its policy for agrarian reform. According to the President of IBRA, the political climate before April 1964 was both sensationalist and demagogic, but the "revolutionary government . . . opted for a democratic solution based on stimulating private property, on the rights of the farmer-owner to the fruits of his labor, and, naturally, on increased production, reintegrating property into its natural social function and conditioning its use for the general welfare" (Cantanhede 1967:7). To this end, the first military government under the presidency of General Castelo Branco enacted an agrarian reform bill in 1964, which empowered the federal government to carry out a complete cadastral survey in Brazil, institute a progressive land tax, exercise control over rural labor contracts, survey and demarcate public lands, expropriate land with payment in bonds,[81] colonize and establish cooperatives, and provide general assistance and protection to the rural economy (Cantanhede 1967:12). In addition, Castelo Branco extended the right to strike to rural workers. According to a presidential decree of 1965, every rural worker in the sugarcane zone was entitled to have, after one year of continual service, up to two hectares of land near to his house "sufficient to plant and raise livestock to an extent necessary for his and his family's subsistence" (SORPE 1967).

Nevertheless, the government's stated goals of transforming rural workers, renters, and sharecroppers into a rural middle class, stimulating the development of small properties through cooperatives, and modernizing and democratizing medium and large plantations (Cantanhede 1967:8), are still nowhere in sight. Land speculation and concentration of landholdings continue throughout Brazil—even on the open frontiers (CIDA 1966:104). Commercialization in agriculture moves faster than government planning, and peasants are still being evicted from their land, thus "abandoning subsistance agriculture which supplies foodstuffs to the market places . . ." (*Jornal de Comercio* 8/13/67:13). The agricultural sector of the Brazilian economy continues in a cycle which the government appears unable or unwilling to break.

EPILOGUE: RURAL POLITICS AND THE MAKING OF THE ADMINISTRATIVE STATE

If, as Oliveria Vianna argues, ". . . the decade of the Regency had taught Pedro II the dangers of local autonomy, of the incurable personalism of our politicians, and of our party organization" (1938:313), the decades of the Second Republic had been similarly instructive. The military acted quickly after the coup d'état of 1964 to institutionalize the historic tendency toward authoritarian rule, purging the system of its "semi-competitiveness" and its "populism" (Schmitter 1971b:15).[82] Within a few short years, a dozen institutional acts, more than five dozen complementary acts, a new constitution (in 1967), and tens of thousands of decrees and laws undercut all legitimate opposition and guaranteed the authority of the administrative state.

Brazil abandoned politics in the interest of governing. By doing away with direct elections for the president, and also by retaining both veto power over and the ultimate right to close Congress and state assemblies, the regime effectively eliminated the impasse between the legislative and executive branches that had immobilized civilian government in the last days of the Second Republic. By appointing interventors in some states and nominating candidates for governor to other legislative assemblies, it completely undermined the importance of the states in national political life. By restructuring the multi-party system into a majority government party, the National Renovating Alliance (ARENA), and a "token" minority

opposition, the Brazilian Democratic Movement (MDB), it monopolized all legal channels to political power.

Not surprisingly, a number of elements highly reminiscent of
the Second Empire and the Estado Novo can be discerned in
this latest reordering of the Brazilian polity. The striking difference is in their effect, for the Brazilian military, in the 1970s,
has demonstrated its intent to accomplish the thoroughgoing
centralization of the State. By ". . . intensive concentration of
decisional resources at the *center* and extensive penetration of
government agencies of the *periphery"* Schmitter 1971b:42),
they have shown themselves capable of transforming the political life of the nation. Yet, perhaps their most significant break
with the past is the conspicuous lack of the spirit of conciliation
and compromise that characterized previous regimes. Through
the unprecedented use of arbitrary arrest, imprisonment, and
torture, the cancellation of mandates and the nullification of political rights, the total disregard for the rights of free speech and
assembly, the mass dismissal of academics, and the purges of
union and associational leaders, three successive military governments have taken control of the Brazilian nation.

Documentation of the full result of these and other measures
at the municipal level, of course will require research at some
future time and in several localities, but a number of tendencies
can already be observed. Foremost among these is the end of
"politics as usual." An editorial in one of Brazil's leading dailies
reporting on an investigation into party politics in the northeastern states in the summer of 1971, bemoaned the indifference of
the governors to the party structure which, it said, "discredited
professional politicians." The states, it lamented, are now
engaged more in administration than in politics (*Jornal do Brasil* 8/15–16/71).

In truth, the demise of the multi-party system in 1965 and the
suspension of direct elections for state governors and the president have depoliticized not only the states, but also the municipalities. In many rural areas, the new two-party system was easily accommodated to prior political structures. The majority
party simply changed its name to ARENA, and the opposition

picked up the pieces of MDB. In others, however, the re-trenched oligarchs modified the "politics of adherence" of the Old Republic, opting for a single-party system in which opposition candidates occasionally ran as *sublegendas,* or alternate slates, under an ARENA listing. In either case, the highly competitive political system of the Second Republic was no longer in evidence. A delightful description of the change in one northeastern municipality appeared in a recent issue of a popular Brazilian magazine:

Until 1964, Propriá (population: 18,386), was one of the most politically agitated cities on the lower São Francisco River. Political assassinations were common, and everyone still remembers the occasion in which a state deputy, a leader of Governor Seixas Doria, kidnapped the governor's father, an old man of more than seventy years, a planter in Propriá, in order to guarantee that Seixas would keep a promise that he had made to workers in the rice fields in the region.

Manuel Fontes de Almeida, nicknamed Zinho, sixty years old, father of six, clerk in the civil registry, reinforces with a hearty laugh his affirmation that all of this has ended:—"Now politics here is less politicized and more civilized. You no longer vote for the party, nor even for the political chief, but for the candidate. Thank God, MDB and ARENA are the exact same thing. Fortunately, we're very well advanced in this sector" (*Realidade,* No. 74, 5/72, p. 167).

The reason for this advancement is clear. The spoils system and the factionalism that goes with it are disappearing from rural Brazilian life. Although prefects and municipal councilmen are still elected by direct popular vote, their election is independent of others, and the resources they have to expend are no longer contingent on getting out the vote. The emphasis in the municípios is on administration *not* on politics, since the military has undertaken the "portugalization" of the countryside (Riegelhaupt 1971; Schmitter 1971b).

The Brazilian State has, once again, assumed the responsibility for local governmental affairs, but this time it has demonstrated both its intent and power to intervene directly in the muncipalities whenever private interests threaten the proper administration of its programs. Perhaps most important, in this regard, are the government's new fiscal policies. Whereas the

Constitution of 1946 had made the municípios financially dependent on the states, the Constitution of 1967 shifted the entire responsibility for municipal taxes—including the all-important property tax—and revenue sharing to the federal government. A series of decrees now require prefects to present plans for the application of revenues to relevant federal agencies before they receive any funds, and to publish full accounts of their expenditures at the end of each fiscal period. Article 23, Institutional Act II (October 27, 1965) [83] declares that:

A prefect's irregular use of the assessed revenue taxes allocated to the municipality by the Federal Union is a crime against the public trust. Criminal prosecution in such cases shall be initiated by the Public Ministry, or by one-third of the members of the municipal council.

Notably, the military seems to be forcing compliance. Newspaper reports and interviews that I conducted in the field in 1971 indicate that the long arm of the law now reaches out to the remotest of municipalities. The government has actually suspended prefects and initiated proceedings against them for "crimes against the public trust." In one well-publicized case, the prefect of a tiny município in distant Piauí was suspended and prosecuted for failing to complete the construction of a county schoolhouse. The threat of federal justice, administered by a strengthened judiciary—both civilian *and* military—makes it far less likely that local potentates would defy tax laws or misuse public funds. Even more significant, from the point of view of the rural masses, is the fact that a reinforced public constabulary has been subordinated to the federal army ministry and is now appointed from outside the município, thereby freeing it from local clientelistic constraints. Private justice is yielding to public power. As the *Manual do Prefeito*, the mayor's handbook, warns: ". . . the prefect is not subordinated to any authority, only to the law" (IBAM 1967:11).

In light of my interpretation of Brazilian political history, it might at first seem paradoxical for the agrarian interests to have acquiesced so readily in the loss of their municipal autonomy. Yet, there is an obvious logic underlying their willing embrace of public authority, since the new landholding class has become the guardian of *order* and the reaper of *progress* in the new Brazilian State. Having decided that it would rather be rich than powerful, it has ". . . willingly exchanged its pretensions to political hegemony for economic security, its 'right to rule' for its 'right to make money' " (Schmitter 1971b:10). In addition, it has won some important concessions from the military, not the least of which is the apparent setting aside of the Land Reform Act of 1964, which had been introduced to stimulate production on or the sale of unused lands by disproportionately taxing unproductive estates (Stepan 1971:233, 236).[84]

When I returned to the município of Guaiamú in the summer of 1971, the owners of the sugar mill promptly disavowed any political activity. None was needed. Sr. L. had lost his political immunity and his political rights. The government had disabused the local bigwigs of their discretionary power, and the usineiros were content to let "politics" run its course. MDB did not function at the municipal level. Instead, opposition candidates ran as *sublegendas* for the prefecture and the municipal council. In the village of Coqueiral, factionalism seemed to have disappeared. The former PSP leader was heir-apparent of the former UDNista, now ARENA, president of the fishermen's guild.

Peace had returned to Guaiamú, and with it, prosperity. The sugar mill was enjoying unprecedented growth. Annual production had increased from 300,000 sacks of sugar in the turbulent years of 1964–65, to 600,000 sacks in 1967, and 1 million in 1971. At the same time, the number of mill workers had been reduced to under 200 as a result of mechanization. While the landholdings of the mill had not increased, independent cane suppliers were gobbling up previous tenant holdings in order to meet the usina's demands. Anticipating the electrification of the state from the Paulo Affonso hydroelectric dam, the usineiros had invested their new-found wealth in a lamppost factory and were selling the concrete piles to "modernizing" villages and hamlets throughout the region. Some of the workers' small stucco houses were even electrified! The 150 kilometers of road from the state capital to the mill town had been paved at the owners' initiative, and an intercity telephone system had been installed for their use. The usineiros and their larger suppliers drove from city to countryside in brand-new, Brazilian-made Chevrolet Impalas and Ford Galaxies, costing nearly $11,000 apiece. *Order* and *progress* had also come to Guaiamú, but with them the discrepancies between rich and poor, haves and have-nots, privileged and under-privileged, became ever more marked. The peasants and agricultural workers reaped none of the benefits.[85]

While there have been significant gains in all sectors of the Brazilian economy since 1964, these have been ". . . countered by social policies which worked against the lower classes . . ." (Stepan 1971:263). Acknowledging that the poorest segments of the population in northeastern cities had been hardest hit by government policies, the president recently stated, "The econ-omy might be doing well, but the majority of the people are still doing poorly" (cited in Schmitter 1971b:24). The rural popula-tion seemed doomed to do poorest of all. The extension of so-cial security benefits to "retired" peasants and agricultural la-borers over sixty-five years of age who can prove that they have worked within the past two years, echoes the social welfarism of the Vargas years and simply palliates the enormous social ills in the countryside. Similarly, the reintroduction of rural worker syndicates, 300 of which were formed in the first year of the new regime (Schmitter 1971a:212), appears to be a deliberate effort to preempt independent organization.[86] Despite federally established quotas for literacy in each município, the impres-sive campaigns of the Basic Education Movement (MEB) were ended, and the major effort now being made in the field of edu-cation is the training of skilled personnel for middle-level trades in urban centers. These trades are apparently out-of-bounds for the rural migrant.

Faced with massive squatter slums ringing the periphery of Brasilia—that monumental symbol of national unity and "in-tegration"—the military was taking steps to quell the torrent of rural-urban migration. "Roadblocks" were established at major routes of access to Brazil's principal southern cities when the drought of 1970–71 caused severe dislocations in the Northeast, and in that region itself some 400,000 peasants are said to have been organized into labor gangs. An advertisement in a Rio de Janeiro newspaper in the summer of 1971, signed by a rather unusual regional migrants' association, offered airfare to anyone expressing willingness to return to his native state.

But the real panacea of the military government is Transamazonica, the incredible highway that promises (threatens?) to open an enormous tropical frontier to mass migrations of peasants and agricultural laborers. It would be open, as well, to latifundiarios whose rampant land speculations should be ample warning that the "regenerative revolution" (Buarque de Hollanda 1936:150) of 1964 might well be reviving the agrarian crisis on a massive scale. Whatever the case, road-building and nation-building proceed hand in hand, while the rural masses hunker at the wayside watching progress march triumphantly by.

Chapter six—
The Politics of Despair:
Popular Religion and
Movements of Social Protest

The study of peasant political participation projects us immediately into the uncompromising debate surrounding the significance of peasant political action. Numerous statements have been advanced about the revolutionary "potential" of peasants the world over. To some, peasants are inherently conservative; that is, they are said to be characterized by a deep-rooted fatalism that explains their inability or unwillingness to act in the face of an objective exploitation. To others, peasants are essentially revolutionary, needing only the rhetorical formula of some willful leader to catalyze them to action. Each of these philosophies epitomizes a doctrinal extreme that often reflects more of the ideological bent of the social scientist himself than the actual mood or state of consciousness of the peasantry in question.[1] Both err, of course, in their enunciation of facile judgments about the general condition of the peasant mind, undifferentiated statements about peasant mentalities, about political attitudes (or the lack of them), often incompletely supported by the hard facts of history.

Unfortunately, the study of peasant political participation in Brazil has suffered from the same sets of expectations. Episodic protest has been welcomed as the harbinger of a great revolution to come, or it has been dismissed as the fanatical outcry of a

degenerate and unrepentant mob. The day-to-day behavior of
the rural masses has been viewed as essentially nonpolitical,
the peasant's entry into the political arena being mediated and
qualified by encompassing social relations of the patron-dependent sort, or the rural worker has been seen as a willing and ar-
dent partisan in a highly competitive political field. Yet, the
simple truth is that neither of these polar interpretations is adequate, although ample empirical verification for both can be
found within the long and changing Brazilian past. That the
mass of rural Brazilians is *outside of* electoral politics is not to
be questioned. That a number of others have come to voluntar-
ily engage in partisan politics is also ethnographic fact. That
large numbers of peasants and rural workers have pillaged and
burned, rioted and struck, is seared upon the pages of Brazilian
history. That millions of others have quietly watched the brutal-
ity and slaughter of centuries inflicted on these, their compeers,
cannot be denied. To count the numbers of people at the urns,
or carrying banners, or shouting *vivas*, then, is perhaps to know
the *extent* but certainly not the *significance* of political participation.

Clearly, the way to a fuller understanding of Brazilian peasant
political participation is not through an examination of their
manifest behavior alone. Nor, for that matter, can it be gleaned
from a survey of political attitudes. To really apprehend the nature and quality of peasant political participation in Brazil
requires an examination of a cultural dimension as well; that is,
of ". . . the structures of meaning through which men give
shape to their [in this case, political] experience . . ." (Geertz
1972:320). Now, that political experience doubtless takes a variety of forms, particularly as different socioeconomic types develop ideologies reflective of the specific sets of relationships in
which they are cast and expressive of the specific sets of needs
and expectations peculiar to each. Thus, while generalizations
about a uniform peasant political experience are inaccurate at
best, as evidenced by the case of the Brazilian peasant league
and rural syndicalist movements, there is, nonetheless, a common cultural base throughout rural Brazil which, when properly

understood, will enable us to make more correct statements about political experience in each of these instances.

In this chapter, I propose to examine this cultural dimension of peasant politics in Brazil, particularly the place of religion in the formation of a popular ideology.[2] I will do so by inquiring into the belief systems of the participants in several kinds of rural protest movements (Heberle 1968): social banditry, in which individuals joined together largely to avenge personal transgressions; millenarianism and messianism, in which groups of people organized into religious communities for the satisfaction of social demands; and contemporary political and syndicalist organizations, through which peasants and rural workers effectively sought economic redress. By concentrating on an analysis of the belief systems of the membership of these movements, as opposed to the ideology of the leadership (often manipulative, and whose rhetoric is too often confused with the ideology of the movement itself), I believe I will be better able to assess the significance of their participation in each case, as well as how it has or has not changed in the course of two centuries of endemic peasant protest.

For example, the adherence of masses of peasants to political "leagues" and to Church-run rural unions in the 1950s and 1960s, and the increased radicalization of their demands before the seemingly receptive "populist" government of deposed President Jango Goulart, represent to some a radical departure from traditional forms of peasant political action. They argue that traditionally the Brazilian peasant has been a religious and not a political being at all, that recent political involvement is suggestive of a new kind of ideology—the emergence of a political consciousness closely related to class that has hitherto been lacking. To others, these recent manifestations of peasant discontent are only slightly modified versions of former patron-dependent loyalties, now represented in the collective guise of a "following" that is content still to leave politics in the hands of a beneficent patrão.[3]

Once again, neither of these interpretations of events and attitudes is complete or fully accurate. There is no question that the recent political movements in Brazil lacked the "revolutionary fervor" that adverse publicity attached to them. In that respect, they were quite similar to earlier Brazilian protest movements, whose enemies also exaggerated their dangers to the State. At the same time, however, since the mode of attachment to political leadership in each of the Brazilian movements—whether millenarian or syndicalist—was collective and charismatic, each represents an important departure from the individualistic, exchange relationships that characterized traditional forms of patron-dependency.

As we have already seen, these dyadic relationships, with their mutual expectations of proper behavior and vague understandings about some sort of equivalency in reciprocal exchanges, have long been superimposed upon basic contractual land/labor arrangements, not simply offsetting the asymmetry of the economic exchanges by creating ties of affect and loyalty (which also align peasants and rural workers into factions across class lines), but also providing the ideology that reaffirms, legitimizes, and justifies the authority of the landed class as a group, despite the tenuousness of the individual economic dyads. The most striking aspect of these asymmetrical exchange relationships is the sense of submissiveness and obligation that the peasant bears, a phenomenon that is sanctified in the religious sphere in a general way through the peasant's belief in an omnipotent and omnipresent God upon whose will all things depend and specifically through a *somewhat* analogous exchange relationship between devotees and their patron saints.

If, as I believe, breach of the economic contract, resulting from changes in the general socioeconomic condition of agrarian society, is the immediate cause that led peasants to seek redress, mass political participation in movements of a supra-local character followed only upon the "breakdown" of these patron-dependent relationships, a process closely tied to the inflated competition in national and state electoral politics. Yet, if any identifiable change in popular ideology accompanied this shift in social alignment, then it only recently began to develop as a part of the movements themselves, that is, as a dialectical process that took place within the context of the rural masses' interaction with the movements' leaders, with the State, with *each other*, and with the landowning elites, who began to violently manifest their opposition to legal and systematic forms of social change.

In attempting to trace the development of consciousness, or *conscientizacão*, among the Brazilian peasants with whom he has worked so closely in literacy campaigns, the educator and revolutionary philosopher Paulo Freire has defined "a culture of silence," which derives from the interplay of structural relationships between subordinate and superordinate sectors of the social system. In the culture of silence, ". . . to exist is only to live. The body carries out orders from above. Thinking is difficult, speaking the word, forbidden". (Freire 1970a:22). To understand this culture of silence, writes Freire, ". . . presupposes an analysis of dependence as a relational phenomenon which gives rise to different forms of being, of thinking, of expression, those of the culture of silence and those of the culture which 'has a voice' " (*ibid.*, 32–33). The dependent segment of society ". . . cannot objectify the facts and problematical situations of daily life," and attributes the ". . . sources of such facts and situations in their lives either to some super-reality or to something within themselves" (*ibid.*, 37).

The culture of silence, then, is characterized by a mode of consciousness that is "semi-intransitive," in which the contradictions are apparent but which prevents the peasant from acting politically upon them. This mode of consciousness, the persistent form of resignation among Brazilian peasants that borders on revolt but is rarely so expressed, is vividly portrayed by Fabiano, the emasculated hero of Graciliano Ramos' excellent novel of peasant life in the backlands of Northeast Brazil, *Barren Lives*, who wants to strike out against the landlord who cheats him, and take vengeance on the policeman who had him unfairly beaten, but instead seeks explanations which redirect blame away from the socioeconomic realities of his everyday life and justify his inevitable inaction.

An understanding of this phenomenon must, of course, go beyond an explanation constructed solely in terms of the structure of dependency relations and a theory of exploitation, for in many ways it is Fabiano's tortured self-evaluation that determines his own inaction. I do not intend to understate the importance of economic and political power in maintaining the dependency relationships that characterize rural Brazilian social structure, nor to recast our discussion in psychological terms. To be sure, the law is one among many means of overt social control available to the landowning class in the Brazilian countryside, and legal and extra-legal force is often employed to stay a restive peasant. Yet, it would be wrong to assume that the Brazilian peasantry lives under constant repressive force, even if the threat of such force might well be enough to impede political action in many cases.

In truth, the use of raw power is usually unnecessary or, at worst, is needed only as a reminder. As is the case with Fabiano, sufficient self-control among Brazilian peasants is generated through constant self-depreciation (Freire 1970b), in keeping with a dominant set of cultural norms about proper conduct in interclass situations. It is precisely in this complex intersect between social structure and man's own interpretation and explanation of his place in it that religion begins to play a critical role in the formation of a popular ideology.

Religion has always played a paramount but ambiguous role in the thoughts and actions of Brazilian peasants. It has both nurtured the "culture of silence" and given voice to its discontent. Both as institution and belief system, it has come together with social structure and social organization to produce an ideology which at times, indeed, acts as an opiate, to the point of impeding direct political action on the part of the peasantry, but which at other times is redirected into explicit and devastating expressions of social protest. It is, thus, both a source of social control and a means of social mobilization.

Certainly, in earlier manifestations of social protest it is often difficult to know precisely where religious zeal left off and political action began. This statement is not simply an echo of the Brazilian peasant leader now-in-exile, Francisco Julião, who writes that ". . . the mark of religiosity is on every bandit and the mark of banditry is on every holy man" (1968:61), but rather an assertion that social banditry, to a lesser extent, and millenarianism, particularly, manifested varying degrees of religiosity and secularism at a time when religious dissension seemed to be the only alternative to acts of violent outrage.

Even in the most secularized of contemporary political movements, religious beliefs continue to play a dual role. Thus, the enlistment of peasants and rural workers into the recent political and syndicalist associations and their mobilization for direct political action required their organizers to successfully manipulate religious symbols and to give new shape to the meanings that attach to them, in order to maneuver past the conventionalized understandings of what their proper behavior in interclass situations should be. At the same time, the religious message reinforced the peasant's sense of dependence and obligation. For example, it is reported that

At an organizational meeting of the rural union, with only humble folk present, several people presented their complaints. One family man . . . complained of everything that there was in the way of injustice and human exploitation in the countryside, and finished by saying: 'If God were not so good a father, we would have died some time ago.' (Leers 1967:36)

More importantly, while significant changes might have occurred in the course of a protracted movement, this brief episode seems not to have had a lasting effect on peasant ideology itself. The movements were stilled by the arrest and isolation of their leaders and the disbanding of the formal organizations. What remains in the quiet aftermath of two decades of political agitation are only the peasants' demands and their silent prayers that these demands might yet be met. Just as they dominated earlier protest movements in Brazil, religion and other popular beliefs continue to reaffirm the peasants' dependent social status and to reinforce a "politics of despair." When the majority of Brazilian peasants was finally confronted with that all-important question, "What is to be done?", their only audible reply was "As God wills!"

POPULAR RELIGION

Catholicism is the national religion in Brazil. Well over 90 percent of the Brazilian population is considered to be and considers itself to be Catholic, even though the Church has never held complete sway over the people who at least tacitly adhere to its teachings. The rural masses, particularly, are limited in the degree to which they participate in the formal religion, just as their participation in the political, economic, and social life of the nation is also limited.

While there have never been enough priests to effectively serve the large population spread throughout the vast countryside, the cleavage between the teachings of the Church and popular religions that began as early as the seventeenth century (Vallier 1967:195; 1970) and is now very evident, has more to do with social and political structures than with sheer numbers. Those priests who celebrated mass in the plantation chapels during the colonial period were subject to the economic and social hegemony of the landed gentry to whose needs they primarily ministered (Freyre 1959; 1946). Some of their teachings reached resident slave and free-laboring populations as a matter of course and sometimes as a matter of policy (Bastide 1960; de Kadt 1967:194), but the Church's attentions were directed almost exclusively to the interests of the landed class. Even today, many of the priests located in the rural county seats spend a considerable part of their time at the plantation chapel. The remainder of their time is spent in relative comfort at their home parish or seeking new comforts at the seat of the bishopric. Only rarely is a priest seen making his way on horseback, mule, or by jeep to the innumerable rural neighborhoods and peasant villages where untended chapels have come to play an increasingly important role in a distinctly peasant belief system.

In this peasant belief system, a dominant overlay of Catholic religious tradition is infused with elements of Afro-Brazilian and Amerindian cultism.[4] As such, it is hardly a faithful rendition of Church doctrine.[5] Formal Catholicism is the religion of cathedrals and priests, of orthodoxy and dogma. Folk Catholicism is a mixture of this-worldly manipulation and mystical asceticism.[6] Peasants are told to accept the teachings of the Church, but they are confronted with an institutional framework of closed chapels and occasional itinerant priests. They are left with a religion of household altars and personal saints, and they are forced to reinterpret and redefine the formal teachings of the Church within the context of their own needs and capabilities. Many of their ideas about religion and religious events come to them through the *literatura de cordel,* troubador songs that are now printed in pamphlet form and strung out at the local marketplaces for sale to peasants who themselves become disseminators of the Word.[7]

Their most apparent concern is for this world and not for an afterlife, a seeming paradox in a setting in which death is the constant theme.[8] Openly, it is true, they worry neither about sin nor salvation, directing their energies instead to the satisfaction of their daily needs. At the same time, however, their attempts to understand, explain, and cope with their own worldly position through the mediation of the supernatural endows their belief system with an imposing spiritual element as well. This spirituality is characterized by a devout and total submission to an omnipotent and omnipresent God who, while distant and little understood, is believed to be the embodiment of all good. Interaction with this God is mediated through a hierarchy of personal saints, whose potential for achieving miracles is the primary focus of peasant religious behavior.

Popular religion in Brazil, then, operates on public and private levels that must be viewed together. The first is concerned with ritual acts; the second with individual belief systems. Unfortunately, the more directly observable behavioral manifestations of public and private acts of devotion have taken precedence over the study of the meanings derived from them in the ethnographic accounts of "folk" religion. Thus, while there are some fine descriptions of saints day celebrations [9] and religious pilgrimages,[10] the meanings attaching to these activities are still little understood.

More significantly, perhaps, many of the masses' most fundamental religious beliefs do not always find expression in ritual form, and thereby fail to get special notice in the literature. For example, the receiving of sacraments is often made impossible either because of the lack of money or of priests. Peasants often forego baptism, confirmation, and sometimes even the final rites of the Church. Yet, the failure to perform in these formally prescribed ways does not necessarily mean that the ideas and beliefs about these life crises have any less import in the lives of Brazilian peasants. Thus, a peasant may be buried without the final rites of the Church, but his pallbearers take care to lay the coffin at the foot of the cross outside the chapel and to remove their hats before proceeding to the burial ground, and doors will be closed in silent respect of death as the cortege moves slowly through the village streets. Even when a priest does reside in a local community, the financial cost of religious participation is usually far too much for the peasant to bear. Very few Brazilians can afford the luxury of the tolling of the bells for a deceased family member, let alone the celebrating of an individual mass. Nevertheless, concern is obviously great, as is demonstrated, somewhat paradoxically, by mutual aid societies guaranteeing funeral costs and death benefits to their members—one of the first nonfamily-based organizations to be established in rural Brazil.

At the core of this peasant "theology" is a fundamental and deep belief in an all-powerful God who is at the center of all occurrences, good and bad, and to whose will each individual must submit completely and unquestioningly. The Brazilian peasant expects little from life, and he asks for little. He will tell you, with not a slight degree of melancholy and anguish, that he was born into this world to suffer in his particular condition as an act of God—"We work and suffer quietly, following the route that God laid out" (Leers 1967:38)—and it is upon God's will that he waits. Statements such as "That's the way

God wants it to be" (Está do jeito que Deus quer), "God's will is done" (Que Deus está servido), and "If God wills" (Se Deus quizer) punctuate seemingly endless expressions of resignation. Unexpected events and contretemps that further reduce the marginality of an already impoverished existence simply are accepted as extra punishment with no other explanation required. A peasant expresses it best himself in the idiom of exchange, when he states, "God pays us what we deserve, penny for penny" (*ibid.*, 39).

Yet, the Brazilian peasant's resignation is not complete, and through an ongoing exchange relationship with one or another saint, he undertakes to mitigate some of the harsher circumstances of his life. These saints take on the aspect of mediators between the secular and sacred worlds. Each individual devotes himself to the personal saint whose name he bears and with whom he closely identifies. He is expected to be a sincere devotee of his particular saint, to remember and commemorate his saint day, to light candles to him, and to propitiate him in countless other ways. The relationship is supposed to be one of steadfast devotion and unequivocal loyalty. Occasionally, a peasant might actively cultivate the attention of another saint by transferring his acts of devotion. However, the basic bond between saint and devotee is never broken completely, and more often than not the peasant is content to manipulate the existing relationship, constantly restating his faith in the power and goodness of his personal saint.

A popular song, recorded in the literatura de cordel, emphasizes the importance of saint-devotee relationships. It tells of a peasant in the backlands of the northeast state of Paraiba who dreamed that he should become a devotee of Saint Anthony. Accepting his dream as a vision, the peasant became a religious zealot, fulfilling all of his obligations to the saint. However, his faith was badly shaken when his horse, his son, and finally his wife all died in rapid succession. In half-crazed fury the peasant ran away, only to meet, in his flight down a lonely country road, St. Anthony disguised as a priest. "I have lost my faith in St. Anthony," he confessed to the priest, threatening all the while to commit suicide. The priest took from his cassock a picture of the peasant dead at the foot of his horse, from which he had evidently been thrown. "St. Anthony, like the good saint he is, killed him and took him out of his agony," he explained. He then showed the peasant a picture of his son being taken off to jail, and another of his wife making love to another man, offering the same explanation for each event in its turn. He prevailed upon the peasant not to take his own life, but to return home and pray to St. Anthony. The peasant lowered his gaze to think, and when he looked up, the priest was gone. He returned home, prayed to St. Anthony, and "lived until he was seventy years old, when he found salvation" (Mota 1962:195–200).

The great proliferation of personal, associational, community, and national patron saints is testimony to the importance of these sacred bonds. At the apex of this saintly hierarchy, in which some saints are believed to be more powerful than others or to specialize in some particular benefice, are the multiple manifestations of the Virgin Mary,[11] and of Jesus. Jesus himself is considered a saint, and his name, like the others, is given to children born on his own calendric days of devotion. Virtually every home has an altar on which it proudly displays its saints and fetishes. Household prayer meetings are called to honor a personal saint, who is feted with wine and dancing after a brief liturgy.

Although each individual has his own patron saint, often a large group of people will venerate the same household image. For example, when a statuette of St. Anthony was seen to leave a glass enclosure and walk across a household altar in the northeastern village of Coqueiral (Forman 1970), a chapel was built and dedicated to him. The statuette still belonged to the particular household, but the chapel was consecrated through the faith of one village faction, which maintains it with cash contributions.[12]

These saints are believed to be capable of performing miracles, and in addition to a generalized concept of protection in exchange for fealty, peasants assume specific obligations toward a particular saint in repayment for specific benefactions that were requested and received. For example, a peasant might seek advice or material aid, usually of the most immediate sort, and make a vow, a *promessa*, which is a promise to fulfill a stated obligation once the benefaction is received. The means of fulfilling the vow is always stated in the form of an offer, "If you do such and such for me, I will do. . . ," and the vow is kept only when the saint has upheld his part of the presumed bargain. Thus, if a bountiful crop is requested, the *promessa* is discharged only at harvest time; and a vow in the case of illness is kept only after the cure is made.

The nature of the obligation is carefully weighed against the nature of the request. It is common to light fireworks for a lesser obligation, while a cure usually is remembered by placing an *ex voto* in a popular sanctuary. These *ex votos*, carved from wood or molded in clay or wax in the shape of the diseased organ, are invariably dedicated to the particular saint to whom the appeal was made and who is accredited with performing the miracle, thereby thanking him publicly and spreading the word of his goodness and power. Peasants take these obligations very seriously and say that a saint is angered if a vow is not kept.

There are occasional reports that a saint's image may be punished when he does not perform according to his devotee's expectations, and statues of saints are said to have been found immersed in tubs of water or exiled from their altars until such time as their performance improves. Yet these cases are rare, and most peasants express horror at any thought of defiling the sacred. On the contrary, the constant expression of faith enhances the probability of effective protection and aid, and a peasant's belief in his saint's ultimate ability to act on his behalf rarely wanes. The failure to receive a saintly benefice is more likely to be taken as another personal failing, and a disappointed peasant will usually try to satisfy his saint with an improved offer.

There is no recourse to higher saintly authority. An individual might initially make a vow to a more powerful saint, such as the patron saint of a pilgrimage shrine, or to one who specializes in the kind of benefice he is seeking, if he thinks that particular saint is more capable than his own patron saint of acting on his behalf on that particular occasion. However, the idea of viewing this sacred arena as a competitive marketplace in which peasants bargain for maximum result (de Kadt 1967:196) would hardly do justice to the peasant belief system. Keeping the vow is an act of devotion. The element of debt is obviously high (Gross 1970), but it should be viewed as the fulfillment of a sacred debt of gratitude rather than as a simple repayment for services rendered.

In an important and informative article on "Religion, the Church, and Social Change in Brazil," Emanuel de Kadt asserts that this "hand-to-mouth supernaturalism" (1967:198) is

. . . exclusively a means of establishing control over nature . . . of overcoming adversities which man cannot cope with in a human temporal manner. It is wholly concerned with the satisfaction of man's 'natural' daily needs . . . which it attempts to ensure by means of near-magical rites, thought to have intrinsic value and inherent efficacy." (*Ibid.*, 195)

He goes on to stress the similarity of the character of the relationships between saint and devotee and patron and dependent:

There, also, the *patrão* takes it upon himself to pursue, as a favour, the peasant's immediate interests in return for specific services and a general show of respect on the part of the peasant. There too the peasant will look forward to a secular miracle in the form of very special favours. In short, the key concepts of folk Catholicism are very nearly identical to the key concepts operating in the traditional socio-political sphere. (*Ibid.*, 196)

For de Kadt, this means that the peasant, both as dependent and as devotee, is a supplicant seeking a miracle at the hand of a benefactor. He views both relationships as purely manipulative and directed toward this-worldly satisfactions, a fact which contributes further to the maintenance of the status quo. "By channelling their efforts into continuous invocations of the supernatural the peasants in effect buttress the existing social, economic, and political relations" (*Ibid.*, 197). In this way, ". . . religion has indeed contributed to keeping the masses politically ineffective" (*Ibid.*, 194).

It is not uncommon to discuss peasants' religious behavior in the idiom of exchange and to suggest a direct correspondence between sacred and secular relationships (Foster 1963; Gross 1971). Popular Catholicism does mold the religious hierarchy to the form of secular society, and it is quite possible to draw parallels between the peasant's views of the Holy Family and his patrão and patroa. Superficially, there is also a striking resemblance between the peasant's behavior vis-à-vis his saint and the reciprocal obligations that exist between patron and dependent. God, Himself, is sometimes looked upon as an "Almighty Patron" (Gross 1971), not simply as the Divine Father, but also as the "bom pai da gente," a reference to "our good Father" that has also been used in a political context and carries with it the expectation of patronage and all the affective weight of personalism.

Yet, there are also significant differences in the nature of these sacred and secular relationships. Whereas a clearly stipulated economic contract usually underlies the patron-dependent bond, the making of a vow in exchange for a particular supernatural benefice only follows upon the prior establishment of a more general relationship between saint and devotee. The social exchange dimension of the relationship between patron and dependent is superimposed upon basically temporary economic exchanges between real individuals, and the transitory expression of loyalty is hardly equivalent to the underlying expression of faith that characterizes the enduring bond between saint and devotee.

In my view, the real congruence in these relationships is to be found in the basic principles derived from them rather than in the structure of the relationships themselves. An extraordinary sense of submissiveness to authority and obligation to meet debt informs the peasant's behavior in both the sacred and secular domains. The patron's authority is paramount while the relationship exists, even though the slate can be wiped clean and the relationship terminated through the repayment of debt. The relationship between saint and devotee is not so easily terminated. A peasant may switch allegiance to another saint, but the bond between him and his patron saint is never really broken. At the same time, the sacred debt of gratitude expressed in the keeping of a vow is not unending. The vow itself must be fulfilled, usually through some actual expenditure of a material or a physical sort—fireworks, *ex votos*, or ascending *via cruces*. Rather than some metaphysical understanding of piety, loyalty, and a life of ethical response to an acknowledged never-ending debt, the necessity for immediate dismissal of obligation through repayment of debt orients the Brazilian peasant to the realities of survival in a secular world in which he is a thoroughly dependent being.

In one important way at least, the ritual extension of nonkin social bonds corroborates this view. When they do participate in religious rituals surrounding life crises, many peasants do so as much for the socioeconomic relationships established through the accompanying compadrio institution as for participation in the rites of the Church alone.[13] With each of these *rites de passage* an individual builds up a network of godparents (*padrinhos*) and co-parents (compadres) with whom he establishes strong reciprocal bonds marked by a particular mix of sentimentality and respect. Godparents and co-parents are often sought from among persons of higher socioeconomic status, and children are socialized early on into the system of patronage and rewards for correct behavior. Even when entering adulthood at the time of marriage, an individual is given a new set of godparents to whom he defers in countless ways, such as asking for a blessing, and to whom he can turn in time of need. These interactions follow the formal patterns of behavior of patron-dependent relations, with the additional sanctification provided by their ritual basis. It is notable, in this regard, that a religion premised on personal salvation has become characterized by community involvement and the strengthening of interpersonal bonds, which reinforce those notions of submissiveness and obligation that mark Brazilian peasant ideology.

It is in this way that religion nourishes the "culture of silence" and contributes to a politics of despair. Religion does not necessarily mask life's contradictions, nor does it provide simply a parallel (sacred) structure as a model for correct behavior in the secular world. Rather, by affirming the correctness of the notions of submissiveness and obligation, it gives credence to man's assessment of his own incapacity, providing him with an order of explanation that negates the necessity of his taking direct action on his own behalf. The existence of man's superiors and his relationship to them are rendered understandable. Responsibility, both as to the source of the problematical situation and its possible resolution, is fixed.

Historically, the search for solutions has led the peasant away from the institutional structure of the Church (de Kadt 1967:200–2). Its inability to fulfill the spiritual and psychological needs of the rural masses has resulted in a wide range of religious dissension, leading to Protestant conversion and adherence to a variety of spirit cults of Afro-Brazilian and caboclo, or Amerindian, types.[14] These spirit cults and Protestant sects are now found throughout rural and urban Brazil (Willems 1967).[15] Their success is due, in no small part, to the failure of the Church to minister to the pressing spiritual and material needs of the people. A negligent clergy which primarily serves the upper classes, the constant demand for payment for services rendered, and a lack of sympathy for the peasant belief system have all alienated a sizable segment of the flock.

The Church, in its insistence on doctrinal purity, has failed to understand the social and psychological functions performed by peasant religion and, in its rigidity, has failed to appreciate the flexibility and adaptability of its own teachings. Church leaders frown on popular catholicism and spiritualism in any form. Diversion from orthodoxy is seen as dissent, and African and Amerindian syncretic elements are forcefully—and sometimes forcibly—discouraged. At best, these cults are held up to ridicule. At worst, they are suppressed by civil authorities on the instigation of Church leaders. Even at the village level, there is little sympathy among parish priests and local elites for the religious needs of the peasants, whose belief system is often publicly derided. Much of the derision follows along race and class lines. Thus, the peasant is chided as an ignorant fool who cannot be properly instructed. He is told that his household altar is antireligious and that his saints are powerless. When a young black boy named Antonio appealed to his patron saint to make him grow older more quickly so that he could be admitted to the local movie house, the manager responded that St. Anthony could not possibly be of service to him and that he had best direct his request to São Benedito, the black saint. Here, too, as in the Amazon community of Itá, São Benedito is pictured ". . . as of dark skin and as a slave in the house of the lord—of the same color and status of the ancestors of most of the lower-class people" (Wagley 1964:220n).

It is of little wonder, then, that the peasant is shy of the Church. In physical structure, often opulent and imposing, it emphasizes his humbleness, contributing to his feeling of discomfort and unworthiness (Ramos 1965). As an institution with which he has had very limited direct contact, it is as forbidding as any other national bureaucracy. The peasant views the Church as an instrument of the upper classes, with whom the priest is also closely identified. He is the itinerant agent of the Church, who comes to town for a paid baptism or wedding, en masse, or to bless the many graves dug since the last year's visit. From the peasants' perspective, he appears in the village not so much to cater to their spiritual needs as to catch up on the business of the Church. In sharp contrast to his neglect of the needs of the peasantry, he baptizes the landlord's son, performs the shopkeeper's daughter's marriage, and celebrates mass for the tax collector's soul. Often, the priest himself is the landlord, assuming the role of patrão, and collecting rents— however nominal—on lands long ago bequeathed by the faithful to the Church. Much of the oppressive economic behavior of the dominant classes is associated with priest and Church. Few peasants want to participate in rituals that often accompany exploitation in everyday life. Thus, fishermen in the village of Coqueiral refused to attend the blessing of the newly constructed building which is used by the tax collector to weigh their fish, but which they are forbidden to enter (Forman 1970).

The Church, of course, takes an active role in national politics, and it is not unusual to find priests as candidates for a variety of local offices. Their political ideologies span a broad spectrum, and some priests expend considerable energy on behalf of peasants, as has that segment of the Church which is active in the organization of rural unions for agricultural laborers (de Kadt 1967:204ff.; 1970).[16] Nevertheless, there is a popular stereotype of the priest who acts as political agent for local landowners. On one occasion, I watched a rural priest as he directed the townspeople in mass violence against a group of peasants who had gathered in the town square for a rally organized by the peasant leagues. From the sanctity of the Church, he harangued his parishioners by loudspeaker on the evils of communism and protestantism and incited first the schoolchildren and later the hired guns of local landowners to action against the peasants. The mass hysteria which he deliberately created culminated in the wounding of several people and the death of at least one child (Forman 1963). Not surprising, then, that peasants are wary of the political activities of priests and often react with outright condemnation. For example, speaking about the priest-turned-mayor of this same county, one informant declared simply: "Father F. became mayor because he ran out of ways to make money as a priest." [17]

MOVEMENTS OF SOCIAL PROTEST

Emphasizing the role of religion in the formation of an ideology that is said to effectively immobilize the rural masses is not to suggest that they cannot be mobilized in specific cases. Two centuries of often violent upheaval makes this a statement of the obvious, and it is not terribly difficult to discover the specific conditions that led to their mobilization in each case (Forman 1971). As we have already noted, popular religion in Brazil has a double aspect: it is both a source of social control and a means of social mobilization. An examination of the peasant belief system in relation to movements of social protest, then, enables us to better understand why these acts of protest were not more generalized, why their occurrence most always required organizational efforts from outside, why these organizational efforts assumed the particular form they did, what was the likelihood of forging a common ideological base between the leadership and the membership at large, and finally, what was the quality of peasant participation within the movements themselves.

The expression of rural discontent in Brazil is not a recent phenomenon. Protest movements have recurred throughout Brazilian history. During the nineteenth and twentieth centuries, millenarian and messianic cults sprang up across the Brazilian hinterland, and bandit groups—now immortalized in the traditional songs of marketplace troubadors and in recent songs of social protest—roamed the Brazilian countryside. These two manifestations of rural discontent have often been lumped together as variants of social movements. Yet, they differ markedly in origin, in form, and in function.[18]

Social banditry represents a quest on the part of individuals for redress of grievances inflicted upon them by members of the dominant social order. It addresses itself directly to the secular authorities and merchant class in rural Brazil. Bands of *cangaceiros*, or bandits, led by men like Antonio Silvino and Lampião, ravaged the Brazilian countryside, particularly the Northeast, in the early decades of this century, attacking towns and plantations. They were fashioned from the mold of traditional Brazilian backland society, redirecting the violence characteristic of the interfamilial political struggles among the landed classes against those of its members whom they did not serve.[19] The Brazilian *cangaceiro* was more often than not an outlaw of good family who began his career as a bandit after some act in defense of his own or his family's honor (Souza 1972:110, 117). He banded together with others like himself for protection against the police, the agents of richer and more powerful men with whom he was not aligned. Later, he was able to recruit small numbers of displaced peasants and rural workers attracted to him by his offer of protection, the promise of spoils, and his acts of defiance against civil authority.[20] At a time when political dominance among the local oligarchs was assured by force, the blunderbuss also represented the great social equalizer.

This is in no way intended to phrase the phenomenon of social banditry in the idiom of the class struggle (Facó 1963, passim). As Souza has noted,

The very environment in which the *cangaço* thrived prevented it from making effective revolt for the following reasons: first, because the *cangaceiros* catered to the peasants' support in exchange for protection, thus restructuring the traditional dependence and subordination relations between the bands and the rural masses; second, because the *cangaço* had no political aims radically opposed to those of the dominant order (1972:131).

The bandit was not seeking a new social order, but merely—and momentarily—trying to punish those whom he blamed for personal transgressions. He always chose up political sides, aligning himself with one or another dominant political faction in the areas of the hinterland that his band traversed. The very perpetration of violence was both socially and culturally sanctioned within the ongoing system.[21] Lampião, in 1926, actually accepted a commission in the Brazilian federal army, as well as federal arms and money, in exchange for a promise that he would march against the Prestes column, a force of dissident army officers and their adherents who were being led on a long march through the northeast countryside by Luis Carlos Prestes, later leader of the Brazilian Communist Party. That battle was never joined, for Lampião chose to sojourn instead with Padre Cicero, the messianic leader of Joazeiro, who was then engaged in his own political struggle.

Despite Lampião's resurrection as a hero by some members of the Brazilian Left, the peasant's attitude toward the bandit is decidedly ambivalent.[22] He has been taught for centuries to respect and fear the rich and the powerful, and he looks upon the *cangaceiro* as a complex mix of both saint and sinner, to be protected at times, but also to be informed upon. The tales of backland heroism in the literatura de cordel are, once again, a significant source of data. In each of these moralizing stories, the bandit is represented as a hero who acts on behalf of defenseless and humbled peasants. Nonetheless, there are also constant reminders that the bandit hero was properly punished by the law, sometimes mercifully but oftentimes violently. The mediating circumstance appears to be the bandit's degree of religiosity. Thus, a popular song about Antonio Silvino emphasizes that he was indeed a religious man, who was released after a short jail sentence to live out his life on a peasant farm. The pamphlet ends in the following way: "Attention: Antonio Silvino did not die a tragic death, but peacefully, demonstrating that the good things he did outweighed the bad" (Camilo n.d.). And another popular verse, entitled "The Arrival of Lampião in Hell," recounts how he defeated the forces of Satan who refused him entry to Hell upon his death at the hands of the "legal forces" (Silva 1963). The troubador terminates his song: "I cannot tell you the resolution of this story about Lampião. He did not stay in Hell, but he also never arrived in Heaven. In all certainty he is still somewhere in the Backlands" (Pacheco 1949). Francisco Julião has a more plausible version. "The death of any one of them does not raise the level of frustration," he writes, "because hope is not wiped away; it transforms itself into the miracle of resurrection. In the minds of the most ingenious and desperate peasant masses, Lampião is not dead. He was called by Padre Cicero of Joazeiro" (1968:61).

The Padre Cicero movement is only one among many messianic and millenarian cults which have been a conspicuous part of the Brazilian rural scene in the nineteenth and twentieth centuries. These movements are multiple and varied, as the following brief descriptions of them will show. Nonetheless, an examination of some of their main features demonstrates certain consistent patterns and enables us to make some general statements about ritual expressions of this kind. Before proceeding to the descriptions, however, let me emphasize one important fact. None of these social movements was simply an isolated instance of religious fanaticism, in which bands of malcontents wandered through the countryside flagellating themselves in penance for the sins that they believed must have caused their desperate plight. Like the bandit groups just discussed, millenarian and messianic movements must be viewed against a backdrop of the complex political and economic struggles that characterized rural Brazil at the time of these occurrences. The historian, Ralph della Cava, examining two of the best known of these movements, those of Padre Cicero in Joazeiro and of Antonio Conselheiro in Canudos, makes clear their relationship to the national political and ecclesiastical structures which were then penetrating the Brazilian hinterland (1968). In point of fact, each of the twelve or more movements of this type for which we have adequate documentation was intricately involved in regional power struggles. Each manifested a complex mix of secularism and religiosity in its attempts at community organization and economic development. In all cases, success or failure in the simple matter of survival against hostile civil and religious authorities depended upon the willingness of the movement to accommodate to the political and economic structures that then dominated rural Brazil.

THE CITY OF HEAVEN ON EARTH, 1817–1820

Late in the second decade of the nineteenth century, an illiterate ex-soldier, Silvestre José dos Santos, gathered some four hundred followers at Mount Rodeador, in the backlands of the northeastern state of Pernambuco, where he established the Cidade do Paraiso Terreste, the City of Heaven on Earth.[23] There he constructed a chapel in which he and an assistant, also an ex-soldier, allegedly heard a saint promise that Sebastian, the venerated King of Portugal,[24] would emerge from a rock and transform ". . . the two leaders into princes; the poor into rich men; and augment the riches of the fortunate" (Perreira de Queiroz 1965a:198).

The community was organized into religious, civil, and paramilitary groupings. Silvestre formed a brotherhood with himself as leader, an assistant, and twelve "apostles" known as *os sabidos*, or the wise men. The rest of the faithful were called *os ensinados*, or the learned ones. Initiation into the brotherhood consisted of the confession of the neophyte, who pledged before two sword-wielding "brothers" to maintain secrecy and to die in the defense of Jesus Christ and King Sebastian. Common evening prayer meetings were held, followed by a nightly *saintly march* around the encampment. Women were not permitted to participate in these rites.

For a time, the community seems to have lived peaceably, subsisting on the agricultural endeavors of its adherents. However, while he never broke openly with the Church, Silvestre soon incurred the wrath of local ecclesiastical authorities when he began to administer confession. The Governor of the state of Pernambuco, advised of the potential danger of a sizeable encampment of this type, dispatched troops to Mt. Rodeador on October 25, 1820. In the ensuing battle, all of the adherents were massacred, with the exception of Silvestre, who escaped into the hinterland.

THE ENCHANTED KINGDOM, 1836–1838

In 1838, in the backland region of Flores, in the same state of Pernambuco, a thaumaturge called João Antonio Santos, began to preach that King Sebastian was going to be disenchanted and bring riches to those who believed in him. Substantial numbers of followers started to gather around him, with the result that a priest was sent to dissuade him from these heretical teachings. João Antonio agreed to leave the region. Two years later, however, his brother-in-law, João Ferreira, picked up the standard.

João Ferreira declared himself King of over three hundred followers,[25] to whom he preached that Sebastian would appear with his court at the entrance to the Enchanted Kingdom, marked by two massive monoliths that rose up starkly in the barren sertão. He told his followers that the disenchantment of King Sebastian would require considerable human blood, but that once he reappeared, the sacrificial victims ". . . would return rich, powerful, and immortal; white as the moon if they were black men, and young girls if they were old women" (Pereira de Queiroz 1965a:200–1).

João Ferreira's father offered himself up as the first sacrifice on May 14, 1838. Within three days, he was joined by thirty children, twelve men, eleven women, and fourteen dogs. Still, King Sebastian did not come, and on the fourth day, João Ferreira was himself sacrificed, while another brother-in-law assumed his throne. Forced to move his kingdom because of the stench of the decaying corpses at the base of the rock, the new king led his followers to a new site. On their way, they encountered state troops who had been called to the area by alarmed residents. A battle took place in which twenty-two of the devotees were killed, while the remainder dispersed and fled into the surrounding countryside.

THE NEW JERUSALEM, 1893–1897

. . . and so there appeared in Baia the somber anchorite with hair down to his shoulders, a long tangled beard, an emaciated face, and a piercing eye—a monstrous being clad in a blue canvas garment and leaning on the classic staff which is used to stay the pilgrim's tottering steps. (1944:127)

Thus, Euclides da Cunha introduces Antonio Conselheiro, Anthony the Counselor, in his brilliant historical novel, *Rebellion in the Backlands.*[26] Beyond this description, little is known about the early days of Antonio Vicente Mendes Macial, except that he was born to a rural middle-class family, engaged in commerce in the state of Ceará.[27] Da Cunha portrays Antonio as a quiet, introspective young man who worked as a cashier in his father's business. A bad marriage appears to have contributed to a life of religious devotion, which gave way to wanderings and pilgrimages shortly after he was abandoned by his wife. While roaming the countryside, preaching the coming of the end of the world, Antonio was joined by a permanent following of disaffected peasants, who settled in Itapicurú, Bahia, where they built a chapel. Almost immediately, however, trouble began with local authorities, and in 1876, the Counselor was arrested and returned to his native state of Ceará. Released soon thereafter, he returned to the state of Bahia, where he continued his wanderings until 1887.

The Counselor and his followers went from town to town

building chapels, repairing cemeteries, and burning the "excessive luxuries" of the devout who joined them. People sought him out for advice and cures, and his fame grew with the persistent rumors of the miracles which he allegedly performed. He was thought to be a saint and later likened to Christ himself by his followers. He claimed only to be a messenger of God, a prophet. He spoke of the coming of the millennium and of the return of King Sebastian, who would usher in the Kingdom of Heaven on Earth in a new land of Canaan. He required the faithful to abandon their riches, to practice chastity, humility, and abstinence, and to sorrow and do penance for their sins in order to hasten the coming of the millennium. Euclides da Cunha writes of him: "Like his correspondents of the past, Antonio Conselheiro was a pietist longing for the promised kingdom of God, which was always being put off . . . His teachings were no more than an approach to a Catholicism which he did not thoroughly understand" (1944:136).

The Counselor respected the Church and local church leaders, and he consistently refused to perform any priestly duties (Perreira de Queiroz 1965a:206). His attitude toward secular authority was far more rigid, particularly after the proclamation of the republic in 1889. He openly opposed the republic as an antichrist government which prefaced an end to the world (Perreira de Queiroz 1965a:204). When the municípios were granted autonomy and new tax regulations promulgated, he burned the decrees in the public square on market day, inviting an attack by the local police whom his followers easily routed. Nevertheless, the incident caused their retreat into the backlands where, in 1893, the Counselor established Belo Monte at Canudos. This site, a cattle ranch abandoned to the drought, was to become the New Jerusalem where the faithful could await the Final Judgment.

At the height of this adventure some eight thousand followers gathered around Antonio Conselheiro in the New Jerusalem (Perreira de Queiroz 1965a:207). Most of them were families from the drought-ridden sertão. Drawn from among cowboys, small farmers, and squatters, all were said to have had some material wealth which they left behind. Moreover, they were required to turn over one-third of their possessions to the Counselor upon their arrival in Canudos for the sustenance of the community. The community itself was internally stratified between rich and poor, but everyone strictly observed the teachings of its leader. The Counselor organized his followers into several groups with himself at the apex. The commanders of civil, military, and economic units, along with a religious assistant, served as his four apostles. In addition, a brotherhood called the Santa Companhia, which required that its members turn over all their possessions to the community, held prayer meetings and organized saints' day processions.

Canudos was not an isolated community. The residents maintained relations with neighboring towns, and there was a bustling commerce which brought them into contact with Brazilian society at large. It was the form of attachment which ultimately led to their demise. Local landowners initially had been pleased to support the community, which supplied them with a ready labor force. Their preoccupation grew, however, when people began to abandon their farms and collect permanently around the prophet. He formed political alliances with some of the landowners, who sought him out for the votes and labor which he had come to control. However, in so doing, he made both political friends and political enemies, increasing the displeasure of the latter by sanctioning raids on their plantations.[28] Although he always seemed to have good relations with the local backland clergy, the Church leadership also began to react strongly as his following increased. As early as 1882, a pastoral letter had forbidden him to preach (Cunha 1944:137), and a Church emissary had failed in an attempt at reconciliation in 1895 when he tried to convince the faithful to disperse (*ibid.*, 164). What seems obvious is that the local clergy and fazendeiros alike begrudgingly accepted the Counselor's presence while his work proved useful to them, but that they eventually yielded to Church authority and political pressures which eventually combined to bring about his downfall.[29]

Four expeditions were sent against Canudos between No-

vember, 1896, and October 5, 1897, when the city finally fell to
besieging troops. Cunha says that only four defenders were left
to face an army of from 5,000 to 6,000 men (1944:475). For more
than a year, the followers of Antonio Conselheiro had held off a
well-equipped army totaling more than 12,000 soldiers (Facó
1965:121). An armed struggle of the masses against the army of
the republic had supplanted the promises of salvation and hap-
piness in the Kingdom of Heaven on Earth (Facó 1965:103–4).

THE MUCKERS, 1872–1898

These movements of social protest were not confined to rural
populations in the Northeast. A messianic movement also arose
among German colonizers in the state of Rio Grande do Sul in
the extreme south of Brazil in 1872. It occurred in a zone of
small farms marked by economic progress where, nevertheless,
religious and secular teachings were still quite limited in scope.
The local population began to seek out João Jorge Maurer, a
curandeiro, and his wife, Jacobina, an epileptic who read and
interpreted the Bible to them. Within a short time, regular
meetings were being held, during which Jacobina appeared in
flowing white robes with a crown on her head, singing Protestant hymns and blessing everyone present.

On May 19, 1872, Jacobina declared that she was the reincarnation of Christ, whose words she spoke. She predicted the end
of the world and promised everlasting life to the faithful. From
among the thirty-four families who joined her, she chose twelve
apostles, starting with her husband, João Jorge. She also appointed a Secret Council. Her followers were forbidden to attend Catholic or Protestant church services, to drink, play
games, or dance. Children were not allowed to attend school.
Jacobina reserved to herself the right to make and to break mar-
riages.

Violence erupted within the community when Jacobina
changed husbands and ordered all others to do the same. A
number of adherents left the sect, and reprisals were exacted
against them. Several of the faithful were killed. Local political
chiefs, with whom Jacobina refused to cooperate, began to de-

nounce the group for any bad occurrences in the area. Jacobina and her followers reacted with more violence to this persecution. Eventually, government troops were ordered into action against the Muckers, but were defeated in their first encounter. The community's Church and fort were burned, however, and Jacobina and her followers retreated into the countryside where, allegedly, all children under five years of age were to be beheaded. In the face of such a possibility, the troops attacked again, this time killing the seventeen people who remained with Jacobina.

In 1887, Jacobina's daughter began to preach in the same region and continued to do so until 1898 with a small following.

JOAZEIRO DE PADRE CICERO, 1872–1934

Cicero Romão Batista, the revered Padre Cicero, was ordained in 1870 and sent shortly thereafter to the town of Joazeiro, a small interior post in the Valley of Cariri, Ceará. Cariri, at that time, was a rich and fertile valley of large plantations. It was also the scene of much oligarchic strife, a refuge for victims of the drought, and a breeding ground for insurrectionist movements which radiated out from the urban centers of the Northeast (Facó 1965:126ff.). The valley was highly integrated into the economic and political life of the surrounding states and, under the aegis of the Padre, was to grow into one of the major commercial centers of the Brazilian hinterland.

During his early years in Joazeiro, and particularly during the great drought of 1877–79, Padre Cicero distinguished himself as a dedicated country priest, earning the title of the *pai dos pobres*, the father of the poor.[30] Refugees traveled in great numbers to Joazeiro to seek his help and advice. His reputation as champion of the poor and friend to the needy was soon enhanced by the popular belief in his miraculous powers. In 1889, the *beata* Maria de Araujo spat blood as she took the host from Padre Cicero's hand, and the first of a series of alleged miracles was performed. A commission sent by the bishop of Ceará upheld the idea of a miracle, but the bishop himself reversed its decision and attributed the event to natural causes.[31] The case was argued in subsequent investigations and in a series of pastoral letters which culminated in the suspension of Padre Cicero from all his clerical duties. In 1898, the padre traveled to Rome, where he hoped to plead his case before Pope Leo XIII, but to no apparent avail. He returned to Ceará with hope for absolution, but the bishop still refused to authorize his preaching in churches, taking confession, or administering baptism except at death. He was allowed, however, to celebrate mass outside of Joazeiro itself, and he continued to give lectures of a religious nature to the throngs who gathered outside the window of his home (Montenegro 1959:29–30).

Padre Cicero's fame continued to spread throughout the Brazilian countryside, largely owing to the testimony of pilgrims to Joazeiro, to the songs of troubadours, and to the sale of religious memorabilia in the marketplaces. Between 1904 and 1909, the town itself grew tremendously, with immigrants coming from all of the surrounding states. Joazeiro became the commercial and agricultural center of the sertão, and Padre Cicero participated in the supply of labor to nearby plantations (Facó 1965:163). In 1907, he began to collaborate with Floro Bartolomeu, a doctor from the state of Bahia who came to Joazeiro to survey a copper mine on lands purchased for the Church by Padre Cicero.

In an armed clash with the previous owner, Floro defended the Padre's rights to the land in an event that marks the prelate's entry into political affairs. In 1911, Joazeiro was elevated to the status of a *vila de paz* and in 1914 to a city of which Padre Cicero became the first mayor.[32] His political stock rose considerably soon thereafter when he mediated a dispute among political chieftains in the state.[33] He became a political confidant and ally of some of the regional oligarchs and, later, vice-president of the state of Ceará. His friend Floro Bartolomeu was elected a federal congressman.

According to his own testimony, Padre Cicero was "forced to enter into politics in order to avoid having someone else in the political leadership of these people, who would not know how or would not be able to maintain the balance of order which he maintained up to now" (Montenegro 1959:32). However, an alternate explanation is that he did so in order to maintain his own prestige after his suspension from ecclesiastical duties (*ibid.*, 32). Whatever the case, the prelate's political assent clearly enabled him to work out a modus vivendi with the Church. In 1916 the bishop of Crato restored his right to celebrate mass in Joazeiro.

Notwithstanding, as the political and commercial aspects of the movement grew, its religious tenor faded. Padre Cicero limited his own religious activities to blessing pilgrims from the window of his home (Perreira de Queiroz 1965a:236). The *beatos,* followers who had been organized into groups of penitents and a Celestial Court, were disbanded (Montenegro 1959:40,42). Cicero's godson, José Lourenço, a secondary messianic figure who preached the coming of the millennium, was arrested and his Boi Santo, or sacred bull, a Zebu presented to him by Padre Cicero, was ordered killed by Floro Bartolomeu in 1926 (*ibid.*, 59).[34] Furthermore, Floro was well in ascendancy as the priest's principal adviser. José Marrocos, his first assistant and the man who probably engineered the miracle of the host, was shunted to one side (*ibid.*, 33). For all practical purposes, "Joazeiro ceased being a center of heresy in order to become a political fief" (*ibid.*, 53).

THE HOLY WAR OF CONTESTADO, 1910–1916

In the mid eighteenth century, a succession of "monks," known collectively as Monge João Maria and assumed by the local population to be a single individual, wandered in the region of Contestado, in the southern state of Santa Catarina.[35] They preached, practiced "curing," built chapels and erected crosses, and organized solemn processions. They announced the end of the world and demanded penitence. One of them ultimately adopted an antirepublican stance, upholding the monarchy as the true order of God. Word of their alleged miracles spread among the local rural populations, who refused to believe that the last of the *monges* died early in the twentieth century.

In 1911, José Maria, an army deserter, *curandeiro,* and

prophet, appeared in the region, claiming to be the brother of Monge João Maria. Like his predecessors, José Maria was an antirepublican who demanded the restoration of the monarchy. Unlike his predecessors, however, he accepted followers and settled down in a community where they could await the restoration in peace. As was to be expected, the group soon became involved in a political dispute with a local coronel, who denounced them to the governor of the state. Troops were immediately sent to the region, forcing the *monge* and his adherents to withdraw to a sparsely inhabited zone which was in litigation between the states of Santa Catarina and Paraná. Fearing that a land invasion was taking place, the governor of Paraná also dispatched troops to the area. Insisting on their invincibility, José Maria encouraged his followers to resist the troops. He was killed in the ensuing battle. However, the faithful insisted that he would reappear after one year, along with others who had died with him in the battle. It was believed that they would be part of a great Enchanted Army, led by Saint Sebastian, who would then wage a successful holy war against the enemy.

In 1913, a farmer who was a disciple of José Maria claimed that his niece, Teodora, saw visions of the returned "monk," [36] and he established a nucleus of followers in Taquaracu, Santa Catarina, to await the Enchanted Army. Once again, the group became involved in local political affairs, and troops were called in to disperse them. The attackers were routed in an initial battle, but returned two months later to scatter the defending band. Once again, the dissidents regrouped, this time at the remote village of Carauata, a settlement located on a piece of land which was also in litigation, albeit between two individual claimants. One of these men was immediately proclaimed emperor (Perreira de Queiroz 1965a:250). Ensuing intervention on the part of the State grew into a serious military campaign of extermination when, shortly thereafter, the movement issued a proclamation in the form of a monarchist manifesto, calling for the holy war against the republic to begin on September 1, 1914.

There followed a succession of leaders who gathered around

them large numbers of adherents at several hinterland sites. At the height of the movement, some 28,000 kilometers were occupied in the states of Santa Catarina and Paraná alike. Vinhas de Queiroz estimates that there was a total of 20,000 believers, of whom 6,000 were killed in the armed struggle. Some 8,000 men comprised the dissidents' standing army of *jagunços* (armed retainers) (1966:199–200).

Communities, varying in size from 300 to 500 inhabitants and scattered throughout the occupied territories, were organized hierarchically into distinct groups, all of which were subject to the strict disciplinary measures of the Messiah. At the vanguard was *Os Doze Pares de França*, a military elite comprised of the "apostles of Saint Sebastian." There were ministers of war, agriculture, and finance, as well as prayer "commandoes," field commandoes, and the Virgens Inspiradoras, who marched in front of the soldiers on their way to battle. The settlements were also rigidly stratified. Political chiefs and rich farmers assumed positions of power, and private property was maintained. Still, supernatural qualities ultimately were decisive in the succession to supreme leadership, one of the last of the leaders being the swineherd, Adeadato; and there was equality in the mutual quest of all adherents alike for a secure place within a stable society.

SANTA BRIGIDA, 1945—

Contentions to the contrary notwithstanding, a number of messianic and millenarian movements have continued to the present day.[37] One of the more recent of these was led by Pedro Batista da Silva, the Velho Pedro, a former sailor, longshoreman, and soldier, who was found wandering in the interior of the Brazilian Northeast in 1942. For a number of years, he lived as a curer and a penitent, suffering persecution at the hands of local authorities. Eventually, in 1945, he settled down at Santa Brigida, in the município of Jeremoabo, in the semi-arid region of the state of Bahia. The area was very poor, with an economy based largely on subsistence agriculture and a very weak periodic market. There was no road, and the local chapel has been described as a goat corral in which the goatherd actually lived.

Upon his arrival in Santa Brigida, Pedro Batista rented a piece of land from the coronel in Jeremoabo. He agreed to cease his activities as prophet and thaumaturge in exchange for political protection. Nevertheless, his reputation as a holy man continued to attract pilgrims and settlers in large numbers to the area (Perreira de Queiroz 1965a:275). He also began to loan money to these settlers at no interest. Extraordinary agricultural and commercial development followed. Pedro Batista bought two trucks and began to haul local produce to surrounding market towns. Soon Santa Brigida itself became the most important market town in the region. Pedro Batista became the largest single landowner and merchant, establishing cereal and cotton warehouses and purchasing disfibring machines for subcontract. He opened two schools, bought a diesel engine to supply electricity to the town, and gave a plantation to the federal government for a colonization and agricultural experiment station. Upon the death of the coronel in 1963, he established Santa Brigida as the head of its own district, with himself as its mayor.

Pilgrims to Santa Brigida believe that Pedro Batista (who died in 1967) was the reincarnation of Padre Cicero. He claimed only to be a good Catholic, albeit one with some profound spiritist beliefs. He always maintained good relations with local clergymen, who were invited to celebrate mass in the community. However, the Church seems to harbour a degree of enmity because of the heightened religious activity there. Pedro Batista allowed no drinking, smoking, dancing, or games and, while the community is theoretically egalitarian in structure, an established hierarchy of confidants exercise a number of religious and civil charges in which true authority is vested. Thus, while the Pedro Batista movement has undergone a rather considerable transformation over the past two decades, it still manifests certain of the same basic patterns of organization, belief, and response that characterize other social movements in rural Brazil.[38]

PROTEST MOVEMENTS AND SOCIAL STRUCTURE

These millenarian and messianic movements reflect the total integration but partial participation of the populations of rural Brazil in the nation's socioeconomic, political, and cultural processes.[39] They express both the religious and secular needs of masses of peasants and rural workers caught up in the throes of social conflict and unstructured social change. They also decry the inability of the Catholic Church—and the unwillingness of the Brazilian State—to respond to the very real problems which confront them, both historically and at the present time. Drawing upon a tradition which affected them profoundly, the rural masses articulated their needs in the religious idiom of the "folk" society, withdrawing into remote communities where they organized by their own teachings and for their own defense.

Nonetheless, there is no denying that these movements and the ideologies they formulated were a conscious part of the Catholic tradition of rural Brazil, providing one alternative framework through which peasant needs and demands could be expressed. If, basically, they were reflections of economic discontent, and there is considerable evidence that land questions were paramount in the regions in which they developed,[40] it is undeniable that the particular form they took was fashioned out of the cleavage between the Church and popular religion and thrived in the mystical domain that lay between the teachings of orthodox Catholicism and the peasants' own belief system. Their leaders were encouraged by the spiritual revival of the priesthood in the nineteenth century and based the legitimacy of their apocalyptic preachings in such books as the *Missões Abreviadas*, an abridged version of the teachings of seventeenth- and eighteenth-century Jesuit missions to the Brazilian Indians.[41] All of them (save Padre Cicero and Pedro Batista who led the two movements which were transformed within and by the dominant social order into successful political and economic undertakings) preached the end of the world and the salvation of the faithful, leading their followers to some isolated area where they established a community of believers to await the coming of the Kingdom of Heaven on Earth.

While there is no sociological account which tells us precisely from whence the membership of these movements was drawn, it seems to have come from among the peasants and rural laboring classes, smallholders, renters, and sharecroppers, with tenuous control over the land (Perreira de Queiroz 1965a:284, 1965b:64 passim; Vinhas de Queiroz 1966:203).[42] Many of the original adherents were pietists, active in the building and care of Church property. All seemed prepared to translate their day-to-day religious experiences and beliefs into the faith upon which the millenium depended. They accepted their leaders as emissaries of God, as reincarnations of Christ, or as supernatural beings in their own right. They attributed to them saintly powers and accredited them with the performance of a host of miracles. They acquiesced in their secular and religious demands, trusted in their affirmation that the end of the world was at hand, and sacrificed themselves to the ideal of salvation for the faithful in a society made better for everyone. If their stated ideology was to transform the world, it was not to violently turn it upside down. These movements were composed of men who chose to withdraw rather than to stand and fight. They were prepared to fight, and often did to the very last man, but only if attacked. Even then, they did so in the belief that who would come to lead them and make them invincible but Saint Sebastian, the venerated King of Portugal, who died in 1518 in Alcacer Kibir in his own holy war against the Moors.[43]

As to the structure of this new society, it reflected much of the traditional Brazilian social order. In a land made fertile, all men would work harder, and the poor would become rich men, and the rich, richer. Strict order was imposed and moral codes enforced, contributing to a life of austerity and hard work that obviously led to the commercial success of so many of the movements. At the same time, the organization of these heavenly kingdoms was very hierarchical and rigidly authoritarian, reflecting an ideology of greater equity which was hardly egalitarian. The saviors acted as both spokesmen and consciences in the secular and religious affairs of the communities they led. While the bulk of the membership was comprised of displaced peasants and rural workers, the ranks were joined by richer landowners and politicians who sought to manipulate the messiah because of his control over potential sources of labor and votes. If in these kingdoms the Brazilian peasant might have transcended the here and now, he could not transcend his own subjugation.

These public manifestations of religious zeal are, then, both a social statement and a private affirmation of traditional faith. They are social movements only in the sense that an aggregate of individuals has come together to seek their own salvation in a secular world of plenty for everyone. In their vague enunciation of public goals, they appear neither revolutionary nor reformist.[44] Rather, society is restructured according to some alternative model—the backlands turn to seacoast and the seacoast to sertão, black men become white, and old women are made young again—in a set of inversions which are more a denial of the present than a positing of the future. In their condemnation of this present, they suspend time and seek a more just and perfect society in a vague recollection of the past, often invoking the Empire to replace a republican, antichrist government. Yet, this in no way resembles the florescence of a new, action-oriented political consciousness.[45] It is only a remembrance of a better time when a just and noble emperor and his court were benefactors in a land in which the slaves had been set free—and there was no municipal government to levy taxes. At the same time, these movements do not represent a total flight from the secular world, but merely an attempt to come to grips with it by bringing prosperity to the community and renewing local political frameworks (Perreira de Queiroz 1965b:453).[46] Most of them failed to obtain that satisfactory an accommodation, however, either because their leadership opted for religious excesses—sometimes even including human sacrifice—in the expression of their demands or because they played badly at the game of local politics, in either case inviting massacre at the hands of federal troops.

Only two of the movements, those of Padre Cicero and Pedro Batista, showed considerable success, not only in the business of staying alive, but also in stimulating ongoing economic progress and establishing themselves as important regional political figures. These goals were accomplished largely through a denial of their religious zeal, a recapitulation to the dominant values of the society, and a reintegration into the social and political processes of their respective states, in which the leaders of the two movements assumed proper roles of traditional backland political chieftains, in this case, patrons to their devoutly faithful flocks.

RELIGION AND SOCIAL CHANGE

The recruitment of peasants into the diverse political and syndicalist associations of the 1950s and 1960s was likewise accomplished through the invocation of religious symbols and the reshaping of their meanings, either by clerics intent on making social justice work within the fold, or by political organizers who understood well the important place of popular religion in the forging of a common political ideology. In the former instance, "The real sources of Catholic radicalism in Brazil have been the people who elaborated these principles contained in the official doctrines of the Church" (de Kadt 1967:205). As an example of the latter, the former leader of the peasant leagues, Francisco Julião, writes:

Knowing by my own experience the feeling of legality of the peasant, that is his respect for the law, like his religiosity and his ingenious mysticism, two factors that contribute decisively to his immobilization and submission to the existing order of things, we made the Civil Code and the Bible instruments of work and motors of action. (1968:116)

In either case, the actions of the leadership of these movements were directed almost exclusively to secular ends: labor legislation for written contracts, increased salaries, and improved fringe benefits for rural workers; agrarian reform based on the redistribution of agricultural holdings for peasants. Referring the reader to the excellent account of *Catholic Radicals in Brazil* by Emanuel de Kadt (1970), for both the intellectual history and cultural content of the syndicalist and basic education movements, I will now turn briefly to an examination of the peasant leagues.[47]

The message first went forth in the form of a popular verse, Julião's "Letter of Freedom for the Peasant" (Carvalho 1962), a poor and unconvincing imitation of the literatura de cordel, which was intended to propagate the peasant leagues and to explain their organizational form to the masses. It was followed by "The Ten Commandments of the Peasant Leagues for the Liberation of the Peasant from the Oppression of the Latifundia," which included demands for a progressive land tax, a constitutional reform for the expropriation of land with payment in long-term bonds, regulation of rents and crop shares, production and consumption cooperatives, strict limitations on monopolistic land concentration, development of colonization projects, extension of labor legislation to rural workers, elimination of the abuses of the intermediary in the marketing system, restructuring of the sugar economy, and the creation nationally of peasant leagues which "represent Law and Order against the anarchy and disorder which are the Latifundia." Julião's last letter to the peasants, read in January 1964, and called *Benção, Mãe*— Bless me, Mother—emphasized the importance of the peasant leagues over and against the Church-run rural syndicates, insisting that political organization was the only viable alternative for the masses of Brazilian peasants.

And so religion became the bludgeon in the secular struggle for men's souls. Church, State, reformers, and land owners alike shouted the same simple slogans at potential adherents to their cause.[48] At an organizational meeting of Julião's peasant leagues that I attended at Surubim, Pernambuco, in 1962, the following dialogue took place between the student organizer from the state capital and a local landowner:

Landowner: Only God in Heaven resolves the problems of
these people. If God does not make it rain, no one
will come out of this problem.

Organizer: You are not a Christian, sir. Christ said, "Do for
yourself, and I will help you." Christ was not self-
ish. He fought for the people. He is the Son of God who came to
fight, to suffer . . . We do not want to take God from the heart
of anyone. Christianity is first obligation and then devotion.
Nothing will fall from the Heavens. It is not enough to speak in
the name of God or to cross ourselves. Any bandit can do that.
The Church is not a whole tree. It is only some branches which
are the rich priests. Faith is not enough. You must live Christianity. Man must work, fight for justice, equality, dignity.
Christ, too, was a revolutionary. Did he not use the whip to
drive the money lenders from the Temple? We now have
weapons!

Compared to a peasant like this one, sir, you are rich. You
cannot speak in the name of these peasants. You're well fed,
well clothed. We accept your word in the spirit of democracy
and liberty, but not as a peasant dying from hunger. If everyone
were in your state, we wouldn't need the Peasant Leagues. You
ask for salvation for yourself, but forget your brother. This spirit
is contrary to the Leagues. This spirit will bring another flood.
Don't go to the Church and ask for salvation for only yourself
and your family. Ask for your brother!

Audience: By the Grace of God!

As for the members present, Julião's appeal was based on the
same combination of mystique and faith that characterized earlier communities of believers. A tenant farmer at the meeting
told me that he was there for "a defense in life, for medicine, if
one should fall sick among us . . . for advice." His opinion of
Francisco Julião was clear. "He is the Prince of Life, who is
going to give us the resources to live." When asked how this
would be done, he responded: "I don't know because I am ignorant. I am waiting for an explanation, and then I will follow!"

This particular meeting ended abruptly when the hired guns

of local landowners were turned on the crowd gathered in the town square, wounding several peasants and killing one small boy, an episode which I recounted in the introduction to this book. The questions which I then posed with regard to the peasants' ability to rally either economically or politically within the agrarian system can now be approached from another perspective. In the course of the next several years, the peasant political and syndicalist associations in Brazil grew in number and membership to sizable proportions across the nation. Yet, it was a national movement only to the extent that it aggregated a disparate set of local organizations comprised of individuals seeking to redress personal grievances, individuals who were desperate (as opposed to despairing), whose personal and family security was so totally undermined by the threat of eviction or actual physical harm that they began to stare objective reality in the face. In this sense, these recent social movements differed from earlier manifestations of social protest only in the way their leadership was able to articulate their demands as a loud, if not totally coherent, voice. That is, what distinguished these contemporary rural movements from earlier ones in Brazil was not the socioeconomic processes giving rise to them (although these have been accelerated), nor the immediate motives of the peasants who joined them (although they undoubtedly grew significantly in number), nor even the "outlook" (Shils 1968) of the memberships themselves (since they had only then begun to change). Rather, what distinguished the contemporary peasant movements from past ones in Brazil was the capacity of articulate outside leadership to join together to relate a diverse set of local organizations to national political and administrative structures, their capacity to make realistic demands on the social system as spokesmen of a significant national lobby.

It is at this point that we might usefully turn again to Paulo Freire's application of the concept of *cosçcientizaçáo*, that "process in which men, not as recipients, but as knowing subjects, achieve a deepening awareness both of the socio-structural reality which shapes their lives and of their capacity to transform that reality" (1970a:27). This process occurred in Brazil, according to Freire, precisely when "cracks" began to open up in the structure of society with the rapid penetration of commercialization in the hinterland and the subsequent breakdown in traditional patterns of land tenure and forms of social alignment. Certainly, the threat to individual livelihood, the recruitment methods of the organizers of the peasant associations, the very associational aspect of these organizations, apparent government responsiveness to some of their specific demands, and the violent overreaction of the landed classes can all be seen as part of a process of awakening consciousness in which the peasant began to pass out of the "culture of silence."

Silence is no longer seen as an inalterable given, but as the result of a reality which can and must be transformed. . . . In the process of emerging from silence, the capacity of the popular consciousness expands so that men begin to be able to visualize and distinguish what before was not clearly outlined (Freire 1970:38).

But since, in this transition, the "culture of silence" is not broken all at once, the peasant masses could not speak on their own behalf. They became subject to the appeals of populist leadership from the cities which in turn awakened with the first audible cries of the peasantry. This leadership engaged the peasant politically in Brazil, but never gave him power. It manipulated him as part of its own bourgeois political strategy—seeking his votes and cautioning him all the while against the outright use of revolutionary violence. It employed the strike and the demonstration, land invasions and market raids as weapons to apply pressure on the nation, but in so doing filled the landowning classes and an emergent and vulnerable middle class with an overriding fear of "communism and corruption" leading to their strong support of the 1964 military coup d'état and subsequent dictatorship.

The military government which seized the reins of power on April 1, 1964, carried its purge down to the local level of the peasant political movement. The peasant leagues and independent political associations were disbanded, and many of their leaders were arrested. Francisco Julião spent several months in a military prison before making his way into exile in Mexico. The Church-sponsored rural unions were allowed to continue, but with government interventors in leadership roles. The peasants were quickly and easily reintegrated into the "culture of silence." There was little need of force, and the use of the media to disseminate the symbols of nationhood and glorify the military were deemed unnecessary in the countryside, that is, beyond the rather general appeal implicit in the very idea of a "redemptive" revolution.

The political movement of the 1950s and 1960s engaged a large number of peasants partially and fleetingly in the political process, but as an "external" factor which could not be easily accommodated. In an important sense, the extent of their participation far outweighed its significance. At the present time, these peasants continue on the fringes, an agglomerate of despairing people, longing to be saved, still seeking the miracle, and still acquiescing to the will of God.

Notes

1. Introduction

1. In addition to the general anthropological materials on peasant society and culture, Eric Wolf's excellent study of "The Mexican Bajio in the 18th century: an analysis of cultural integration" (1955) and Clifford Geertz's *Agricultural Involution: The Processes of Ecological Change in Indonesia* (1966a) have provided important models for this undertaking. While Wolf's close examination of the economic variables at play in the development of a particular regional sociopolitical complex differs profoundly from Geertz's encompassing view of the effects of the Dutch colonial system on ecological and economic processes in Java, they each influenced in crucial ways my own thinking about the study of the Brazilian peasantry.

2. While I am obviously concerned in this volume with a variety of rural socioeconomic types, the designation of a "peasantry" serves both as a useful shorthand and as a clear referent to a large body of anthropological and other social-scientific literature on the subject.

The basic anthropological definition of a peasant is found in Alfred Kroeber's now classic statement:

> "Peasants are definitely rural—yet live in relation to market towns; they form a class segment of a larger population which usually contains also urban centers, sometimes metropolitan capitals. They constitute part societies with part cultures. They lack the isolation, the political autonomy and the self-sufficiency of tribal populations; but their local units retain much of their old identity, integration and attachments to soils and cults" (1948:284).

The components of this basic definition have been greatly expanded and refined by different writers who have emphasized to varying degrees the cultural, social structural, economic, or political criteria mentioned in Kroeber's brief statement. Many have generalized their discussions to include the artisans and market middlemen who also comprise a peasant society. All anthropological definitions of peasants, or peasant society, fall into two main groupings: those that stress the cultural aspects of the rural way of life and those that concentrate on the social structural and economic attributes of the system.

The cultural school takes off from and is still best represented by the writings of Robert Redfield (1960). Although never excluding the characteristic social relationships which help to define a peasant society, Redfield chose to emphasize the cultural component in describing the peasant way of life. He concerned himself primarily with the traditional aspects of peasant society, focusing his attention on the systems of ideas, ethos, and world view which he thought best identified this social group. He was well aware of the symbiotic social ties that exist between the rural and urban segments of society and included "peasant" as an intermediate category in the process of social change from the "folk" to the "urban." However, he subordinated questions regarding the structure of these relationships to a more general discussion of the peasant's partial share in the cultural traditions of the dominant social group. It was never Redfield's intent to encourage a generation of anthropologists to focus down on the "little community" to the exclusion of the wider social unit of which the village is an intricate part, and he cannot be faulted for the neglect into which this aspect of his work has oftentimes fallen. On the contrary, it is to his lasting credit that his general, if somewhat eclectic, discussions of the multifaceted nature of peasant society serve to remind us of the complexity of the social system with which we are dealing.

A far more rigorous social-structural approach is found in the writings of Eric Wolf, who defines peasants as rural cultivators in a state system in which liens are placed on their production by a dominant social class. A significant aspect of the peasant's dependency is the payment of a *fund of rent,* in money or in kind, for use of the land to someone who stands in a superordinate position (1966:9–10). According to Wolf, peasants are ". . . rural cultivators whose surpluses are transferred to a dominant group of rulers that uses the surpluses both to underwrite its own standard of living and to distribute the remainder to groups in society that do not farm but must be fed for their specific goods and services in turn" (*ibid.,* 3–4).

In his earlier "Types of Latin American Peasantry," Wolf limited his subject to an agricultural producer in effective control of the land who aims at subsistence and not reinvestment (1955:453–54). He offered us important organizational and decision-making criteria for distinguishing among types of peasants, but willingly narrowed his field of inquiry to exclude sharecroppers, tenant farmers, fishermen, and the range of artisans and craftsmen who form an integral part of peasant society. Raymond Firth, on the other hand, offers an extremely broad definition of peasants. He writes that the word peasant refers to a ". . . socio-economic system of small-scale producers with a relatively simple, non-industrial technology" (1964:17). The system is essentially rural and depends upon the existence of a market. Firth's concept involves therefore a "set of structural and social relationships rather than a technological category of persons engaged in the same employment" (*ibid.,* 18). As such a peasant is a peasant not because of the kind of work he does, but because of the visible set of relationships which bind him to the larger society.

In a previous study of innovation and change in a small community in Northeast Brazil, I used such a broad definition of peasants and peasant society to include fishermen and artesans. I found fishermen to be structurally and functionally akin to agriculturalists vis-à-vis the larger society of which they are a part. Fishermen also pay a kind of rent, either in the form of a share of the catch or in a regular percentage paid to local branches of a national fishermen's guild. At the same time handicraft production contributed so much to the successful maintenance of the traditional economy that artisans could not be excluded from the definition of peasant society. My further view of the critical need to internally differentiate the general category of a peasantry will be made clear in chapters 3 and 5.

3. Schmitter (1971a), following Smelser, has applied the concept of integration to Brazil in the Durkheimian sense of increased structural differentiation and the re-constellation of the parts, the coming together of the elements in a new configuration. While I am interested in the character of these new configurations, I am specifically concerned in the present volume with the place of the peasantry within each.

4. Leonard Binder has written that ". . . the political relationship between a modernizing elite and a traditional mass, one of the key political issues in all developing countries . . . is the issue of national integration" (1964:624). But the question of national integration, the relationship between the modernizing elite and the traditional mass, cannot be discussed in relation to politics and in cultural terms alone, as Chandra Jayawardena (1964:907) has pointed out in his review of Geertz, et al., *Old Societies and New States*. The processes of integration occur along multiple dimensions—economic, social, political, and cultural-ideological—and must be examined in that way.

5. See, for example, the excellent discussion of the "multiple" pasts of a particular village in India by Cohn (1961), in which he suggests that there are two kinds of pasts: 1) the traditional past, which is mythological, legendary, and stems from the "sacred traditions" of the people; and 2) the historical past, which is the ideas about events remembered by the people in the region. Both of these have to be seen, in turn, in terms of the various segments of the society present in the locale, i.e., castes in the Indian case. According to Cohn, "The traditional past functions to validate a present social position and to provide a charter for the maintenance of that position or the attempt to improve it. It provides a much wider framework than do the local historical pasts. The traditional past relates particular groups to an extensive social network . . . the historic past explains, supports, or provides a basis for action in the local social system."

6. In no case do I pretend to offer a definite historical account. I am concerned with the problem of the representativeness of local histories and their generalization to a total system, a problem evidenced in both chapters 2 and 4. Moreover, some questions will obviously be raised about the nature of the data employed in the analyses. Limited demographic data and travel accounts, as used in chapter 2, are certainly highly suggestive of the patterns which I believe were emerging, although close analysis of tax and land records, wills, birth, marriage and death certificates, and whatever legal processes occur, would have vastly improved the argument.

7. It is difficult for the anthropologist trained in the inductive method and disciplined in *in situ* studies at the local level to sustain for very long a fully macro-approach to a sociocultural phenomenon, such as a peasantry, which is best understood through the ethnographic medium. Yet, the movement back and forth between the local and the national poses another set of problems that should vex every anthropologist engaged in the study of a complex society: how do we generalize out from the particular field situation and from our own data? Since neither the community nor the region serves as a microcosm of the social system, how do we in this instance justify the use of specific sets of data as the basis for particular assumptions and generalizations? Indeed, can we even posit a unity of population and problem which transcends the localities and is unitable into a single encompassing monograph on the Brazilian peasantry? Obviously, my answer to this final question is *yes!*

8. There have been a number of anthropological attempts to define a distinctly peasant subcultural type. Wagley and Harris (1955) have called attention to a general Latin American peasantry that includes horticulturalists, who are tied to regional and national economies and exhibit an historically derived blend of European, American Indian, and/or African cultural patterns. These peasants are clearly differentiated from modern Indians because of their involvement in and identification with the nation as an entity and from the town-type subcultures that mediate between them and the national culture. Peasants are further distinguished from plantation workers on *engenhos* (the traditional sugar estates) and *usinas* (factories-in-the-field): "it is the dependence and allegiance to the *patrão* (boss), together with the distinctive land tenure, occupational, and communal arrangements peculiar to the monoculture regime which distinguishes *Engenho* plantation subcultures from Peasant subcultures" (*ibid.*, 435).

On the other hand, the centralized administrative control characteristic of the usina-type corporation has resulted in the breakdown of personalistic ties between patron and client, transforming the agricultural worker into a "rural proletariat."

In a later attempt to refine Eric Wolf's (1955) typology of closed corporate and "open" peasant communities in Latin America, Wagley (1963:159ff.) carried the distinction between peasant and plantation neighborhoods in Brazil even further, subdividing his categories according to reginal subsistence or commercial crop activity and related land-tenure patterns (sugar, cacao, cotton, coffee, etc.). However, Wagley is primarily interested in describing the way of life in the local community, and he does not attempt a detailed clarification of the socio-economic nature of peasant society itself. Thus, for example, he finds that the peasant community is less progressive than the plantation community, since the plantation is tied to the outside world by product exportation, while the peasant neighborhood is isolated and with limited communication to the outside. In this way, he attempts to describe the attitudes that emanate from the different organizational principles underlying the two types of agricultural establishments, but fails because he does not systematically account for the integrative mechanisms which define a peasantry, as opposed to a rural proletariat. Compare his view, however, to that of Furtado (1965:130–31) and CIDA (1966:157), which take note of the effects of the world market on plantation workers but report that the plantation is a rather closed and self-contained unit for its workers, since owners and administrators discourage workers from participating in the world outside the immediate community.

9. As we shall see, the agrarian system of which I speak was characterized from colonial times to the present by the production on large plantations of commercial export crops and cattle, and supported by the internal supply of foodstuffs through local and regional markets. The need for labor in both sectors of this single economic system has generated a wide variety of economic arrangements and rural social types including peasants, a wage-laboring rural proletariat, colonist-farmers, and indigenous horticulturalists. This book is about only one segment of the total Brazilian rural work-force, the peasantry. In this category I include sharecroppers, tenant farmers, renters, and smallowners, who are primarily engaged in the production of foodcrops for the internal market. As

we shall see, the precise nature of their attachment to the internal market is crucial to our understanding of peasant society and a basic criteria for distinguishing peasants from other agricultural workers. The exclusion of other rural labor types is not without good reason. I have already stated that this book is about a peasantry and not a general description of life in the Brazilian hinterland. Therefore, I will discuss the Japanese immigrant organized into productive and marketing cooperatives in São Paulo, the Mundurucú horticulturalist/rubber gatherer drawn into the Amazonian economy on the fringe, and/or the salaried laborer on sugar and coffee estates only when their inclusion is required to clarify some point about peasant society itself. Through such specificity and the examination of one limiting case, I hope to cast some light on the peasant phenomenon everywhere.

10. Beyond the mysterious Amazon, the fabled city of Rio de Janeiro, and the imposing architectural structure of Brasilia, the Northeast is perhaps the best known of Brazil's political subdivisions, whose extreme economic and social problems have pushed it to the forefront of international consciousness. It is a region that has received increased attention since 1960 when press reports of conditions there filled American officials and the public with the fear of another Cuba, this time within the hemisphere's second largest and second most populous nation. The Northeast began to receive massive foreign aid after 1961, when President Kennedy formalized the existent channels of giving in his declaration of an Alliance for Progress. In recent years, it, like other undeveloped regions of the world, has reaped the attention of economic developers, and it has offered innumerable examples for theorists of economic growth. It has also drawn the attention of anthropologists, political scientists, and countless others in search of the "traditional" and the "folk," the backward segment of complex human societies which could then be studied "in the process of social change." Significantly, in this regard, it was in the Northeast, as well as in the urban centers of the Rio de Janeiro-São Paulo-Minas Gerais industrial triangle, that the machinations of populist political and religious leaders reverberated on national middle-class consciousness, further encouraging the military coup d'état that wrested civilian authority from President João (Jango) Goulart in April 1964.

11. The most familiar problem of the Northeast is, of course, the periodic droughts that devastate the land, kill the cattle and crops, and dislocate hundreds of thousands of impoverished peasants and landless agricultural laborers in mass migrations to coastal cities and the more viable agricultural areas of the nations. It is said that the drought of 1877–78 took a toll of over 500,000 human lives and dispatched an enormous labor force to the Amazon rubber trails. Nearly one hundred years later, the drought of 1970–71 killed untold numbers of people and provoked the organization of labor gangs for the construction of wells, dams, and roads, a federal strategy for drought relief that fails to recognize the fundamental social, economic, and political problems that are the basic scourge on the landscape.

12. See, for example, Wolf's statement that "Mexico—or any complex system—is . . . the web of group relationships which connect localities and national level institutions. The focus of study is not communities, but groups of people" (1956:52). Wolf goes on to say that we ". . . can achieve greater synthe-

sis in the study of complex societies by focusing our attention on the relationships between different groups operating on different levels of the society, rather than on any one of its isolated segments" (*ibid.*, 63).

13. In his probing inquiry on *Area Research*, Julian Steward wrote, "There are few studies which attempt to show how the larger society affects the community under investigation; and there are no studies which undertake to conceptualize fully and in detail the relationship between the community and the larger whole" (1950:23). Yet, he still advocates the community study approach and wants to "relate the town more explicitly and completely to the larger extracommunity society" (*ibid.*, 31). In a later study, he succumbs to cautioning anthropologists to know their place by yielding the study of national institutions to sociologists, political scientists, and economists, and suggests that the anthropological "contribution" to the study of complex society can be through describing the "manifestations" of national institutions at the local level (1955).

14. The Russian economist A. V. Chayanov (1966) has contributed significantly to our understanding of the organizational aspects of peasant economies. Utilizing data from the pre-revolutionary zemstvo reports, Chayanov describes Russian family labor on peasant farms and contrasts them to commodity farms which operate as speculative business ventures. The transition from the one to the other is characterized by a decisive change in decision-making processes on the farm. The head of the peasant farm makes a subjective evaluation of marginal returns for increased inputs of labor against family consumption needs which are fulfilled largely by production in kind. The commodity-type farm, on the other hand, markets produce for cash, which is used to meet consumer demands. According to Chayanov, business activity on the commodity-type farm, on which hired hands were paid wages in anticipation of a calculable profit, is conducive to quantitative analysis. However, quantitative calculations were not made on the peasant farm which hired no labor and paid no wage. As an alternative, Chayanov suggested the labor-consumer balance, in which peasant decisions are made in terms of subjective evaluations regarding demand satisfaction as compared to the drudgery of labor. The effecting of such a balance, or on-farm equilibrium, led to the successful functioning of the peasant labor farm and, according to Chayanov, to its long-range competitiveness with capitalist farms. "An organizational analysis of peasant family economic activity is our task—a family that does not hire outside labor, has a certain area of land available to it, has its own means of production and is sometimes obliged to expend some of its labor force on nonagricultural craft and trades" (1966:51). Chayanov believed that the organization of these farms into cooperatives would preclude the necessity of collectivization as the only alternative to capitalist land concentration.

15. In adopting this latter approach, Wolf (1968:xv, 276ff., et passim) is able to use commercialization as the catalyst to revolutionary change in peasant societies.

16. Compare this to the statement by Chayanov: "The very advantage or disadvantage of any particular economic initiative on the peasant farm is decided, not by an arithmetic calculation of income and expenditure, but more frequently by intuitively perceiving whether this initiative is economically acceptable or not. In the same way, the peasant farm's organizational plan is con-

structed—not by a system of connected logical structures and reckonings, but by the force of succession and imitation of the experience and selection, over many years and often subconsciously, of successful methods of economic work" (1966:119).

17. This is not to say that acquisitiveness is not a characteristic of peasant societies but that, more often than not, it takes the particular form of possession of material objects, valued in themselves, and used as a hedge against inflation, and manipulated as a form of savings (Forman 1970:105ff., 126).

2. Beyond the Masters and the Slaves: A Peasantry in Brazil

1. Unlike the Indians of Mexico and Peru who became the peasant backbone of post-Conquest development in those countries, the pre-Conquest Indians of Brazil, living in widely scattered settlement with low population density and accustomed to swidden agriculture and hunting practices, did not suit Portugal's agricultural exploitation of her New World colony. Some Indians were, of course, drawn into the commercial economy, but the overwhelming bulk of the agricultural labor force was supplied by African slaves. The Portuguese population itself was too small to supply large numbers of agricultural laborers to the colony.

2. A variety of community and regional studies attests to this fact. See M. Harris, *Town and Country in Brazil* (New York: Columbia University Press, 1956); Harry W. Hutchinson, *Village and Plantation Life in Northeast Brazil* (Seattle: University of Washington Press, 1957); Manuel Diegues Jr., *Regiões Culturais do Brasil* (Rio de Janeiro: Centro de Pesquisas Educacionais, I.N.E.P., 1960); Charles Wagley, *An Introduction to Brazil* (New York: Columbia University Press, 1963); Charles Wagley, ed., *Race and Class in Rural Brazil*, 2d ed. (New York: Columbia University Press, 1963); Manuel Correia de Andrade, *Paisagens e Problemas do Brasil* (São Paulo: Editora Brasiliense, 1968). See also Charles Wagley and Marvin Harris, "Typology of Latin American Subcultures," *American Anthropologist*, LVII, 3 (June 1955), 428–51.

3. It is not our purpose to discuss the nature of slavery in Brazil. There are numerous descriptions of the slave trade and of the economic and social life of the slave plantation based on sugar in such works as Manuel Diegues, Jr. *O Bangue nas Alagoas* (Rio de Janeiro: Edicão do Instituto do Acúcar e Alcool, 1949), and Gilberto Freyre, *The Masters and the Slaves*, trans. by Samuel Putnam (New York: Knopf, 1946). Stanley Stein, *Vassouras* (Cambridge: Harvard University Press, 1957) gives an excellent account of the nineteenth-century economy of slavery in the coffee lands. The Brazilian slave plantation was a radical ecological adaptation to New World conditions. It was neither based on a previous Portuguese model nor organized along feudal principles; it was from its inception a commercial agricultural establishment.

4. Dauril Alden gives figures which indicate a high proportion of freedmen among the general Brazilian population in the colonial era and states that late in the eighteenth century, "Though evidence is lacking, it is likely that manumission was more prevalent in the great plantation captaincies-general of Pernam-

buco and Bahia de Todos os Santos than in Brazil's Far South where slavery had been introduced more recently and involved far fewer numbers. The extent to which manumission was practiced in different parts of Brazil at this time and its effect upon the social structure of the colony deserves to be studied" (1963:198–99).

5. Diegues Jr. estimates the size of sesmarias at between 10,000 and 13,000 hectares and the *data de terra* at 272 hectares (1959a:16). See Schwartz (n.d.:3,53n7).

6. One of the vexing problems in the economic history of Brazil is the question of a labor market. This question is particularly complicated by the issue of slavery. On the one hand, we have the buying and selling of slaves, as capital, used in producing a salable commodity (sugar) by entrepreneurs who made a profit solely in the commerce of humans, and on the other, the well-documented practice of hiring out slaves for production on other people's plantations. In this way, too, they represented a form of capital and were definitely part of the labor market. This practice appears to have been widespread not only on plantations, but also in the cities.

7. See Schwartz (n.d.) for a fascinating account of *lavradores* in sixteenth- and seventeenth-century Bahia.

8. In the English edition, *The Colonial Background of Modern Brazil*, the author writes:

"Another essential outcome of the colonization process . . . was the growing number of people condemned to a marginal existence outside the normal productive activity of colonization. This activity was almost exclusively limited to members of the closed circle of the colony's basic economic and social organization: masters and slaves, the entrepreneurs and administrators of colonization, and their humble tools. As long as there were only masters and slaves, as at the very beginning, everything went well. All the settlers in Brazilian territory had their proper place in the colony's social structure and its activities could develop along normal lines. But gradually other categories began to be formed, composed of people who were not slaves and could not afford to be masters. There was no room for these categories in the colony's system of production. Despite this their numbers began to grow. . . ." (1967:419)

9. Fuentes, Lambert, Sodré, Singer, and Castro line up on the side of feudalism. Scholars like Simonsen, Caio Prado Jr., Furtado, Gunder Frank, and Geiger take the position that the economy was basically capitalistic. Others like Ianni and Cardoso look for intermediate forms.

For a fuller discussion of these positions see Andre Gunder Frank, "The Myth of Feudalism in Brazilian Agriculture," in *Capitalism and Underdevelopment in Latin America* (New York: Monthly Review Press, 1967), pp. 331–77. On the question of feudalism in Latin America, see also Doreen Warriner, *Land Reform in Principle and Practice* (Oxford: Clarendon Press, 1969), pp. 4–10; 226–32.

10. There are of course other distinguishing characteristics including the allegiance of the serf, possibility for mobility, the openness or closedness of the system, etc. On the nature of medieval peasant life see, among other, Eileen Power, "The Peasant Bodo," in *Medieval People* New York: Barnes and Noble,

1966), pp. 18–38.; P. Boissonade, *Life and Work in Medieval Europe* (New York: Harper & Row, 1964); Marc Bloch, *Feudal Society* (Chicago: University of Chicago Press, 1964); F. L. Ganshoff, *Feudalism* (Harper, 1961).

11. According to Marc Bloch, the fundamental features of European feudalism are: "a subject peasantry; widespread use of the service tenement (i.e., the fief) instead of a salary, which was out of the question; the supremacy of a class of specialized warriors; ties of obedience and protection which bind man to man and, within the warrior class, assume the distinctive form called vassalage; fragmentation of authority—leading inevitably to disorder; and, in the midst of all this, the survival of other forms of association, family and State of which the latter, during the second feudal age, was to acquire renewed strength. . . . Like all the phenomena revealed by that science of eternal change which is history, the social structure thus characterized certainly bore the peculiar stamp of an age and an environment. Yet, just as the matrilineal or agnatic clan or even certain types of economic enterprise are found in much the same forms in very different societies, it is by no means impossible that societies very different from our own should have passed through a phase closely resembling that which has just been defined. If so, it is legitimate to call them feudal during that phase" (1966:446).

12. As Carlos Guilherme Mota points out in his account of the forms of thought that lay behind the insurrection of 1817 in the Northeast, "Native rural aristocracy versus Portuguese merchants; landowners versus slaves, this in synthesis, [were] the two basic principal antagonisms. But it would too greatly reduce the arena of social antagonisms, overall if one remembers that a free and poor population began to provoke tensions of a more complex nature . . ." (1972:2).

3. The Nature of Integration I: The Social Dimensions of the Agrarian Crises

1. There is some disagreement over the question of "concentration" versus "atomization" of landholdings in Brazil. The disagreement is, in part, a result of troublesome statistics since laws regarding taxes and expropriation do lead to "fragmentation" into several estates in the recording of many latifundia, which are, in effect, single units. The rate of concentration versus atomization also differs among micro-regions in Brazil and depends largely on the competition between export crops/cattle and foodstuffs (Prado 1960:199–209; see also Johnson 1970).

2. The effective land measure used by IBRA is called a "module" and does not represent a fixed acreage of land. Rather, the quantity of land is determined as the amount necessary to utilize the full-time labor of four working adults and support them at a level consistent with (generally undefined) national goals of well-being. The size varies from state to state and region to region in accord with the minimum wage stipulated for each local area. The minimum wage is, however, usually considerably below what would be required for an adequate standard of living as workers define it. See Ludwig and Taylor (1969) for a further discussion of IBRA's land measure.

3. CIDA estimated the number of underprivileged farm workers in Brazil in

1950 at almost 7.5 million or 59 percent of the total farm labor in the country. This represents approximately 3.5 million, or 65.3 percent of the farm families (1966:132) and reaches nearly 70 percent in the Northeast (ibid., 136). An important discussion of the effect of land consolidation on unemployment in the coffee economy appears in Margolis 1973:77 ff.

4. According to the CIDA study, there are approximately 647,000 owners of family farms in Brazil. A "family-size farm" has sufficient land to support a family at a satisfactory standard of living through the work of its members. Two-to-four people are afforded full-time employment on the farm, with most of the farm work being carried out by members of the farm family. In the 1967 cadastral survey, these "efficient estates" were classified as rural businesses, or *empresas rurais*, but constituted under 10 percent of the total number of rural properties (Ludwig and Taylor 1969:6).

5. There was between 1950 and 1960 an increase of over one million farms on 33.2 million hectares of land. The bulk of these were under 10 hectares each and only 2 percent were over 200 hectares. The 788,000 new small farms occupied an additional 2.9 million hectares, while 21,000 new farms of over 200 *hectares* controlled an additional 14.7 million hectares. Sixty-five new farms of over 5,000 hectares themselves accounted for an added 7.6 million hectares of land (CIDA 1966:90). According to CIDA only 2 percent of the land is used for *lavoura* and 80 percent held in forest in properties of over 100,000 hectares. In properties of 10 hectares, over 60 percent of the land is devoted to agriculture. See pages 333–34 (passim) for discussion of the viability of small farms in Brazil vis-à-vis their aggregate contribution to the domestic diet, intensity of land use, output per hectare, and use of savings for investment (relations between land tenure and land use).

6. For a discussion of Brazilian extension agencies, see Schuh (1970:240ff.), Ribeiro and Wharton (1969), and CIDA (1966).

7. Folkloric descriptions of these rural types are given in a publication of the Instituto Brasileiro de Geografia e Estatistica, *Tipos e Aspectos do Brasil* (1903); see also Diegues Jr. (1960).

8. Andrew Gunder Frank believes that these owner-worker relationships in Brazil are structured within a context of monopoly capitalism in such a way that nonowners and even small owners have to buy access to land by selling their labor. He then classifies forms of sale of labor as:

1. Sale of labor for money wages (wage workers)
2. Sale of labor for product (payment in kind)
3. Sale of labor for using land (tenant), and paying with money (renting), and paying with product (sharecropping), and paying with labor (unpaid, forced labor) (1967:264–65).

Manuel Diegues Jr. offers a similar classification of types of rural labor in Brazil, based on the form of remuneration accruing to each:

1. Those who receive salaries in money and are called *assalariados*, or salaried workers;
2. Those who are remunerated in kind, that is, workers who are paid in foodstuffs, and who can plant some products in order to obtain other resources for their subsistence;
3. Those who are totally or partially remunerated, with permission to plant

subsistence crops, the harvest belongs to them, and, in exchange, they provide the owner with a few days of work in the principal activity of the plantation; and

4. Those who receive a share of production either in product or in money but without the contract that would make it into a strict sharecropping arrangement (1959a:87).

9. Squatters are the most disenfranchised of all the rural types in Brazil. They simply move onto a piece of land whch they cultivate rudimentarily until they are forced to leave or come to terms with the owner, at which point they become retainers on the estate of a patron. *Agregados, of moradores,* as squatters have come to be called, have no rights in the land. They are given a small plot and sometimes allowed to build a house in exchange for their services. A squatter pays no rent, but is required to sell his crop to the landowner. He is also expected to give several days' labor per week—a *condiçao*—for a particular task for which he receives a wage usually lower than the legal minimum.

10. See CIDA (1966:186, 261ff.) and Frank (1967:234ff.) for further discussion of the intermixing of agricultural types in rural Brazil. For an excellent discussion of the effects of land consolidation on varying labor arrangements in the coffee economy, see Margolis 1973:70ff, 127ff).

11. See Johnson (1970) for a description of sharecropping arrangements in the state of Ceará and Candido (1964) for sharecroppers in São Paulo state. For a list of the variety of names by which sharecropping arrangements go in Brazil, see Diegues Junior (1959a:95). For a description of colonos on coffee plantations in Paraná state, see Margolis 1973:133–34.

12. Previously, up to 30 percent rent reduction was allowed, and the cost of rent to an individual tended to increase with his earnings, even though the cost to the landowner remained the same. There is also a possibility that landowner's deducted rent from several workers who live under the same roof (CIDA 1966:275). In addition, deductions up to 25 percent are allowed for food when it is furnished by the employer.

13. According to Fallers, "the primary social structural roots of stratification are to be found in the differentiation of roles within a network of relations and the mutual understandings and expectations about behavior that mediate between them. At the same time, a people's stratification system is also rooted in its culture, in so far as there exist standards of evaluation by which human behavior is judged (1963:162–63).

"Thus, the study of stratification may appropriately begin with a cataloguing of the array of differential roles, with a delineation of cultural definitions of virtue and excellence in human behavior, and with a study of the interaction between these in terms of both cultural differentiation and over-all differential evaluation of roles. This, however, is only the beginning, for the place of actual persons and groups in all this cannot be regarded as a passive one. If persons are assigned to different roles, and if culture evaluates these roles differentially, holding up some as more worthy than others, then the processes by which persons are allocated among roles may be expected to engage the interests and anxieties of persons and groups. Persons and groups may be expected to strive actively to achieve or defend their positions and, in the process, to manipulate, and even create, elements of the culture that evaluates them. A recognition of this "dynamic" element in stratification systems makes it useful to distinguish "secondary structural and cultural aspects" of such systems. By the "secondary structural aspect" of stratification we mean the structures and processes by which persons are allocated among roles, as distinguished from the "primary" differentiation of roles, or division of labor. By "secondary culture" we mean ideas and beliefs *about* stratification—about how and why persons are allocated among roles as they are and about the justice and injustice of this process—as contrasted with the "primary" definitions of excellence and the relative worth of roles" (*ibid.*, 163).

14. See, for example, Celso Furtado's discussion of a static rural versus a changing urban social structure in his discussion, "Brazil: What Kind of Revolution?" (1965). Also Wagley writes: "Thus, it might be said that traditionally there were only two social classes in Brazil: an upper-class consisting of landowners, merchants, professionals, government officials, and bureaucrats, and a lower class of manual laborers and artisans. The upper class consisted of *patrões* (employers), while the lower class included their extra-familial dependents—household servants, field hands, sharecroppers, and other employees. This two-class system is not entirely a thing of the past, but, as indicated above, most Brazilians still fall into one of the two traditional hierarchical categories. . . . Perhaps there has always been a relatively small group in Brazil who might be called middle class, . . . but . . . the development of a large middle class is something new for Brazilian society" (1963:101).

15. A discussion of the so-called "dyadic contract" can be found in Foster (1961, 1963). See also Wolf (1966b). A sizable literature on patron-clientism and political development now exists and will be discussed in chapter 6.

16. For another of many such examples, see Gross's (1970) study of the sisal economy in Northeast Brazil, in which he attempts to reconstruct the lines of social stratification in this remote município in the state of Bahia by following debt and credit relationships and the resultant patron-dependent bonds throughout the local system. Gross admirably demonstrates how the structure of the entire sisal economy—which in the ideology of Brazilian developers was intended to democratize agriculture in the region—is built upon and maintained by patron-client ties.

17. For example, the important volume, *Race and Class in Rural Brazil*, edited by Charles Wagley, describes in detail the particular systems of social stratification and race relations in four communities located in different ecological zones in the Northeast region and in Amazonas. Using standard of living based on income and patterns of consumption as a gross objective measure, two or more rural "classes"—upper, lower, and a possible middle—are delineated and then further refined by more subtle internal rank orderings based on the prestige gradients of racial identity, family affiliation, and education (Wagley et al. 1952).

Owing to its own peculiar constellation of historical socioeconomic features, each of the communities studied manifests some differences in its contemporary patterns of race and class alignments, as demonstrated in Table 5. Nevertheless, an examination of any one of them demonstrates the shortcomings of any attempt to objectify fixed social classes in rural Brazil. Thus, using wealth and occupation as objective criteria, Marvin Harris divides the population of the old mining town of Minas Velhas into two distinct groups, group A and group C.

Group B "[which] was established merely as a statistical residue" of those individuals who fit at neither of the extremes of the social system, is crosscut by a "racial ranking gradient" into two distinct groups, as shown in the diagram. "The term 'average wealth' denotes a position in the upper half of group 'B' and the term 'poor' denotes a position in the lower half of group 'B.' Hence, it is clear that group 'B' is not one but two classes . . ." in which some individuals in group B₂ actually rank higher than others in group B₁ on economic, occupational, and educational scales (Harris 1952:73). Harris concludes: "We are now in a position to assess the true significance of race as a criterion of class. While the racial value gradient is not as decisive as the economic gradient, its effect is sufficient to split the middle class in half and to create four classes where only three would otherwise exist" (*ibid.*).

Social Class in Minas Velhas, Brazil.

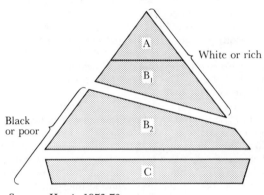

Source: Harris 1952:73

Like Harris, who himself modifies this earlier model of social stratification in Minas Velhas in his later monograph, *Town and Country in Brazil* (1956:96ff.), each of the other studies in *Race and Class in Rural Brazil* is more concerned with the inter- and intraclass patterns of race relations and with the life styles of the various subcultures represented in these highly differentiated municipal seats than with the general pattern of socioeconomic relationships between a dependent peasantry and a landed elite that concern us in this volume. Yet, in his introduction to that volume, Charles Wagley wrote that their research demonstrated that "The most important and most crucial alignment in rural Brazil was that of social classes, and that racial type was generally but one criterion by which individuals were assigned to social class. Race relations, then, must be seen as *an aspect of relations between social classes,* and as part of *a larger set of social patterns which determine the relations between individuals and groups* within the rural Brazilian community" (1952:9). [Emphasis mine]

In the remainder of this chapter, I will examine that "larger set of social patterns which determine the relations between individuals and groups" in rural Brazilian society, particularly the structure and culture of patron-dependent relations.

18. According to Edward Shils, "The cognitive and evaluative map of a stratification system is a differential allocation of deference to a series of aggregates of persons—for the most part anonymous—in accordance with their proximity to the center and thus in accordance with the magnitude of their presumed charisma. The stratification system of a society is the product of imagination working on the hard facts of the unequal allocation of scarce resources and rewards. The charisma is imaginary, but it has the effect of being "real" since it is so widely believed in as "real." Deference which is basically a response to charisma is only a matter of opinion but it is an opinion with profound motivation and a response to profound needs in the grantor and the recipient of deference" (1968).

19. The peasant community . . . may see the rise of wealthy peasants who shoulder aside their less fortunate fellows and move into the power vacuum left by the retreating superior holders of power. In the course of their rise, they frequently violate traditional expectations of how social relations are to be conducted and symbolized—frequently they utilize their newly won power to enrich themselves at the cost of their neighbors (Wolf 1966a:16).

20. Peter Blau suggests that ". . . if the power to command services and compliance is derived from the supply of needed benefits, those subject to power do not necessarily experience their position as disadvantageous . . ." (1964:228).

21. According to Fallers, "The notion of noblesse oblige, for example, expresses the obligation incumbent upon the legitimate occupant of an ascribed role to perform certain definite kinds of behavior. From the point of view of the person assigned by ascription to a low position, the situation is still more complex. For him there is probably always some difficulty in accepting as immutable a definition of himself as unworthy by nature, no matter what he may do. This is not, of course, to argue that he cannot, in some sense, come to accept his position. It does mean that a culture that presents to certain persons very much greater opportunity to occupy the most admired roles must also offer consolation in some form to those thereby deprived of such highly valued opportunity" (1963:164).

4. The Nature of Integration II: The Economic Dimensions of the Agrarian Crises

1. There is a large body of research and literature by anthropologists on peasant market places and traditional marketing systems. The works of Tax (1953), Mintz (1955, 1957, 1959, 1960a, 1960b, 1961), Katzin (1959, 1960), Bohannan and Dalton (1965), Dewey (1962), Belshaw (1965), Nash (1966), Skinner (1964), Wolf (1966), and Ortiz (1967) have all dealt with marketing institutions. Economists are well aware of the role of the market, particularly in Western economic systems. Oddly, they neglect the relevance of the market to peasant economies. With few exceptions, economists have studied the peasantry solely in relation to its role in aggregate economies. Only recently have they begun to ask questions vital to the peasant economy itself (Georgescu-Rogan 1960, Dandekar 1962, Schultz 1964, Mellor 1966, among others). The recent translation of A. V. Chayanov's *The Theory of Peasant Economy* (1967) has greatly enriched the lit-

erature in this field, even though he did not examine the nature of the feedback effects of the market on peasant agriculture.

2. Throughout this paper, marketplace refers to the physical locus for the periodic exchange of goods and services in rural areas. A marketplace network refers to a number of such loci which are connected through the movement of goods and personnel. The marketing system refers to the regional or national movement of goods between rural and urban centers.

3. For an interesting, but controversial treatment of the manner in which the very "underdevelopment" of Northeast Brazil is tied to the "development" of southern Brazil, see A. G. Frank, "The Myth of Feudalism in Brazilian Agriculture," in *Capitalism and Underdevelopment in Latin America* (New York: Monthly Review Press, 1967), pp. 331–77.

4. The first half of this chapter, authored jointly with Professor Rigelhaupt, appears with few modifications, in the *Journal of Comparative Studies in Society and History* (2):188–212.

5. Certain commodities produced in the county of Guaiamú, such as straw baskets, extend beyond this marketing radius, and are sold in urban centers like Rio de Janeiro, Salvador, etc. (Forman 1966). Sugarcane, of course, moves out into the international market. However, we followed only the movement of food staples in the internal marketing system.

6. Distorted statistics are obviously highly functional in traditional agrarian societies toying with the idea of land reform. According to the latest cadastral survey ordered by the President of the Republic in 1967 as part of his overall land reform, the county of Guaiamú has a total of 850 rural establishments with a land area of 81,140 hectares. Of these, 593 are minifundia, representing a land area of 10,839 hectares, or approximately 13 percent; 245 establishments are listed as latifundia with a total land area of 62,216 hectares; 12 properties with a land area of 8,084 hectares are listed as rural business (IBRA, 1967:42). Based on IBRA data, we are at a complete loss to explain the whereabouts of the 15,000-hectare single-property sugar mill.

7. Daniel Gross reports a similar randomness in attendance at fairs in the interior of the state of Bahia. "There are trucks on Friday which go to Coite, a distribution fair, and on Saturday which go to both Valente and Santa Luz. On Sunday there is a feira here, but most people come on foot or mounted. In Monte Santo, people could attend the distribution fair in Euclides da Cunha on Saturday, then go to Cansancao on Monday, Pedro Vermelha on Tuesday, and Monte Santo on Friday" (1968:personal communication).

8. There is more than just food staples flowing back into the countryside from the distribution fairs. A large proportion of handicraft products, such as metalwork and leather goods, have their origins in these market towns.

9. In the state of Alagoas, there are two urban consumers' fairs serving the capital city of Maceió (150,000 people) and the city of Penedo (32,000 people).

10. Michigan State University in cooperation with the Brazilian Agency for the Development of the Northeast (SUDENE) conducted research in the Recife foodshed area from 1966–67. Over 80 people participated in this large research endeavor. We are indebted to Professor Kelly Harrison, Chief of Party, and Dr. Harold Riley, Latin American Market Planning Center, for their cooperation.

11. The exact nature of debt-credit relationships in peasant economies is one

of the most urgent research tasks confronting anthropologists, since data of this kind is crucial to a full understanding of changing rural social stratification in transitional agrarian societies.

12. Chayanov (1966:268–69) noted that even in a system of cooperatives, the pervasiveness of market pressures effects the forms that cooperation will take, leading eventually from selling to processing, and ultimately, to production cooperatives.

13. A fourth alternative for the consolidation of production units might be the grouping of peasants on collective farms with the distribution of foodstuffs through state agencies. Such a system becomes capital intensive through the mobilization of labor; however, it may lead to decreases in production. There is no such system presently in operation in Northeast Brazil, and its development would appear unlikely given the prevailing political ideology.

14. For a full discussion of stated government policy in regard to development, see Ludwig (1969), Schuh (1970), and Weil (1971:391ff.).

15. According to the 1940 census, nearly 600,000 people moved about from farm to farm and village to city within the northeastern states, while well over 400,000 people left the region altogether (Souza Barros 1953:29).

16. For an autobiography of life in a São Paulo squatter settlement, see Maria Carolina de Jesus (1962). The work of Epstein (1969), Pendrell (1969), Leeds (1970), and Brown (ms.) are adding to a growing body of anthropological studies of urban Brazil.

17. A general review of the history of both public and private colonization schemes is to be found in Diegues·Junior (1959a:125ff.). See also, Smith (1963, ch. IX), Azevedo (1961), among others.

18. Diegues Jr. (1959a:184ff.) offers a useful history of cooperativist legislation in Brazil. To date, the cooperative movement has been quite small. Although the general instability of cooperatives and the failure of many to register makes accurate statistics difficult to gather, the 1966 Annuario Estatistico does list 5,893 cooperatives in Brazil with a total membership of 1,278,979 individuals (1966:380). Not surprisingly almost 70 percent of these were located in the south-central and southern states of Rio de Janeiro, Minas Gerais, São Paulo, Santa Catarina, and Paraná, which boast not only the highest degree of economic development in Brazil but also the areas of primary foreign colonization. The largest number of cooperatives within the Northeast occurs in the state of Pernambuco, the most developed state of that region.

5. The Nature of Integration III: Rural Masses and the Brazilian Political Process

1. As we shall see, this theme reemerges in various guises throughout Brazilian history. Except in a few instances, as in its earliest manifestations in the hostility between Creole planters and Portuguese merchants, the question tended to be rhetorical.

2. See, for example, Skidmore (1967:xv); Love (1970:3); Dulles (1968:53ff.).

3. I was guilty of this evasion of 450 years of Brazilian political history when I wrote: "Traditionally, the Brazilian peasant participated only vicariously in

the political process by exchanging his vote for the favor of a patrão. He was insulated from the pressures of the outside world by the attitude of noblesse oblige of the plantation master. Communication was unidirectional, passed down along the rigid lines of the social hierarchy. Alternative courses of action for the rural masses were few. Grievances could only be aired to the patrão or through open rebellion. The recent peasant political movement in Brazil is, at least in part, an attempt to open up new lines of communication where traditional patterns have failed" (1971:5). Obviously, such a superficial characterization fails to adequately describe the nature of a "traditional" system, or the processes of change and integration that have taken place in the course of Brazilian history. In the present endeavor, I make no claim to careful historiography, but merely attempt a thematic interpretation of the struggle among the elites and the consequent inclusion of the masses in the political process.

4. For a discussion of changing forms of legitimacy within patron-client dyads, see Scott (1972b; 1973).

5. At this same time, brokers tend to intercede between patrons and clients, often manipulating to their own advantage the administrative resources that are placed at their disposal. In this way, they themselves can become minor patrons, although they are locked into a system where they remain subject to the authority of the ruling class and in which real advancement is blocked for them. It is at this point that factionalism appears as another local expression of the competitive pursuit of such resources; and factionalism, too, is modified, laid aside, and ultimately destroyed as the system of spoils is regulated from outside.

6. "Massification in Brazil does not mean the fragmentation of those classes which are the bearers of a political and ideological tradition, but rather the incorporation into urban life and the political process of the popular strata from the interior and the countryside. Massification therefore does not mean the dissolution of the collective loyalty of those sectors already integrated into the industrial process, through the widening of their consumption capacity and of techniques of manipulation. Rather, it contributes to the dissolution of loyalties toward the traditional employers in rural areas" (Weffort 1970:395). See also Weffort (1965:164).

7. The reference to "nonpolitics" here is essentially to the relatively nonconsequential nature of decision-making as it often takes place at the village level. I am grateful to Paul Friedrich and Suzanne Berger for the observation that the politics (power components and policy-making components)/nonpolitics (government as administration) distinction, often elaborated in the anthropological literature, is probably misleading insofar as peasant political behavior in the form of overt action usually occurs as a response to some specifically administrative act (like market regulations and taxation). Furthermore, what I am describing in the historical narrative that follows is tremendous *political* activity at the local level—bossism, repression, vote-getting, etc. In fact, if the epilogue to this chapter correctly describes the trends toward the development of an administrative state and a federal government made responsive to the demands of a subject people, then indeed we might expect more, not less, political response at the local level.

8. Relationships within the administrative town or between it and its outly-

ing villages are the focus of most anthropological community studies in Brazil. Few concentrate on the sources of power within those municipalities.

9. Nancy Naro has observed that a close analysis of the transformation of native commercial elites from an offshoot of the landed class, in the person of their sons, to a self-interested economic sector, is in order. She is currently conducting research on related problems in the Brazilian Northeast.

10. As Shirley (1971:74–75) notes, the fragmentation of state power and authority by the planter on his own land "resembled a feudal pattern (but) it was highly integrated with commerce and hence to a large degree nonmilitaristic." On the capitalist and nonfeudal basis of colonial Brazil, see Riegelhaupt and Forman (1970); Johnson (1972).

11. "Representing . . . the only sector where the principle of authority is undisputed, the colonial family furnished the most *normal* idea of power, of respectability, of obedience and of submission" (Buarque de Hollanda 1936:89). For a rich and full discussion of the patriarchal basis of plantation society in colonial Brazil, see Freyre (1946, 1959).

12. On the functioning of municipal councils in colonial Brazil and throughout the Portuguese empire, see Boxer (1965), who also documents the occasional inclusion of mercantilists and craft specialists in the municipal council of Bahia. According to Buarque de Hollanda (1936:50), "The complaints of businessmen, city residents, against the agriculturalist monopoly of power in the powerful municipal Chamber is common in our colonial history." See also Queiroz (1969:14–15), especially her account of antagonisms at the base of the Guerra de Mascates (26ff.).

13. Vieira da Cunha (1963:14) argues that the liberal idea of English parliamentarianism filtered to Brazil through its formulation in France. Bello (1966:33) notes that the immediate inspiration for the constitution is to be found in the writings of Benjamin Constant, particularly his *Constitutional Policy*, whence came the idea of the moderating power of the emperor and a strong centralizing administration. Constant's Brazilian namesake, Benjamin Constant de Magalhaes, was a major figure in the republican movement.

14. In the summer of 1971, as a major symbol of conciliation and of national maturity, the Brazilian and Portuguese governments arranged for the return of the remains of Dom Pedro I for burial in Brazil next to his wife, Dona Leopoldina.

15. The confusing political combinations of the time are echoed by Gilberto Freyre when he writes: ". . . the Empire had functioned as a sort of Imperial Republic, favoring almost a symbiosis between patriarchal liberalism and authoritarian democracy" (1970:167).

16. The Law of 1881 might have been intended to rest power from the latifundiarios as Love suggests (1970:12), but it provided them with opportunity to control the rural vote as well.

17. The idea that an imperial ideology and national unity resulted from the recruitment of officials from a pool of "mandarin-like" elites (Pang and Seckinger 1972) is provocative, but it obscures the fundamental fact that competition and conflict over land and labor (Dean 1971) characterized many of the political machinations of the imperial period in Brazil and the crucial difference that ap-

pointment to office there was not conducted on the basis of an examination system as it was in China.

18. As Poppino (1968:212) notes: "It is one of the paradoxes of Brazilian history that the first sustained surge of industrial growth should occur during the final decades of the empire, when the nation had a highly centralized government whose economic policies were determined by a conservative, rural-oriented elite. In fact, much of the impressive financial and industrial development following the Paraguayan War was an unintentional by-product of the drive to modernize the agricultural economy. It was only a coincidence that occasional fiscal measures approved by the Congress—such as the levying of high import duties on selected manufactures, and the expansion of credit in the late 1860s and again in 1888—stimulated the industrial sector, for this was not the objective of the legislation. The views and values of the dominant rural aristocracy were seldom attuned to the needs of infant industry."

19. Love contends that with the advent of the republic "a democratization of the formal political process occurred . . . [since] . . . the number of elective positions at all levels of government was increased, suffrage was broadened, and authority was decentralized" (1970:7). Yet, the fact that only 2.70 percent of the population was registered to vote in 1898 would appear to belie this position, even given the fact that the literacy rate was only 14.8 percent in the last decade of the empire (*ibid.*, 8). Rather, it would seem that a number of other indicators, such as rates of literacy, responsiveness of government to demand, etc., would better measure the extent of participatory democracy in Brazil and, as Love goes on to note, the republican system was a burlesque which, in the end, simply strengthened the oligarchic stranglehold on the nation.

20. Della Cava divides the First Republic into two periods for the Northeast. The first, the Oligarchic Period (1889–1910), depended on state-based patronage. The second, the Bourgeois Period (1910–30), depended on federal patronage and was characterized by a merchant and landowner coalition (1970:157, 165).

21. "Campos Sales introduced the *política de governadores* to make certain he had congressional support for his fiscal and monetary policies. His most pressing problem was meeting the obligations of the Rothschild funding loan contract of 1889, which consolidated Brazil's external debts and introduced a payments moratorium to restore the nation's credit rating. The contract called for such unpopular measures as increasing taxes, decreasing the currency in circulation and government expenditures, and placing a lien on the Rio customs revenues for the House of Rothschild. In effect, then, the *política de governadores* was simply a response to the reality of Brazil's colonial economy" (Love 1971:96).

22. For a description of control over state electoral machinery in the Old Republic by the Partido Republicano Riograndense, see Love (1971:78–79). Despite the variation from national patterns of *coronelismo* posed by the essentially *coroneis burocratas* in Rio Grande do Sul, Love's description of the consolidation of power by the state Republican Party is invaluable. In that state, the real authority, in the form of local bossism, fell to four subchiefs of police (*ibid.*, 80), who were akin to the *coroneis* of other regions.

23. The outstanding study of *coronelismo* and municipal politics in Brazil is to be found in Leal (1948). For an interesting account of four recent *coroneis*, see Vilaça e Albuquerque (1965). A number of studies of local politics have appeared in the Revista Brasileira de Estudos Politicos, for example, Santos (1961). See also Paulson (1964), Harris (1956), and the general account in Torres (1965).

24. Della Cava describes how local *coroneis* vied with one another for the privilege of supporting the state oligarchy in Ceará, which simply waited for a victor to emerge—and to the victor belonged all of the electoral spoils. These struggles often engaged old-time landowners against newcomer commercial elites (1970:94–95, 142). See also Shirley's detailed account of a doctor who turned to politics in the mountainous município of Cunha, São Paulo, during the Old Republic (1970:80ff.).

25. "During the First Republic the state oligarchy manifested itself in the local community as a monopoly of power by a single political faction. That is not to say that there were no political struggles. To the contrary, this was the usual situation in all of Brazil: two political "clans" (extended families) engaged in fierce struggles and, with their followers, vertically divided society. Basically, however, in any given moment all of the positions of power in the community were controlled by one of the political factions. The political ascension of the other faction, when it occurred, signified a complete change in a short time, and the occupation by the new group of all the local focii of power. The dominant group at any given moment held, locally, the monopoly of power and was supported by the state oligarchy" (Lopes 1971:189).

26. The Great Depression of 1929 presaged the collapse of the coffee economy and strengthened the resolve of the São Paulo planters to retain their control over government fiscal policy. By nominating another *paulista* to succeed him, the presidential incumbent violated the established tradition of alternation and adherence, and laid the basis for a new coalition between the states of Rio Grande do Sul and Minas Gerais, providing civilian support for the military coup d'état that placed Vargas in the presidency. For a thorough account of regional political history in Rio Grande do Sul and the rise of Vargas to power through "traditional" *coronelista* channels, see Love (1971). See also Skidmore (1967, chs. 1–2) for an account of the revolution of 1930.

27. Shirley describes a doctor who arrived in Cunha, São Paulo, just as Vargas was deposing the coffee planters after their abortive counterrevolution in 1932. By careful manipulation, he was able to consolidate his position in the local hierarchy. Shirley refers to him as a patron, but it would be better to view him as a broker between the landed power elites and their clients. Lebanese commercial elites with a new economic resource later became new patrons (1971:81ff., 97ff.).

28. If the Vargas regime represented an alliance of the urban industrial bourgeoisie and the proletariat, it was no less conciliatory to agrarian interests. In fact, Vargas virtually ignored the rural worker and the critical question of agrarian reform throughout his twenty years as chief executive.

29. See Furtado (1965) for the classic explanation of how government support for coffee during the crisis buoyed internal demand and through import substitution created the basis for Brazil's own industrialization.

30. Proportion (percent) of total population voting

	1950	1954	1958	% Urban (1960)	% Literate (1960)
Northeast	13.7	14.1	14.4	20	30
Southeast	17.7	19.1	24.6	45	65

Source: Soares (1964:169–70, 182).

31. Schmitter's excellent account of syndicalization in the Vargas era argues convincingly that there was a clear set of continuities in political culture and practice from previous constitutional regimes (1971a:123ff.). "Getulio Vargas was perhaps so preoccupied with self-preservation that he had little left for other goals, although his daughter claimed that his basic conception of his role was that of tutoring the polity" (ibid., 75). For a quite different view of the Vargas era as the inception of a populist democracy that lasted until the military coup d'etat in 1964, see Ianni (1970).

32. A close examination of the data suggests the limits actually imposed on suffrage by the literacy requirement. Sodre, for example, demonstrates that out of some 31 million potential voters over eighteen years of age in 1950, only 13.8 million, or about 44 percent were actually registered to vote in the election of 1958. If we consider that only 15 million out of a potential 45 million voters were registered in 1962, we discover a drop in the size of the electorate to 34 percent relative to the eligible population (1967:220–21). On the injustice of denying the vote to illiterates, see Weffort (1965:165).

33. The importance of this vote in presidential and gubernatorial elections is demonstrable, beginning with a populist candidate's conquest of the São Paulo statehouse in 1947. It is reflected again in Vargas' electoral victory for his second presidency in 1950 and in the fact that his disciple, former Labor Minister João Goulart, won more votes as vice-presidential candidate than Kubitschek did for the presidency in 1955, when he lost votes to populist Adhemar de Barros (Skidmore 1967:149). Again, Janio Quadros' victory in the presidential election of 1960 defied standard party alignments (Weffort 1970:390ff.), although perhaps the most significant testimony to the independence of urban voters was the fact that a rhinoceros in the São Paulo zoo won 90,000 votes in the 1959 mayoralty election in that city. The phenomenon was not confined to the Southeast. In fact, perhaps the most indicative of this trend was the election of Miguel Arraes in 1962 as governor of the northeastern state of Pernambuco, where industrialization was just taking hold and the capital city of Recife had grown to over one million people (de Kadt 1970:48).

34. Even if they had been intent on agrarian reform, which their compromise with agrarian interests makes unlikely, successive presidents until Jango Goulart (1961–64) hesitated to use their decree powers for fear of alienating Congress whose support was necessary for other measures. See Skidmore (1967:169, 379–80 n.15).

35. Schmitter (1971a:29–30) suggests that the system moved from semicompetitive (competition at the local level) to fully competitive (competition at the local and national levels) during the Goulart regime.

36. The revolution of 1930 toppled the sugar aristocracy that had dominated the state in the Old Republic. Through a series of state and municipal interven-

ters, the Goes Monteiro family consolidated its hold over the state. For nearly two decades, they wielded unchallenged power while their opposition was brutally silenced or enmeshed in the enormous patronage network established under the Estado Novo. I am indebted to Rosemary Messick, University of California, San José, for the information on state politics in Alagoas in the Second Republic (personal communication).

37. See Sodre (1967:187ff.) for a discussion of "Who are the People in Brazil?" (*Quem e o povo no Brasil*).

38. The rural land tax was among the most important of revenues collected by the state. In 1961, it was shifted to the county and then back to the federal government in 1964 "where it was even more likely to be collected and less likely to be redistributed in favor of local government" (Schmitter 1971a:271).

39. The number of municípios in Brazil as a whole doubled during the Second Republic. In the state of Minas Gerais, the number grew from 16 in the colonial period to 95 under the empire and then 316 in 1948, 388 in 1953, 405 in 1958, 722 in 1963 (Burns 1970:329)—in each case quite soon after the congressional elections. For a fascinating account of the making of a new município, see Della Cava (1971).

40. Singer defines a *cabo eleitoral* as ". . . a local leader who has some tens or at maximum a few hundred votes, an insufficient number to permit him to run for office himself. He is a sort of administrative lawyer of his community, that could be a village, a slum, an association, or a recreational club" (1965:74).

41. In a fascinating account of local-level politics in the northeastern state of Paraiba, Blondel reports an increase of 56 percent in registered voters between 1945–50 while the overall population growth in the state was only 11 percent in the same period. These figures suggest considerable vote fraud, since the number of registered voters exceeds the estimated number of illiterates above fifteen years of age by some 60,000. Voting age at the time was eighteen years (1957:73–74).

42. Singer has distinguished three types of professional politicians in Brazil: the coronel, the representative of an economic group, and the clientelist politician who ". . . differs from the representative of an economic group principally by not being tied to definitive economic interests" (1965:77). Clearly the usineiros fit neither of these categories, although *their congressman* would be a good example of the economic group representative. Muniz Falcao is an excellent example of the clientelist politician.

43. This agitation reached its peak during the turbulent years of the Goulart presidency. The reader should not mistake Sr. L.'s desperate quest for a return to power for popular agitation, just as the mill owners' turning of the plantation house into a citadel should not be mistaken as an act of repression.

44. The degree to which factionalism in village politics perverts democratic processes, saps political energies, and pervades social and economic life has been described in a number of community studies. An excellent account is to be found in Harris (1956:186ff.). See also Shirley (1971). For a general discussion of factionalism, see Nicholas (1965).

45. A complete account of this associational rivalry and the economic and political outcomes related to it is to be found in Forman (1970).

46. While the UDN won most elections in the município, there is every like-lihood that they were rigged, and interviews conducted in the field suggest that there were large numbers of defectors to PSP candidates among peasants and agricultural laborers not resident in the mill town or on mill lands.

47. See Sodre (1967:221–22) for a discussion of vote-buying in the elections of 1958. In one case, the political spoils of drought relief were actually used for the purchase of votes in the state of Ceará rather than for traditional largesse. See also Blondel (1957).

48. See Shirley (1971:84–85, 106ff.) for a detailed discussion of how the ex-tension of the bureaucracy into Cunha, São Paulo, undermined the traditional authority of the landed elites, largely through the ascension of metropolitan law over personal law.

49. The urban population grew from 31.2 percent in 1940 to 45 percent in 1960 (CIDA 1966:61). The rural population grew at a considerably lower rate.

50. A common explanation for the failure of the peasant leagues to make inroads in the state of Alagoas is that the plantation owners are resident there and that the patrão system prevails. Yet, the foregoing account, as well as the facts that Alagoan history is replete with social banditry and that Alagoans swelled the ranks of the religious pilgrims to Juazeiro, renders such an explana-tion less than tenable. I suggest that the failure of the peasant leagues to make headway in Alagoas reflects the attenuated development of the internal market-ing system in that state as compared with others, meaning that tenure on the land was generally more secure. Church-sponsored rural unions did make some inroads among the rural proletariat in the northernmost part of the state. Since voter patterns appear to change in areas where syndicates and leagues were not operant, as in Alagoas, we could hypothesize that formal mobilization into polit-ical organizations follows upon the raising of a certain level of consciousness, a suggestion born out by de Kadt's study of MEB.

51. For reports on several of these state and national conventions, see Silva (1961), Vera (1961, 1962), *I Congresso* (1961).

52. A law of rural unionization was passed as early as 1903, but only thirteen unions resulted from this legislation (Price 1964:6). Moreover, these unions had little meaning with regard to the formulation of demands since they grouped employers and employees together in the same associations (Wilkie 1964:5). See Freitas Marcondes (1962) for a discussion of rural labor legislation in Brazil. Price (1964) offers the most complete account of rural labor legislation and unionization.

53. The National Confederation was made up of 10 federations with 270 unions, but 33 more federations with 557 unions were waiting for recognition at the time (SUPRA 1963:17). Huizer (1965:129) says that the Confederation in-cludes 29 federations from 19 states and 743 rural unions. In addition, there were an inestimable number of peasants who were obviously sympathetic but feared to join the movement.

54. This breakdown corresponds substantially to a typology of peasant politi-cal movements in Latin America elaborated by Obregon (1967). Noting that his classification might be lacking in empirical underpinnings, Obregon proceeds

to treat the peasant leagues in Brazil as a monolithic organization, including them in all three categories of peasant movements (Obregon 1967:308). We have already noted that the peasant leagues are definitely not a monolithic organization and that the name is best treated as a generic rather than a specific referent for the movement as a whole.

55. Julião believed the landed peasant to be more effective than the rural proletariat because under Brazilian law his rights fell under the civil code exempting him from the rigid bureaucracy of the Labor Ministry, because he could pay for legal defense with the fruits of his labor, and because he could take the offensive in a struggle by occupying land and withholding rents and shares (1962:58–62). Judicial proceedings proved ineffective in protecting the rights of salaried workers who lacked the financial resources for legal defense and the minimal economic conditions necessary to resist the landowner (1962:5–57). Furthermore, while the relationship between salaried worker and employer is essentially economic, since it is based on a wage, the relationship between peasant and landowner concerns itself with rights and thus assumes a political character from the beginning (1962:64). Nevertheless, Julião also appealed to rural salaried workers to join unions, although he recognized a fundamental difference between urban and rural workers and believed that the model for urban trade unionism could not simply be transplanted to the countryside (1962:46–47).

56. It has been noted that one of the prime incentives to the consolidation of landholdings throughout Brazil was the growing market for cattle (CIDA 1966:24; Schattan 1961:75).

57. Some additional references on the peasant leagues of Julião not cited elsewhere in this book, are Leda Barreto (1963); Callado (1967); Gondim da Fonseca (1962); Julião (1962a, 1963); and Sodre (1963).

58. João Pedro Teixeira was shot and killed on April 2, 1962, and the new owner of the plantation on which he lived was implicated in the crime (Carneiro, in CIDA 1966:338). A large manifestation was organized in the state capital on May 1, 1962, to honor him.

59. Obregon (1967:21) contends correctly that the confederation of peasant "bands" in Brazil grew out of strength in the countryside. However, there is no doubt that the movement was organized by urban elites. Carneiro tells us that the organizers of the league in Sapé were not peasants but workers with union experience in the cities, although the movement later came to be run almost exclusively by the peasants themselves (CIDA 1966:338).

60. Labor legislation in Brazil was always concerned primarily with the urban worker (Freitas Marcondes 1951:399), and the unionization of rural workers was inevitably to bear the mark of Vargas' syndicalist state. The rigid hierarchical organization of territorially based, noncompeting unions into state federations and a national confederation of rural workers subordinated to the Ministry of Labor, placed control over the unions in the hands of the government bureaucracy.

61. Callado (1967) contends that Julião was willing to use violent means but, in an interview with league organizers in 1962, I was told that Francisco Julião believed in the possibility of peaceful "revolution." There is an indication that

once in exile from Brazil, his position became more radical. In a recent statement from Mexico, he writes: "We believe that you cannot win the peasant masses from the top down, from the city to the country. You must live with the peasants, undergo the same problems they meet everyday, fight with them as one of them" (1966:167).

62. Julião noted that there were about 40 million peasants in Brazil and only about 5 million rural salaried workers (1962:67). In the 1958 elections for state assembly, he polled 3,216 votes while in the 1962 election for the federal chamber of deputies he won an easy victory with 16,200 votes (Price 1964:42–43). According to Andrade (1963:250), there were some 30- to 35,000 league members in the state of Pernambuco in 1963 and some 80,000 in the Northeast. Wilkie (1964:7) estimates some 40,000 members in 1964 in Pernambuco. For a fruitful discussion of the peasant movement in Brazil as a reflection of the mass appeal of "new guard" politics, see Leeds (1964). Leeds contends that the movement merely substitutes new patrons for the old. Another discussion of the paternalistic aspects of the movement can be found in Galjart (1964) and in a reply by Huizer (1965). A refutation of this position can be found in Obregon (1967:329ff.). For a complete account of national political events in Brazil since 1930, see Skidmore (1967).

63. Julião eventually broke with the leader of the Paraiba league at Sapé, Assis Lemos, because of a political question which arose between them. Lemos critized Julião's violent stand, but the real issue seems to have been the control over the League (CIDA 1966:330–40). Part of the attraction was certainly the strength of the Sapé league which boasted some 10,000 members in the state, which had some 40,000 members at large (CIDA 1966:341).

64. A good deal has been said about Communist Party infiltration in the peasant movement. While the Communist Party would certainly like to take credit for the movement (Borges 1962:260), and their influence cannot be denied in some areas, it would be blatantly wrong to generally classify the independent peasant associations as communist.

65. Obviously, the communist orientation to rural salaried workers was a reflection of their bias for an urban proletarian revolution. They criticized Julião for making the workers' movement an appendage of the peasant movement and excluding the Communist Party from a role in the direction of the movement (Borges 1962:259).

66. These first peasant leagues died out when the Brazilian Communist Party was declared illegal in 1947. However, the Communist activity in rural areas began again in 1962 (Borges 1962:253). In 1954, the Communist Party founded ULTAB (Union of Agricultural Laborers and Rural Workers of Brazil), which is active in the states of São Paulo and Ceara. In São Paulo it is aligned with the Agrarian Front, a radical Catholic group (Price 1957–58).

67. The principal influence of the Communist Party in Pernambuco seems to have been in the largest labor unions of the sugarcane zone, where they were better organized than the Church (Price 1964:51–52). The Church, the Communist Party, and the peasant leagues sometimes appear to have been in competition in the same area. However, it seems that they were appealing to different population segments (socioeconomic types) within that area. Further research

into the precise composition of the membership of various peasant unions and leagues would throw important light on this issue.

68. The Communist Party might well have feared another crackdown since one had shut down an earlier movement in 1945–46, and also in Paraná in 1951 (Silva 1961:56–57). Celso Furtado said after the 1964 military coup d'état that the communists also criticized Goulart for moving too fast, for fear that he might provoke the military into action (personal communication). Skidmore (1967:225) notes that "The Brazilian Communist Party was working to force a more nationalist and democratic government within the existing structure."

69. The rural unions actually had their origin in the state of Rio Grande do Norte in 1949 when Bishop Eugenio Sales founded the Rural Assistance Service. By 1963, there were 48 rural unions in the state, with a total of 48,000 members (Price 1964:49). According to Wilkie (1964:7) 61 out of 62 rural unions in the Pernambucan Federation, which claims some 200,000 members, are Church-sponsored. Feitosa Martins (1962:136–37) reports tremendous growth in the movement in São Paulo between 1961–62. See also Martins (1962).

70. For a statement of the mixture of social, religious, and economic goals of Church-sponsored rural unions in São Paulo state, see Frei Celso (1963) and Feitosa Martins (1962). Dumoulin (1965:16) notes that the primary stress of the unions in Rio Grande do Norte was on basic education, agricultural extension, and the development of good citizenship. Their interest in processing land disputes was so slight that they employed only one lawyer. A further statement of the goals of the movement and its nonpolitical nature can be found in Calazans' (1961) Syndical Primer for the Rural Worker in Rio Grande do Norte.

For an excellent general account of the activities of Catholics-on-the-Left, particularly their role in the Basic Education Movement's (MEB) adult literacy program, see de Kadt (1970). The movement's "primer" which was ultimately supplanted by one with less "political" content carried the following message: "What are elections like in Brazil? Many voters vote for the candidate of the patrão. Many give their vote in exchange for shoes, clothes, or medicines, others for a job or for money. Should this situation continue? The vote means consciousness. It means freedom. Consciousness can't be sold. Freedom can't be bought" (cited in de Kadt, p. 159). The primer was entitled Viver é Lutar (To Live Is to Struggle). The above is from Lesson 20.

71. In 1943, the Consolidation of Labor Laws extended to rural workers the minimum wage, the right to annual vacations, regulation of the labor contract, provisions regarding the payment of salaries and the right to prior notification of termination of the labor contract (Price 1964:7–8). The serious problem is to see that such legislation is made effective in the countryside.

72. In the same interview, Padre Melo sharply criticized Bishop Dom Helder and Padre Paulo Crespo, spokesman for the Church-sponsored Rural Orientation Service of Pernambuco (SORPE), for their policy of directing rural unionism from above, working primarily with the leaders on the movement and not with the peasants, themselves. See Crespo (1963) and Mitchell (1967) for further insights into the different positions of these two men. Everywhere the rural unions have attempted to train local leaders (Wilkie 1964:8; Feitosa Martins 1962:139). However, Wilkie notes the continuing importance of outside leader-

ship among the rural unions in Pernambuco and that the federation's administrative assessor even recommended candidates for the president and council at the time of elections (1964:10).

73. This distinction was used by Lenin, who believed that the middle peasant would be swept away in the capitalist economy, leaving the extreme groups of rural proletariat and capitalist farmers (1960b:181). Lenin also notes that the market is a key factor in the ability of the small farm to compete with the highly capitalized farm (1960a:37). For an application of this typology to rural São Paulo state, see Vinhas (1963). From a strictly empirical perspective this typology might be considered insufficient. In reality, these rural types are constantly intermixed, so that one man may be an owner, renter, sharecropper, employee, and wage earner at the same time on different agricultural properties. Souza (1956:289) found six different types of renters in the São Francisco Valley and three different types in São Paulo state. CIDA (1966:192ff.) offers a description of the variety of peasant types in rural Brazil. There are also regional variations.

74. I suggest that it is the local middleman who is being forced out of the internal marketing system by commercial elites, and who shares common goals with the peasant whose tenure on the land is being threatened. Years of tension between peasant fishermen and local elites in the county of Coruripé, Alagoas, in Northeast Brazil, erupted into armed conflict when policemen tried to force them to sell their fish to consumers directly on the beach at lower prices. The village women, led by a fishhawker, attacked and killed eight policemen, thereby ensuring their place in the local market (Forman 1970).

75. According to Harding (1964:36), "Combative peasant organizations appeared not in vital coffee, cacao, sugar, and cattle sectors, but where paternalism had broken down and the conflict was most intense between peasant and landowner: in marginal fazendas that were hard-pressed to compete with more modernized commercial sectors in agriculture; and in frontier areas and land near cities where, because of the rise in land values, speculators and commercial farmers were moving in to grab land from squatters who had cleared and farmed the land."

76. The manifesto of the meeting in Natal called for a radical reform based in the expropriation of land payable in government bonds over a long term and calculated on the declared tax value of the property. Additional demands included voting rights for illiterates, establishment of cooperatives and price guarantees for production and warehousing, long-term credit arrangements, and the extension of social security benefits to all rural workers (*I Convenção* 1963).

77. From 1946 to 1960 only six rural unions received the recognition of the Ministry of Labor (Freitas Marcondes 1966:54). Under the government of João Goulart, 266 rural unions were recognized (SUPRA 1963:18). While it is obvious that formal recognition of the unions, depended on the receptivity of national political leaders, the movement was evidently well under way prior to Goulart's taking office. He by no means created the demands of peasantry, but capitalized on them when they became highly audible.

78. For detailed accounts of the events leading to the overthrow of the Goulart regime, see Skidmore (1963), Bello (1966), Schneider (1972), and Stepan (1971). The Rural Labor Statute was essentially a complement to the consoli-

dation of Labor Laws of 1943 (Price 1964:7–8). It has a long history in Brazilian congressional committees, having originated in a bill sent to Congress by President Getulio Vargas as early as 1954 (Price 1964:9–10). Ferrari (1963) recounts the legislative events surrounding the presentation of the bill. For conditions leading up to and an explanation of the Rural Labor Statute, see Campanhole (1963) and Vianna (1963).

79. This association came to be known as the National Confederation of Agriculture after the Rural Labor Statute was passed in 1963. It has been argued that the movement was a weak organization. However, at the end of 1961 there were 1711 such associations with 240,120 members, mostly in the south, east and northeast (*Desenvolvimento e Conjuntura* 1964a:33).

80. Padre Melo's rural union in Cabo, Pernambuco, was left untouched because, according to the priest, "the military is afraid of his tongue." In 1966 the movement returned to clerical leadership, but the government maintains strict control. The weakening of the rural unions is evidenced by the fact that collections from rural workers toward the unions fell considerably. In 1964–65, 1,691 patrons collected union contributions from their workers, while in 1966–67 only 555 collections were made (SORPE 1967).

81. Skidmore (1967:318) notes that ample protection was provided for the landowners, including guarantees against currency depreciation for the holders of government bonds.

82. For an extremely insightful discussion of the Brazilian sociopolitical system, *o sistema*, before the 1964 coup, see Schmitter (1971a). For a brilliant indictment of the regime's overall performance since 1964, see Schmitter (1971b). An alternate view of the regime is to be found in Schneider (1972).

83. The texts of the Institutional Acts are appended in Burns (1972). For acts and decrees specifically related to the municipalities, see IBAM (1967a and 1967b).

84. The Agrarian Reform Act of 1964 empowered the federal government to carry out a complete cadastral survey in Brazil, institute a progressive land tax, exercise control over rural labor contracts, survey and demarcate public lands, expropriate land with payment in bonds (with guarantees against currency depreciation), colonize and establish cooperatives, and provide general assistance and protection to the rural economy. Perhaps the most significant aspect of the agrarian reform bill was the beginning of the Brazilian Institute of Agrarian Reform's (IBRA) cadastral survey in 1965.

85. As Harris (1956:103) notes, rural Brazilians see all progress as dependent on actions of *o governo* irrespective of what the progress represents, who the beneficiaries are, or who initiated it. The current regime is credited for having brought progress to Guaiamú, although very few individuals have actually benefited from it.

86. Significantly, the Federation of Rural Unions in Pernambuco, originally comprised almost exclusively of rural workers, was reported to have split after 1964 into three federations, one of wage earners, one of sharecroppers and fixed tenants, and one of smallholders who are not employees.

6. The Politics of Despair: Popular Religion
and Movements of Social Protest

1. See discussion of actor versus observer ideologies of exploitation by Sydel Silverman (1970).

2. In discussing this cultural dimension, I do not mean to argue against the primacy of the socioeconomic conditions that give rise to this set of movements. In the last chapter I sought to explain precisely those socioeconomic variables that served to establish the preconditions out of which the most recent mass movements were formed. I do, however, want to distinguish this cultural level of analysis from the sociological and also from the sociopsychological, or the analysis of the motivations, deduced from such concepts as "relative deprivation," that make possible the recruitment of peasants into mass movements. The specific motivations of the members of the diverse syndicalist and political associations and the stated ideology of their leaders are discussed briefly in chapter 5.

3. Leeds (1964) contends that the movement merely substitutes new patrons for the old. Another discussion of the paternalistic aspects of the movement can be found in Galjart (1964). For the alternate position, see the reply by Huizer (1965) and the general discussion in Obregon (1967).

4. Folk religion in Brazil is a syncretic mix of Catholicism and Amerindian and African cultism. It contains a strong element of supernatural beliefs of a magical nature. A peasant may incant the spirit of an old Indian caboclo or an African god at a Saturday night cult meeting and fulfill a vow to his saint before Sunday mass. He believes fully in his saint, but he believes equally as much in the werewolf, the evil eye, and the harmful effects of "the wind." He might acknowledge the priest and treat him with respect, but he is more likely to turn to a saint, a *curandeiro*, or a *mãe de santo* (the mother of the saints—i.e., a cult priestess) in times of need.

5. The Brazilian anthropologist, Thales de Azevedo, emphasizes five elements in which folk Catholicism differs from the formal dogma of the Catholic Church in Brazil: 1) the lack of a concept of salvation; 2) the lack of a concept of sin; 3) indifference to the sacraments and to the priest, who appears in a service role for the Church rather than as a mediator for God; 4) adherence to the cult of the saints; and 5) the use of domestic liturgies as opposed to formal rites. He suggests that the folk religion is of therapeutic value rather than a path to salvation since it is the way in which the peasant expresses his search for fulfillment of worldly expectations rather than some other-worldly satisfactions (1963:3).

6. Wolf notes that peasant religion has two functions. On the one hand, it ". . . functions to support and balance the peasant ecosystem and social organization" primarily by means of ceremonials which serve to validate the particular household units in peasant society and the relations between them (1966a:100). On the other hand, peasant religion ties the peasant to a wider ideological order. This latter function is far more complex than the validating function performed by ceremonials since, rather than merely validating local beliefs, the teachings of the dominant religious order may have to be reinterpreted at the local level in order to be congruent with local beliefs. There is a sizable mystical element in Brazilian popular religion, as evidenced in the following repre-

sentation of an illiterate bard's belief. The diagram was drawn for the author in the sands of a northeastern beach, the points named, and the poem recited.

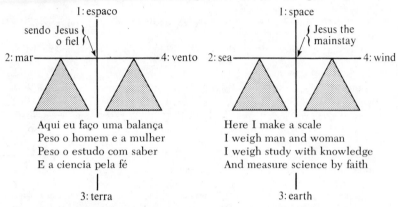

Aqui eu faço uma balança	Here I make a scale
Peso o homem e a mulher	I weigh man and woman
Peso o estudo com saber	I weigh study with knowledge
E a ciencia pela fé	And measure science by faith

7. Peasant society in Brazil is, of course, not entirely silent. The ideology of peasant culture is manifest in a rich variety of folk games and dramas, and in the massive and diverse literature of troubadours' tales, the literatura de cordel, so-called because of the manner in which it is strung out for sale on cords in the rural market places. These expressions of Brazilian peasant culture are replete with symbolic content that underlies peasant ideology and as such are much in need of anthropological analysis and interpretation, a task which I am unprepared to undertake in the present volume. There are a number of sources, however, through which such an undertaking could be begun (Mota n.d. c. 1961, 1962, 1965; Casa de Rui Barbosa 1961, 1964; Souza ms.).

8. It is difficult to know the peasants' feelings about death. They know of a heaven and a "land of Satan" both presided over by God, but there seems to be no great concern with entering one as opposed to the other. Children, it is believed, become angels that accompany "Our Lady." However, there is no notion that a good life on earth will lead to everlasting peace in heaven. The greater concern seems to be with the creation of Heaven on Earth, a phenomenon to be discussed below in connection with millenarianism. Souls are known to exist, and people sometimes communicate with the dead in spirit cult meetings, in visions, and in dreams, but most often to seek advice and resolve this-worldly problems. The "other world" into which one passes upon death is ill-defined ("Sei lá o que é, compadre"—How should I know what it is, compadre?). What happens at death? "A vida escapa" (Life escapes). The village midwife, shortly before her own death, began to have premonitions and expressed two overriding concerns—she wanted to die literate and to be buried in a coffin rather than be lowered by hammock into a pauper's grave "to be eaten by worms."

9. One of the most interesting expressions of the distinctly peasant religious tradition in Brazil is the celebration of saints' days. Brazilian communities lack the civil-religious hierarchies so well described for the fiesta pattern in Spanish-American communities, but the *dia do santo* is nonetheless an important part of

rural life. It is marked not so much by its heightened religious activity as by festive display and the solidifying of interpersonal bonds. Indeed, there may well be more ritual content in the celebrations for the goddess of the sea, Iemanjá, on February 2, when Afro-Brazilian cults celebrate her day of devotion. The nationally celebrated saints' days of São João, São Pedro, and Santo Antonio, and the local festivals in honor of a village's own patron saint are all occasions of individual gaiety and community spirit begun by the early morning tolling of the church bells and culminating in a village dance. There are, of course, the traditional novenas and religious processions in which an image of the saint is borne through the streets of the village on the shoulders of young men or women dressed in their finery for the occasion. There are also prayer meetings in the village homes, and the chapel is opened for the singing of the Ave Maria. If a priest is at hand, a mass will be celebrated. However, the spirit of the occasion is usually marked by the accompanying fireworks, dances, and folk performances, or by the fair with its games of chance and stands selling religious objects. These are days of genuine community pride, and the status of a village is greatly enhanced by their festa "to which people come from miles around." The best known of the Brazilian Saints' Days is undoubtedly the festival of St. John, *dia de São João*, on June 24, when rural Brazil pays homage to its favorite saint. Rural villages come alive with bonfires in front of every house, and balloons light the sky as they rise from the heat of kerosene wicks. São João is the festival of roasted corn and genipap liqueur, manioc cakes and the *buchada*, the stuffed intestines of a sheep. Young people dance the latest city fad in the *sede social*, while outside the old folk revive the traditional *coco* and the *base da chinela*. It is in this festive atmosphere that friends join hands and jump over bonfires, thereby establishing a bond of *compadrio*, while they recite some version or other of a popular refrain:

> *São João dormiu*
> *São João acordou*
> *Vamos ser compadres*
> *Porque São João mandou.*

10. Millions of peasants take part in the yearly mass pilgrimages to the many shrines that dot the Brazilian countryside. Some of these, such as Bom Jesus de Lapa (Gross 1971) and Monte Santo, in the state of Bahia, Joazeiro do Norte in Ceará, and Congonhas de Campo, Minas Gerais, are famous and attract people from throughout the nation. However, Brazil is also full of lesser-known scenes of miracles, such as Poxim, in the state of Alagoas, where for nine days in February, the faithful come in droves to pray for their sins, cure their sicknesses, and spend their meager savings at the stands of saints and sinners alike. It is in these shrines that the Brazilian peasant seeks to fulfill his ultimate religious obligation and to satisfy his most pressing human needs. The Church supports many of these shrines, and usually a priest is resident to supervise activities, control "excesses," and collect the gifts of the faithful. In 1961, I traveled on the crowded train from Rio de Janeiro to Congonhas de Campo to join the hundreds of thousands of pilgrims who gather for the first fifteen days of the month of September at that famous shrine. There the fair stalls were rented out by the Church to businessmen who set up games of chance and sell religious

objects. Tents lined the streets of the small city where years before Aleijadinho, "the little cripple," carved his beautiful statues of the disciples and the stations of the cross, first with the stumps of his hands and later with his feet. On that occasion, as on other visits to shrines, I was struck not so much by the ecclesiastical ritual, which was limited, as by the economics of the event and by the tremendous expression of faith of the masses gathered there.

11. For example, Our Mother of God, Nossa Senhora de O', do Bom Parto, da Guia, do Rosario, do Carmo, de Desterro, das Candeias, do Bom Conselho, do Perpetuo Socorro, das Dores, da Piedade, Aparecida, Imaculada Conceição, Assunção, de Lourdes, de Fatima (Leers 1967:16).

12. Political factionalism carries over even into religious life. The dominant political party in the village is part of a patronage network that flows through the sugar mill in the county, from where much local church support is derived. The opposition party, then, does not frequent the village church when the priest is present, but holds prayer meetings in the small chapel dedicated to Saint Anthony.

13. For an excellent historical analysis of the *campadrazgo* system, see Wolf and Mintz (1950). An interesting structural analysis of the same system is to be found in Gudeman (1972).

14. There is an enormous literature on spirit cults in Brazil, especially of the Afro-Brazilian variety.

15. Protestantism has been far more successful in urban than in rural areas. In many rural localities, the reception of Protestants is poor, and itinerant preachers are often ridiculed and sometimes even stoned. This is not because peasants are unwilling to dissent from the Catholic Church, but because local priests often preach against protestantism and communism in the same way and portray preachers as a kind of collective evil. The easier reception of spiritism probably derives from the fact that protestantism requires a sharp break with Catholic dogma and traditional social behavior (e.g., smoking, drinking, dancing, and sports), which is not necessary for members of spirit cults. See Willems' (1967) account of protestantism in Brazil. See also de Kadt (1967:200–1).

16. Discussing the effect of social encyclicals on Church policy in Brazil, de Kadt notes, "the importance attached to 'solidarism' and the right to private property, and the strong denunciation of socialism and class conflict have tended to turn them, in the Brazilian context, into tools more appropriate to those with conservative interests than to basic reformers" (1967:205, 208). He also notes that the great majority of Catholic leaders in Brazil are rigidly conservative (206). See also his discussion of Church-run rural syndicates in chapter 5.

17. All of this contributes to a great deal of anticlericalism in rural Brazil, most marked among men who rarely go to church. There is a rich lore which attributes rather particular sexual prowess to local prelates and perpetuates such anticlericalism. Peasants are often heard to make bitter derogatory remarks such as "You can't trust a man who wears a skirt!" or to offer explanations for the use of the habit ". . . so he can hide his guns and prophylactics!" One of the troubadour songs relates a rather typical story about a handsome young woman who is orphaned and left quite alone in the world. At confession, a priest makes a pass at her. She agrees to give him dinner at her home at 7 p.m. and then goes on to confess to another priest. He also makes a pass, and receives a dinner invitation for 8 p.m. Finally, she confesses to a very elderly priest, who also sum-

mons his sexual energies, and is invited to dine at 9 p.m. The young woman successively feeds, invites to her bedroom, and slays each of the priests, and then asks the village idiot to bury them, telling him that it is her own father returned from the grave each time. She finally rids herself of the village idiot by throwing excrement in his face, and he wanders into the street where he tells his tale to a disbelieving policeman. The young woman, her virginity intact, meets and marries a rich young landowner and lives happily ever after (Santos n.d.).

18. The reader's attention is called to Hobsbawm's excellent account of prepolitical social movements (1959). In one sense, I include social banditry here simply out of convention, since I do not believe, in the Brazilian context at least, that it constitutes a social movement comprised of an organized set of activities by a group of people in pursuit of a public goal or, as Gusfield (1968) suggests, "socially shared demands for change in some aspect of the social order." Nonetheless, a discussion of social banditry enables us to confirm a number of points about the quality of peasant participation in movements of social protest.

19. Facó (1965) suggests that much of the strife in the Brazilian countryside at this time stemmed from the challenge of new commercial elites to the dominant social, economic, and political position of traditional landed elites.

20. Drawing upon the astute political analysis of Nunes Leal, Souza argues that banditry became professionalized at "the historical moment when two lines of development—the decay of the private power of the landlords and the expansion of the regulative capabilities of the state—intersected, creating a point of indifference when neither of them was strong enough to offset the other." See quote, p. 131.

21. "It is safe to assume that, at least in colonial and imperial Brazil, violence was a cultural norm shared by all members of the patriarchal communes; landlords and peasants alike resorted to violent actions as a prescribed response to a wide range of social situations, especially those involving one's character as a man, his family, and sexual honor. Notwithstanding, this value system was also structured along another dimension, namely, subordination and deference to the upper stratum. If and when a tenant worker was compelled to respond violently to people in a superordinate position, quite often public officers, his action had to be sponsored by the chieftain" (Souza 1972:116).

22. Hobsbawm notes that, generally speaking, social bandits are "peasant outlaws whom the lord and state regard as criminals, but who remain within peasant society, and are considered by their people as heroes, as champions, avengers, fighters for justice, perhaps even leaders of liberation, and in any case as men to be admired, helped and supported" (1969:13), but goes on to note that Lampião was an ambiguous hero to the rural masses (ibid., 52).

23. Perreira de Queiroz writes that the followers were shoemakers, farm workers, blacksmiths, and deserters from the militia. See also, the account of R. Ribeiro, "O episodio da Serra do Rodeador (1818–1820): um movimento milenar e sebastionista," *Revista de Anthropologia* 8 (2).

24. Dom Sebastião, king of Portugal, was killed in Alcecer-Kibir during a holy war against the Moors. Belief in his return spread to Brazil from Portugal during early colonization.

25. Peasants and cowboys joined the group led by King João Ferreira and

members of his family. Converts and food were sought among the local plantations. It is reported that the group ate little and drank a lot, that prayer meetings
and marriage ceremonies were held frequently, and that polygamy prevailed.

26. De Cunha's account is a magnificent rendering of history, which contains
a great deal of detail and excellent descriptions of local color, despite the geographic and racial determinism which leads him to attribute these events to
miscegenation and the harshness of the sertão.

27. The Macial family had long been involved in a feud with one of the powerful families of the region. What effect this might have had on Antonio Conselheiro is not known.

28. See Della Cava (1968:13) for an attempt to link Conselheiro's alliances to
national political events.

29. Della Cava tries to refute Facó's contention that this movement arose
from lower-class alienation against Church authority by attempting to show that
the Northeast Church began to reform in the mid-nineteenth century. A three-
fold reform was intended to reorganize and revitalize the Church and return it
"to the people, especially the lower classes" (Della Cava 1968:3ff.). Such an
argument does not, however, refute the suggestion of alienation. It seems, on
the contrary, to add to the evidence that the Church was reaching out to touch,
but not embrace the rural masses.

30. For a full historical account of Joazeiro de Padre Cicero and his life and
works, see Della Cava (1970).

31. Della Cava states that the idea of a miracle was conjured up and perpetu-
ated within the ranks of the clergy (1967:9 passim). The bishop himself later
claimed that Padre Cicero had told him that Maria de Araujo had been subject
to convulsions and vomited blood since childhood (Montenegro 1959:28). It
would not be the first time that priests in Brazil had allegedly manipulated a
miracle:

> "Senhor Gama related a circumstance which occurred during his ouvidorship
> here, that affords a tolerably strong evidence of the deep subtlety practiced by
> some, at least, of the Brazilian holy fathers, for their personal benefit. A fe-
> male, residing at no great distance from Sabará, whose mind was darkened by
> bigotry, and who was particularly rigid in all religious observances, no saint
> day passing without her exhibiting the utmost devotion, mortified herself in a
> peculiar degree on all occasions of fasting, and during Lent always refrained
> from eating, with such resolution, that she acquired the honour of being con-
> sidered a saint. So strongly was her mind influenced by this delusion, that she
> communicated her self-working inspirations to two or three padres, who lived
> near. They immediately inflamed her wild imagination by their countenance,
> and gave public weight to the notion, by affirming that her soul would ascend
> to heaven on a certain day. Contributions were already talked of for forming
> an establishment to be dedicated to Santa Harmonica, the name of the female.
> The priests were, of course, to have the administration of the funds. Good
> Friday was the appointed day for the consummation of this important event.
> The machinery hitherto worked well, and her exhausted appearance, from
> continued fasting, warranted the conclusion that her dissolution was near. It
> was a subject of general interest, and being introduced where the ouvidor was
> present on the evening preceding the intended conclusion of the drama, he

stated that he had not faith in anything so ridiculous; and in the event of the female's death, he would summon a species of inquest to be held upon the body. A friend or coadjutor of the priests was present; he left the party and hastened on horseback to communicate this determination of the ouvidor to the holy brothers. An effect very contrary to the expectation of her devoted worshipers was thus produced. She speedily recovered from her saintly indisposition, and remains, if not in mental, at least in bodily health to this day. It was ascertained to have been the intention of these priests, founded on the wicked purpose of deriving advantages from the contemplated establishment of Santa Harmonica, to have produced by some means, a gradual exhaustion of life by the appointed time." (Henderson 1821:277)

32. Della Cava states that Padre Cicero was anxious to elevate Joazeiro to prominence so that it would become the seat of a bishopric then being contemplated for the region (1968:18). See also Della Cava (1972).

33. Political haggling between backland chieftains increased with economic prosperity in the region. Facó (1965) suggests that the rivalries were between traditional and new commercial elites rather than between the established oligarchs.

34. He was released on the padre's orders and sent to a fazenda called Caldeirão, which became the center of religious pilgrimages in the area after Padre Cicero's death in 1934. Caldeirão was organized into a brotherhood, and cooperative labor turned the plantation into a model farm. Disagreement with neighboring landlords led in 1938 to an armed conflict with federal troops and the end of this movement.

35. They were called "monks" although they did not belong to any religious order. The first reportedly was an Italian immigrant; the second possibly a Syrian (Vinhas de Queiroz 1966:49). The reader is referred to this excellent study for a detailed account of the events at Contestado.

36. According to Vinhas de Queiroz, Teodora's visions were faked (1966:122).

37. See the account of "The Millenium That Never Came," by Rene Ribeiro, in R. Chilcote, ed., *Protest and Resistance in Angola and Brazil*. Berkeley: University of California Press.

38. At the time of this writing, a graduate student in the Anthropology Department at the University of Chicago, Patricia Pessar, was preparing to undertake research on the transformation of symbols in the context of the Santa Brigida movement, as it underwent change from a heightened millenarian ideology to a developmentalist one.

39. Proceeding from the well-known "dual society" thesis elaborated for Latin America by Jacques Lambert (1959), the Brazilian sociologist M. I. Perreira de Queiroz suggests that messianic movements in Brazil have resulted from social disorganization and anomie which accompany the incursions of the urban sector on the "rustic." Messianic movements, she argues, serve as a counterbalance to the total disruption in the lives of peasants who live in an essentially closed social system, one which has minimal reciprocal influence on the urban sector with which it *coexists* (1965b:318, 327 passim). These "rustic" movements are assigned to two subcategories. Depending on whether social disorganization is due to exogenous or endogenous factors, they are either re-

formist or conservative, but never revolutionary. In an earlier paper, she suggests that these movements occur where peasants live in a closed economy, but rejects Bastide's (1961) notion that the movements are a reaction against change and progress. On the contrary, she says that the Messiah is an intermediary between the traditional subsistence economy and the export-oriented monocultural economy who helps peasants to make the transition by stimulating the production of cereals for the internal market. Messianism is, thus, transitional between archaic and modern, closed and open economies (1963). Obviously, I disagree with the dual society explanation of the genesis and form of millenarian and messianic movements. In the first case, messianic leadership did not always aim at opposing urban society and its institutions as several of the movements demonstrate. Second, the symbiotic relationship between the agrarian and urban sectors of the socioeconomic system has been established, and the infringement of commercialization in agriculture is certainly one of the root causes of disaffection among peasants.

40. There is an obvious correlation between aspects of commercialization and the advent of millenarian and messianic movements. Contestado, for example, occurred on lands under litigation and was radicalized by competition for land posed by the granting of enormous holdings to Germans and Poles for lumbering operations, as well as by foreign colonization in general. Vinhas de Queiroz records an oft-heard complaint: "We don't have any rights to land, which is all for the people of Oropa!" (1966:202). The great droughts of 1877 drove vast numbers of landless peasants into the humid valley of Cariri, the most commercialized zone in the region. In addition, Padre Cicero was joined by thousands of disaffected peasants who had made the long journey to the rubber fields of the Amazon, only to return to the Northeast in search of land. Caldeirão, the plantation to which Padre Cicero's godson and his followers were sent, grew with discontented peasants who were not a direct part of the commercialization of Joazeiro fostered by the prelate. There is some indication that Padre Cicero had them removed to Caldeirão in order to drain off the excess population at Joazeiro itself (Perreira de Queiroz 1965:261; Facó 1965:200ff.). A growing commercial bourgeoisie in the urban center nearest the Mucker community was bringing about incipient social stratification in the German colony, heightening tensions among poorer constituents (Perreira de Queiroz 1965b:228). At the other end, landless agricultural laborers were obviously attracted to these new settlements by their significant economic progress. In some cases, such as Canudos, Joazeiro, Caldeirão, and Santa Brigida, economic development was the conscious policy of the movements' leaders (Perreira de Queiroz 1965a) who strove for agricultural development, encouraged planting, developed handicraft industries, and sought markets. In others, it was a by-product of a life of ascetic denial and hard work.

41. I am grateful to Dr. Theo Brandão, the Universidade de Alagoas, for this reference. As Norman Cohn points out, messianism and millenarianism are very much a part of the Judeo-Christian tradition (1957). According to Worsely, "The greatest single agency for the world-wide spreading of millenarism has been the Christian mission" (1957:245). It would indeed be an important anthropological task to trace historically the transformation of this tradition through such sources

as the *Missões Abbreviadas*. Unfortunately, copies of it are extremely rare, and I have thus far been unable to consult it.

42. "Among those who grouped themselves around the *monge* were a good number of those who, evicted from their land and with no fixed domicile, were without sources of work or income" (Vinhas de Queiroz 1966:88). Perreira de Queiroz thinks no movements occurred along the littoral because plantation society had a greater stability than backland society (1965a:300). It is hard to identify members of the movements who might have come from large coastal plantations, and nowhere are there references to them. However, I would suspect that greater religious and social control prevailed on sugar plantations than in the backlands. Della Cava notes that Padre Cicero movement originated with the ecclesiastic hierarchy and only later came to attract the populace (1967:10).

43. Saint Sebastian and King Sebastian seem to become confused in the Brazilian popular ideology, particularly in the context of these protest movements. Joyce Riegelhaupt and I are now undertaking a comparative study of Sebastianism in Portugal and Brazil in which we hope to work out this and other problems in the popular belief systems over time.

44. "Modern revolutionary movements have—implicitly or explicitly—certain fairly definite ideas on how the old society is to be replaced by the new, the most crucial of which concerns what we may call the 'transfer of power.' . . . But the 'pure' millenarian movement operates quite differently, whether because of the inexperience of its members or the narrowness of their horizons, or because of the effect of millenarian ideologies and preconceptions. Its followers are not makers of revolution. They expect it to make itself, by divine revelation, by an announcement from on high, by a miracle—they expect it to happen somehow. The part of the people before the change is to gather together, to prepare itself, to watch the signs of the coming doom, to listen to the prophets who predict the coming of the great day, and perhaps to undertake certain ritual measures against the moment of decision and change, or to purify themselves, shedding the dress of the bad world of the present so as to be able to enter the new world in shining purity. Between the two extremes of the 'pure' millenarian and the 'pure' political revolutionary all manner of intermediate positions are possible" (Hobsbawm 1959:58–59).

45. Clearly a utopic outlook, the formulation of an *ideal histórico*, as opposed to an historical consciousness, a *consciencia histórica*, which understands the present "as a result of the past and as a potentiality for the future" (de Kadt 1970:87). Historical consciousness informs man "about the contradictions, conflicts, and *un*desirable aspects of reality, as much as about man's hopes or ideals, or the highly valued aspects of his concrete existence." It "emerges when man starts looking critically at his world, and becomes aware of the fact that 'history unfolds in an empirical time-span, which is given substance by the action of man in the form of historical initiative; action, that is, which transforms the world' " (*ibid.*, 87–88).

46. As Vinhas de Queiroz remarks, the majority of these movements do not follow irrational routes. "Sooner or later, due to internal and external factors, the movement tends to re-adapt itself to the world, even when it remains hostile to it" (1966:290). An accolyte of one of the most recently reported movements

resigned his commission as a civil specialist at the airbase in Recife in order to devote himself fully to the work of God. He wrote to the brigadier commander of the II Air Zone, explaining that he was following

"the Voice of Jehovah, God of Abraham and of the Prophets as well as the Voice of his Divine Master, King and Judge, Jesus Christ who is now coming and who is speaking to the Earth to form a pact of Peace, Love, Life, and Fraternity with the Brazilian Government so that it can be united to the Cosmic Government and to the Planetary Government to found a New Jerusalem and to place the World a step ahead in the understanding of God. . . . In case the Brazilian Government accepts the alliance with the Cosmic or Celestial Government, the King of Jerusalem will pay the debts of Brazil in about twenty years and will open the doors of its dispensation so that all Brazilians might be satisfied in their needs and glorify God who is in Heaven." (Ribeiro 1972:165)

47. See de Kadt's (1970:156ff.) discussion of the content of *Viver é Lutar*, the primer of the Basic Education Movement:

"*Viver é Lutar* was part of a *conjunto didáctico*—an educational ensemble. The actual textbook consisted of thirty lessons, realistically illustrated with photographs, geared to the experience of the peasant and his actual life situation. The rest of the *conjunto* was made up of a further three mimeographed booklets, meant only for those who were engaged in the production of MEB's radiophonic programmes. The first was called *Mensagem*, which elaborated the spiritual message of *Viver é Lutar*, referring to texts from the Gospels and making suggestions for links with programmes of catechization. This booklet was the most overtly Christian publication ever to come from MEB."

48. Francisco Julião offers the following personal account of the overt struggle for the peasants' minds:

"A relative of mine, a rich landowner, upon learning that some of his moradores had joined a league, called them together, more than a hundred with women and children, organized a procession in honor of his patron saint, and marched in front, rosary in hand, reciting the 'Our Father' and the 'Ave Maria' to the patio of the plantation house. There he asked, in the name of Christ, that they gather around him while he preached a long sermon whose central thesis was the following: 'The land where you live, I inherited from my father. And you, what did you inherit? Nothing. Therefore, I cannot be blamed for being rich nor you for being poor. All of this was preordained by God. He knows what he's doing. If he gave me lands and denied them to you, all of you who don't conform to this are rebelling against Him. This rebellion is a mortal sin. Accept God's decision so you won't incur his wrath and lose your soul. The poor man lives in the grace of God. The rich man does not. In this way, you are happier than I am, since you are closer to Heaven. Then, why do you detour from the path, refuse to pay the corvee and the raise in rent? Isn't that our agreement? Perhaps I invented these obligations, or did they already exist when Adam and Eve were expelled from Paradise? Listen to what I say and follow my advice: whoever has already joined the League, quit it. The same demon that tempted Christ tempts the Christian. The League has a pact with the Devil because it eyes land that does not belong to it. It wants to turn the people from the path that leads to salvation . . .' Two weeks later, when none of the moradores already enrolled in the League had heeded the sermon, my relative had the municipal constable arrest them all. I had to get a habeas corpus writ to free them. It was an evident sign that the hunger for liberty had greater force than a sermon; that the League had begun to gain ground." (1970:111–12)

Bibliography

Adams, Richard. 1964. "Rural labor." In John J. Johnson, ed., *Continuity and Change in Latin America*. Stanford, Calif.: Stanford University Press.

Alden, Dauril. 1963. "The population of Brazil in the late eighteenth century: a preliminary study," *Hispanic American Historical Review* 43:173–205.

Almeida Prado, J. F. de. 1941. *Pernambuco e as capitanias do norte do Brazil 1530–1630*. Tomo II. Rio de Janeiro: Brasiliana.

Andrade, Manuel Correia de. 1959. *Os Rios-do-Acucar do Nordeste Oriental*. (Os Rios Coruripe, Jiquiá e São Miguel), Vol. IV. Recife: Instituto Joaquim Nabuco de Pesquisas Sociais.

—— 1964. *A Terra e o Homem no Nordeste*. 2d ed. São Paulo: Editora Brasiliense.

—— 1968. *Paisajens e Problemas do Brasil*. São Paulo: Editora Brasiliense.

Antonil, Andre João (João Antonio Andreoni). 1967. *Cultura e Opulencia do Brasil* (1711). São Paulo: Compania Editora Nacional.

Azevedo, Fernando de. 1950. *Brazilian Culture*. New York: Macmillan.

Azevedo, Thales de. 1953. "Catholicism in Brazil: a personal evaluation," *Thought* (Fordham University Quarterly). 28 (Summer):253–74.

—— 1961. "Italian colonization in Southern Brazil," *Anthropological Quarterly* 34:60–68.

—— 1963a. "Problemas metodológicos da sociologia do Catolicismo no Brasil," *Revista do Museu Paulista* 14:345–76.

—— 1963b. *Social Change in Brazil*. Gainesville: University of Florida Press.

Banfield, Edward. 1958. *The Moral Basis of a Backward Society*. Glencoe: Free Press.

Barnes, J. A. 1954. "Class and Committees in a Norwegian Island Parish," *Human Relations* 7:39–58.

Bastide, Roger. 1960. *Les Religions Africaines du Brésil*. Paris: Presses Universitaires de France.

Bauer, P. T. 1954. *West African Trade*. Cambridge: Cambridge University Press.

Bello, Jose Maria. 1966. *A History of Modern Brazil, 1889–1964*. Stanford, Calif.: Stanford University Press.

Belshaw, C. 1965. *Traditional Exchange and Modern Market*. Englewood Cliffs, N.J.: Prentice-Hall.

Bernades, Nilo. 1967. "Condições geograficas de colonização em Alagoas," *Revista Brasileira de geografia* 29(2):65–83.

Beuchler, Hans C., and Beuchler, Judith-Maria. 1971. *The Bolivian Aymara*. New York: Holt, Rinehart and Winston.

Binder, Leonard. 1964. "National integration and political development," *American Political Science Review* 58:622–31.

Blau, Peter. 1964. *Exchange and Power in Social Life.* New York: John Wiley.

Bloch, Marc. 1964. *Feudal Society.* Chicago: University of Chicago Press.

Blondel, Jean. 1957. *As condições da Vida Politica no Estado da Paraiba.* Rio de Janeiro: Instituto de Direito Publico e Ciencia Politica.

Bohannon, Paul and George Dalton. 1965. *Markets in Africa.* Garden City, N.Y.: Doubleday.

Boissonade, P. 1964. *Life and Work in Medieval Europe.* New York: Harper and Row.

Borges, Fragman Carlos. 1962. "O movimento camponês no nordeste," *Estudos Sociais* 14 (15):248–60.

Boxer, Charles. 1965. *Portuguese Society in the Tropics.* Madison: University of Wisconsin Press.

Brasil. 1962. Ministerio do Trabalho. *Sindicalização rural.* Portaria ministerial No. 335-A.

—— 1963. Superintendencia de Politica Agraria (SUPRA). *Sindicatos rurais.* Relação No. 1. December 31.

—— 1966–68. Superintendencia de Desenvolvimento do Nordeste. III *Plano Director de Desenvolvimento Economico e Social do Nordeste.*

—— 1967a. *Instituto Brasileiro de Reforma Agraria (IBRA).A Estrutura Agraria Brasileira.* Rio de Janeiro.

——1967b. Instituto Brasileiro de Reforma Agraria (IBRA). Plano Decenal de Desenvolvimento Economico e Social. Tomo IV: *Agricultura e Abastimento;* Vol. I: *Agricultura e Reforma Agraria.*

Brito, Rodrigues de. n.d. *A economia Brasileira no Alvorecer do Seculo XIX.* Salvador, Bahia: Livraria Progresso Editora.

Buarque de Holanda, Sergio. 1936. *Raizes do Brazil.* Rio de Janeiro: José Olympio.

Burns, E. Bradford. 1970. *A History of Brazil.* New York: Columbia University Press.

Calazans, Julieta. 1961. *Cartilha sindical do trabalhador rural.* Natal: Editora Servico de Assistencia Rural.

Caldeira, Clovis. 1956. *Mutirão: formas de ajuda mutua no meio rural.* São Paulo: Compania Editora Nacional.

Callado, Antonio. 1960. *As Industriais da Seca e os Galileus de Pernambuco.* Rio de Janeiro: Editora Civilizaçôo Brasileira.

—— 1967. "Les Ligues Paysannes," *Les Temps Moderns* 23:751–60.

Camargo, José F. de. 1960. *Exodo Rural no Brasil.* Rio de Janeiro: Editora Conquista.

Camilo, Manuel. n.d. *Antonio Silvino.* Campina Grande, Paraiba: A Estrella da Poesia.

Campanhole, Adriane. 1963. *Legislação do Trabalhador Rural e Estatute da Terra.* São Paulo: Editora Atlas, S.A.

Canabrava, A. P. 1967. "Introduction." In A. J. Antonil, *Cultura e Opulencia do Brasil.* São Paulo: Compania Editora Nacional.

Candido, Antonio. 1964. *Os Parceiros do Rio Bonito.* Rio de Janeiro: José Olympio.

Carvalho, Rafael de. 1962. *Carta de Alforria do Campones*. São Paulo: Editora Jotape.

Casa de Rui Barbosa. 1961. *Literatura Popular em Verso: Catálogo*. Rio de Janeiro: Ministerio da Educação e Cultura.

—— 1964. *Literatura Popular em Verso: Antologia*. Rio de Janeiro: Ministerio da Educação e Cultura.

Castro, Josué de. 1966. *Death in the Northeast*. New York: Random House.

Catanhede, Cesar. 1967. *Palestra Proferida na Escola Superior de Guerra*. Rio de Janeiro: Instituto Brasileira da Reforma Agraria.

Censo Escolar. 1964. *Estado de Alagoas*. Maceió: Ministério de Educação.

Chayanov, A. V. 1966. *The Theory of Peasant Economy*. (First Published in Russian in 1925.) Homewood, Ill.: Richard D. Irwin.

Cohn, Bernard S. 1961. "The pasts of an Indian Village," *Comparative Studies in Society and History* 3:241–49.

Cohn, Bernard S. and M. Marriott. 1958. "Networks and centers in the integration of Indian civilization," *Journal of Social Research* 1:1–9.

Cohn, Norman. 1957. *The Pursuit of the Millenium*. London: Secker and Warburg.

Comite Interamericano de Desenvolvimento Agricola (CIDA). 1966. *Posse e Uso da Terra e Desenvolvimento Socio-Economico do Setor Agricola*. Washington, D.C.: Pan-American Union.

I Congresso Nacional dos Lavradores e Trabalhadores Agricolas. 1961. "Declaraçâo sôbre o carater da reforma agraria: Belo Horizonte. Nov. 17." *Estudos Sociais* 3 (12):433–37.

I Convençâo Brasileira de Sindicatos Rurais. 1963. "*Mensagem*-Conclusões (July 15–20)." Rio Grande do Norte, Natal.

Correa, Roberto Lobato. 1963. "A Colonia Pindorama: uma modificação na paisagem agraria dos tabuleiros alagoanas," *Revista Brasileira de Geografia* 25(4):479–84.

Costa Pinto, Luiz de Aguiar. 1942–43. "Lutas de familia no Brasil," *Revista do Archivo Municipal*, ano VIII, vol. 87–88, pp. 7–125.

Crespo, Pe. Paulo. 1963. "O problema camponês no nordeste brasileiro," *Sintese* 17:55–66.

Cruz Costa, Joao. 1964. *A History of Ideas in Brazil*. Berkeley: University of California Press.

Cunha, Euclides da. 1944. *Rebellion in the Backlands*. Chicago. University of Chicago Press.

Dalton, George. 1967a. "Traditional production in primitive African economics." In G. Dalton, ed., *Tribal and Peasant Economies*. Garden City, N.Y.: Natural History Press.

—— 1967b. "The development of subsistence and peasant economies in Africa." In G. Dalton, ed. *Tribal and Peasant Economies*. Garden City, N.Y.: Natural History Press.

Dandekar, V. M. 1962. "Economic Theory and Agrarian Reform," *Oxford Economic Papers* 14:69–80.

Dean, Warren. 1971. "Latifundia and land policy in nineteenth-century Brazil," *Hispanic American Historical Review* 51(4):606–25.

de Kadt, Emanuel. 1967. "Religion, the Church, and social change in Brazil." In

Claudio Veliz, ed., *The Politics of Conformity in Latin America*. London and New York: Oxford University Press.

—— 1970. *Catholic Radicals in Brazil*. London and New York: Oxford University Press.

Della Cava, Ralph. 1968. "Brazilian messianism and national institutions: a reappraisal of Canudos and Joaseiro," *Hispanic American Historical Review* 48(3);402–20.

—— 1970. *Miracle at Joazeiro*. New York: Columbia University Press.

—— 1972. "The entry of Padre Cicero into partisan politics, 1907–1909." In R. Chilcote, ed., *Protest and Resistance in Angola and Brazil*. Berkeley: University of California Press.

Desenvolvimento e Conjuntura. 1964a. "A situação social da agricultura em 1963." Ano VIII, No. 2 (Feb.).

—— 1964b. "O problema do abastecimento alimentar." Ano VIII, No. 12 (Dec.).

Dewey, Alice. 1962. *Peasant Marketing in Java*. Glencoe: Free Press.

Diegues Jr., Manuel. 1949. *O Bangue nas Alagoas*. Rio de Janeiro: Edição do Instituto de Açucas e Alcool.

—— 1952. *O Engenho de Açucar no Nordeste*. Rio de Janeiro: Serviço de Informação Agricola.

—— 1959a. *População e Propriedade da Terra no Brasil*. Washington, D.C.: Pan-American Union.

—— 1959b. "Land tenure and use in the Brazilian Plantation System." In *Plantation Systems of the New World*. Washington, D.C.: Pan American Union, Social Science Monograph VII.

—— 1960. *Regiões Culturais no Brasil*. Rio de Janeiro: Centro Brasileiro de Pesquisas Educacionais.

Donald, Carr L. 1959. "The politics of local government financing in Brazil," *Inter-American Economic Affairs*, 8(1), 21–38.

Dulles, John W. F. 1966. "Post-Dictatorship Brazil, 1945–1965." In Eric N. Baklanoff, ed., *New Perspectives of Brazil*. Nashville, Tenn.: Vanderbilt University Press.

Dumoulin, Diana. 1965. *The Rural Labor Movement in Brazil*. Mimeographed. Madison, Wisc.: The Land Tenure Center.

Epstein, David. 1969. *Planned and Spontaneous Urban Settlement in Brazilia*. Ph.D. dissertation, Columbia University.

Espindola, Tomas. 1871. *Geographia Alagoana ou descripção physico, politico, e historico da provincia das Alagoas*. Maceió: Typografia do Liberal.

Facó, Rui. 1965. *Cangaceiros e Fanaticos*. Rio de Janeiro: Editora Civilização Brasileira.

Fallers, Lloyd. 1963. "Equality, modernity, and democracy in the new states." In C. Geertz, ed., *Old Societies and New States*. Chicago: University of Chicago Press.

Feitosa Martins, Araguaya. 1962. "Alguns aspectos da inquietação trabalhista no campo." *Revista Brasiliense* 40:132–46.

Ferrari, Fernando. 1963. *Escravos da Terra*. Porto Alegre: Editora Globo.

Firth, R. 1964. "Capital, Saving and Credit in Peasant Societies: A Viewpoint from Economic Anthropology." In Raymond Firth and B. S. Yamey, eds., *Capital, Saving and Credit in Peasant Societies*. Chicago: Aldine.

Forman, Leona Shluger. 1970. "Education in Brazil." In *Your Child*. London: IPC Magazines.

Forman, Shepard. 1963a. "Os sinos de São José dobraram em Surubim," *Cadernos Brasileiros* 5(5):48–54.

—— 1963b. "Up from the parrot's perch." In R. Klein, ed., *Young Americans Abroad*. New York: Harper and Row.

—— 1970. *The Raft Fishermen: Tradition and Change in the Brazilian Peasant Economy*. Bloomington: Indiana University Press.

—— 1971. "Disunity and discontent: a study of peasant political movements in Brazil." *Journal of Latin American Studies* 3(1):3–24.

Forman, Shepard and Joyce Riegelhaupt. 1970. "Market place and marketing system: toward a theory of peasant economic integration," *Comparative Studies in Society and History* 12(2):188–212.

Foster, George. 1961. "The dyadic contract: a model for the social structure of a Mexican peasant village," *American Anthropologist* 63:1173–92.

—— 1963. "The dyadic contract in Tzintzuntzan: patron-client relationship," *American Anthropologist* 65:1280–94.

—— 1965. "Peasant society and the image of limited good," *American Anthropologist* 67:293–315.

Frank, Andre Gunder. 1967. *Capitalism and Underdevelopment in Latin America*. New York: Monthly Review Press.

Frei Calso de São Paulo. 1963. *Os Cristãos e o sindicato na cidade e no campo*. São Paulo: Editora Saraiva.

Freire, Paulo. 1970a. *Cultural Action for Freedom*. Cambridge, Mass.: Center for the Study of Development and Social Change.

—— 1970b. *Pedagogy of the Oppressed*. New York: Herder and Herder.

Freitas Marcondes, J. V. 1948. "Mutirao or mutual aid," *Rural Sociology* 13:374–84.

—— 1951. "Social legislation in Brazil." In T. Lynn Smith and Alexander Marchant, eds., *Brazil: Portrait of Half a Continent*. New York: Dryden Press.

—— 1962. *First Brazilian Legislation Relating to Rural Labor Unions: A Sociological Study*. The Latin American Monograph Series, No. 20. Gainesville: University of Florida Press.

—— 1963. "O estatuto do trabalhador rural e o problema da terra," *Cadernos Brasileiros* 4:55–59.

—— 1966. "O sindicalismo rural e a reforma agraria," *Revista Brasileira de Estudos Politicos* 20:49–58.

Freyre, Gilberto. 1946. *The Masters and the Slaves: A Study in the Development of Brazilian Civilization*. New York: Knopf.

—— 1959. *New World in the Tropics*. New York: Knopf.

—— 1963. *The Mansions and the Shanties: The Making of Modern Brazil*. New York: Knopf.

—— 1964. "The patriarchal basis of Brazilian society." In Maier and Weatherhead, eds., *Politics of Change in Latin America*. New York: Praeger.

—— 1970. *Order and Progress*. New York: Knopf.

Furtado, Celso. 1963. *The Economic Growth of Brazil*. Berkeley: University of California Press.

—— 1965a. *Diagnosis of the Brazilian Crisis.* Berkeley: University of California Press.

—— 1965b. "Brazil: What kind of revolution," *Foreign Affairs* 41:526–35.

Galjart, Benno. 1964. "Class and 'following' in rural Brazil," *America Latina* 7(3):3–24.

—— 1965. "Turnover of farmers in a land settlement in Brazil," *America Latina* 8(2):48–65.

—— 1967. *Itaguaí: Old Habits and New Patterns in a Brazilian Land Settlement.* Wageningen, The Netherlands: Centre for Agricultural Publishing and Documentation.

Galvão, Helio. 1959. *O Mutirâo no Nordeste.* Rio de Janeiro: Servico de Informaçao Agricola.

Ganshoff, F. L. 1961. *Feudalism.* New York: Harper and Row.

Gardner, George. 1849. *Travels in Brazil,* London. Translated as *Viagens no Brasil,* by Albertino Pinheiro. Rio de Janeiro: Editora Nacional, 1942.

Geertz, Clifford. 1960. "The Javanese *Kijaji:* The changing role of a culture broker," *Comparative Studies in Society and History* 2:228–49.

—— 1966a. *Agricultural Involution: The Processes of Ecological Change in Indonesia.* Berkeley: University of California Press.

—— 1966b. "Religion as a cultural system." In Michael Banton, ed., *Anthropological Approaches to the Study of Religion.* ASA Monograph 3, pp. 1–46. London: Tavistock.

—— 1972. "Afterword: the politics of meaning." In Claire Holt, ed., *Culture and Politics in Indonesia.* Ithaca, N.Y.: Cornell University Press.

Geertz, Clifford et al. 1963. *Old Societies and New States.* New York: Free Press.

Georgescu-Rogen, N. 1960. "Economic Theory and Agrarian Economics." *Oxford Economic Papers* 12:1–40.

Gondim da Fonseca. 1962. *Assim Falou Juliao.* São Paulo: Editora Fulger.

Gross, Daniel R. 1970. *Sisal and Social Structure in Northeast Brazil.* Ph.D. dissertation, Columbia University.

—— 1971. "Ritual and conformity: a religious pilgrimage to Northeast Brazil," *Ethnology* 10:129–48.

Gudeman, Stephan. 1972. "The *compadrazgo* as a reflection of the natural and spiritual person." Proceedings of the Royal Anthropological Institute of Great Britain and Ireland, pp. 45–71. London: Royal Anthropological Institute.

Gusfield, Joseph. 1968. "The study of social movements." In David Sills, ed. *International Encyclopedia of the Social Sciences.* Vol. 14. New York: Macmillan.

Harding, Timothy. 1964. "Revolution tomorrow: the failure of the left in Brazil," *Studies on the Left* 4(4):30–54.

Haring, C. H. 1958. *Empire in Brazil.* Cambridge: Harvard University Press.

Harris, Marvin. 1952. "Race relations in Minas Velhas." In Charles Wagley et al., *Race and Class in Rural Brazil.* New York: UNESCO.

—— 1956. *Town and Country in Brazil.* New York: Columbia University Press.

Heberle, Rudolf. 1968. "Types and functions of social movements." In David Sills, ed., *International Encyclopedia of the Social Sciences,* Vol. 14. New York: Macmillan.

Henderson, James. 1821. *A History of Brazil, Comprising its Geography, Commerce, Colonization, Aboriginal Inhabitants*. London: Longman, Hurst, Rees, Orme and Brown.
Hobsbawm, E. J. 1959. *Primitive Rebels*. New York: Horton.
—— 1969. *Bandits*. New York: Delacorte Press.
Horowitz, Irving Lewis. 1964. *Revolution in Brazil*. New York: Dutton.
Huizer, Gerrit. 1965. "Some notes on community development and rural social research," *America Latina* 8(3):128–44.
Hutchinson, Bertram. 1966. "The patron-dependent relationship in Brazil: a preliminary examination," *Sociologia Ruralis* 1:3–30.
Hutchinson, H. W. 1957. *Village and Plantation in Northeast Brazil*. Seattle: University of Washington Press.
Ianni, Octavio. 1965. "Processo politico a desenvolvimento economico." In Ianni et al., *Politica e Revolução Social no Brasil*. Rio de Janeiro: Editora Civilização Brasileira.
—— 1970. *Crisis in Brazil*. New York: Columbia University Press.
Instituto Brasileiro de Administração Municipal. 1967a. *Manual de Prefeito*. Rio de Janeiro.
—— 1967b. *O Municipio na Constituição de 1967*. Rio de Janeiro.
Instituto Brasileiro de Geografia e Estatística. 1903. *Tipos e Aspectos do Brasil*. Rio de Janeiro.
—— 1966. *Anuario Estatístico do Brasil*. Rio de Janeiro: IBGE-Conselho Nacional de Estatística.
Instituto Brasileiro de Reforma Agraria. 1967. *Cadastro de Imoveis Rurais-Alagoas*. Rio de Janeiro.
Jaguaribe, Helio. 1964. "A renuncia do Presidente Quadros e a crise politica brasileira." In Irving L. Horowitz, *Revolution in Brazil*. New York: Dutton.
—— 1968. *Economic and Political Development: A Theoretical Approach and a Brazilian Case Study*. Cambridge: Harvard University Press.
—— 1969. "Political strategies of national development in Brazil." In Irving L. Horowitz et al., eds., *Latin American Radicalism*. New York: Random House.
Jayawardena, Chandra. 1964. "Review of Clifford Geertz, et al., *Old Societies and New States*," *American Anthropologist* 66:906–8.
Jesus, Maria Carolina de. 1962. *Child of the Dark*. New York: Signet.
Johnson, Allen. 1972. *Sharecroppers of the Sertão*. Stanford, Calif.: Stanford University Press.
Johnson, H. B. 1972. "The donatary captaincy in perspective: Portuguese backgrounds to the settlement of Brazil," *Hispanic American Historical Review* 52(2):203–14.
Julião, Francisco. 1962. *Que São as Ligas Camponesas?* Rio de Janeiro: Editora Civilização Brasileira.
—— 1962a. *Escucha campesino*. Montevideo: Editora Presente.
—— 1963. "Brazil, a Christian Country." In Carlos Fuentes, ed., *Whither Latin America?* New York: Monthly Review Press.
—— 1966. "Interview with Alfonso Gortaire Iturralde," *CIF Reports*, Vol. 5, No. 21 (Nov. 1). Translated from *Comunidad* I (3) Sept. 1966.
—— 1968. *Cambão: La Cara Oculta de Brasil*. Mexico: Siglo Veintiuno.

Katzin, Margaret F. 1959. "The Jamaican Country Higgler," *Social and Economic Studies* 8(4):421–35.
—— 1960. "The business of higgling in Jamaica," *Social and Economic Studies* 9:267–331.
Koster, Henry. 1816. *Travels in Brazil*. London. Translated as *Viajem ao Nordeste do Brasil* by Luiz da Camara Cascudo. Rio de Janeiro: Editora Nacional, 1942.
Kottak, Conrad. 1966. *The Structure of Equality in a Brazilian Coastal Village*. Ph.D. dissertation, Columbia University.
Kroeber, Alfred L. 1948. *Anthropology*. New York: Harper and Row.
Lambert, Jacques. 1959. *Os Dois Brasis*. Rio de Janeiro: Centro Brasileiro de Perquisas Educacionais.
LAMP (Latin American Market Planning Center). 1968. *Market Processes in the Recife Area of Northeast Brazil*. Mimeographed. Lansing: Michigan State University. Research report.
Leal, Victor Nunes. 1948. *Coronelismo: Enxada e Voto* (Alternatively titled *O Municipio e o Regime Representativo no Brasil*). Rio de Janeiro: n.p.
Leda Barreto. 1963. *Juliâo, Nordeste, Revolucao*. Rio de Janeiro: Civilização Brasileira.
Leeds, Anthony. 1964. "Brazil and the myth of Francisco Juliâo." In Joseph Meier and Richard Weatherhead, eds., *Politics of Change in Latin America*. New York: Praeger.
Leers, Frei Bernardo, O.F.M. 1967. "Religiosidade Rural." *Igrega Hoje* 14:16–36. Petropolis: Editora Vozes Ltda.
Lenin, V. I. 1960a. "New economic developments in peasant life." In *Collected Works*, Vol. I. Moscow: Foreign Languages Publishing House.
—— 1960b. "The differentiation of the peasantry." In *Collected Works*, Vol. III. Moscow: Foreign Languages Publishing House.
Lockhart, James. 1972. "The social history of colonial Spanish America: Evolution and potential," *Latin American Research Review* 7(1):6–46.
Lopes, Juarez R. B. 1966. "Some basic developments in Brazilian politics and society." In Eric N. Baklanoff, ed., *New Perspectives of Brazil*. Nashville, Tenn.: Vanderbilt University Press.
—— 1967. *A Crise do Brasil Arcaico*. São Paulo: Compania Editora Nacional.
—— 1971. *Desenvolvimento e Mudança Social*. São Paulo: Compania Editora Nacional.
Lourenço Filho. 1929. *Joaseiro do Padre Cicero*. São Paulo.
Love, Joseph L. 1970. "Political participation in Brazil, 1881–1969," *Luso-Brazilian Review* 7(2):3–24.
—— 1971. *Rio Grande do Sul and Brazilian Regionalism, 1882–1930*. Stanford, Calif.: Stanford University Press.
Ludwig, Armin K. and H. W. Taylor. 1969. *Brazil's New Agrarian Reform*. New York: Praeger.
Margolis, Maxine. 1973. *The Moving Frontier: Social and Economic Change in a Southern Brazilian Community*. Gainesville: University of Florida Press.
Martins, Toiapa. 1962. "Proletariado e inquietaçâo rural," *Revista Brasiliense* 42:62–81.
Mayer, Adrian C. 1966. "The significance of quasi-groups in the study of com-

plex societies." In Michael Banton, ed., *The Social Anthropology of Complex Societies*. ASA Monograph 4. London: Tavistock.

Mellor, John W. 1966. *The Economics of Agricultural Development*. Ithaca, N.Y.: Cornell University Press.

Mintz, Sidney. 1955. "The Jamaican Internal Marketing Pattern: some notes and hypotheses," *Social and Economic Studies* 4(1):95–103.

—— 1957. "The Role of the Middleman in the Internal Distribution System of a Caribbean Peasant Economy," *Human Organization* 15(2):18–23.

—— 1959. "Internal Market Systems as Mechanisms of Social Articulation," *Proceedings of the Annual Spring Meeting, American Ethnological Society,* pp. 20–30.

—— 1960a. "Peasant Markets," *Scientific American* 203(2):112–18.

—— 1960b. "A Tentative Typology of Eight Haitian Market Places," *Revista de Ciencias Sociales* 4(1):15–58.

—— 1961. "Pratik: Haitian Personal Economic Relationships." *Proceedings of the Annual Spring Meetings, American Ethnological Society,* pp. 54–63.

Mintz, S. W. and E. R. Wolf. 1950. "An analysis of ritual coparenthood (*Compadrazgo*)," *Southwest Journal of Anthropology* 6:341–68.

Miracle, Marvin. 1968. "Subsistence agriculture: analytical problems and alternate concepts," *American Journal of Agricultural Economics* 50(2):292–310.

Mitchell, Fanny. 1967. "Padre Crespo and Padre Melo: Two approaches to reform." Institute of Current World Affairs, Letter FM-17(Nov. 9).

Montenegro, Abelardo. 1959. *Historia do Fanaticismo Religioso no Ceará*. Fortaleza: Batista Fontenele.

Moore, Barrington. 1966. *The Social Origins of Dictatorship and Democracy*. Boston: Beacon Press.

Morse, Richard. 1962. "Some themes of Brazilian history," *South Atlantic Quarterly* 61:2.

Mota, Carlos Guilherme. 1972. *Nordeste: 1817*. São Paulo: Editora da Universidade.

Mota, Leonardo. 1961. *Cantadores*. Fortaleza: Imprensa Universitaria do Ceará.

—— 1962. *Violeiros do Norte*. Fortaleza: Imprensa Universitaria do Ceará.

—— 1965. *Sertão Alegre*. Fortaleza: Imprensa Universitaria do Ceará.

Nash, Manning. 1965. *The Golden Road to Modernity*. New York: Wiley.

—— 1966. *Primitive and Peasant Economic Systems*. San Francisco: Chandler.

Nicholas, Ralph W. 1965. "Factions: a comparative analysis." In Michael Benton, ed., *Political Systems and the Distribution of Power*. London: Tavistock.

Nunes Leal, Victor. 1949. *Coronelismo, enxada e voto*. Rio de Janeiro: Editora Forense.

Oberg, Kalervo. 1965. "The marginal peasant in Brazil." *American Anthropologist* 67:1417–1427.

Obregon, Anibal Quijano. 1967. "Contemporary peasant movements." In Seymour Martin Lipset and Aldo Solari, eds., *Elites in Latin America*. New York: Oxford University Press.

Oliveira Vianna. 1933. *A Evolução do Povo Brasileiro*. São Paulo: Companhia Editôra Nacional.

—— 1938. *Populacoes Meridionaes do Brasil*. São Paulo: Companhia Editora Nacional.

—— 1955. *Instituições Politicas Brasileiras.* Vols. I and II. Rio de Janeiro: José Olympio.

Ortiz, Sutti. 1967. "Colombian rural market organization: An exploratory model," *Man* (n.s.) 2:393–414.

Pacheco, José. 1949. *A Chegada de Lampiâo no Inferno.* Joazeiro de Norte: Editora Proprietârio.

Palmeira, Moacir. 1966. "Nordeste: mudancas politicas no seculo xx," *Quadernos Brasileiros* 8:67–78.

Pang, Eul-Soo and Ron L. Seckinger. 1972. "The Mandarins of Imperial Brazil," *Comparative Studies in Society and History* 14(2):215–44.

Paulson, Beldon. 1964. *Local Political Patterns in Northeast Brazil.* Research Paper #12. Madison, Wisc.: Land Tenure Center.

Pendrell, Nan. 1969. *Squatting in Salvador.* Ph.D. dissertation, Columbia University.

Pereira de Queiros, Maria Isaura. 1963. "Movements, messianique et dévelopement economique au Brésil." *Archive de Sociologie des Religions* 16:109–21.

—— 1965a. *O Messianismo no Brasil e no Mundo.* São Paulo: Universidade de São Paulo.

—— 1965b. "Messiahs in Brazil," *Past and Present* 31:62–110.

—— 1969. *O Mandonismo Local na Vida Politica Brasileira.* São Paulo.

Poppino, Rollie. 1968. *Brazil: The Land and People.* London and New York: Oxford University Press.

Powell, John Duncan. 1970. "Peasant society and clientelist politics," *American Political Science Review* 64 (June:411–25.

Power, Eileen. 1966. "The peasant Bodo: life on a country estate in the time of Charlemagne." In *Medieval People*, rev. ed. New York: Barnes and Noble.

Prado, Caio Jr. 1957a. *Historia Economica do Brasil.* São Paulo: Editora Brasiliense.

—— 1957b. *Evolução Politica do Brasil.* São Paulo: Editora Brasiliense.

—— 1963. "O estatuto do trabalhador rural," *Revista Brasiliense* 47:1–13.

—— 1964. "The agrarian question in Brazil," *Studies on the Left* 4(4):77–84.

—— 1965. *Formação do Brasil Contemporâneo.* São Paulo: Editora Brasiliense.

—— 1966. *A Revolução Brasileira.* São Paulo: Editora Brasiliense.

—— 1967. *The Colonial Background of Modern Brazil.* Berkeley: University of California Press.

Price, Robert. 1964. *Rural Unionization in Brazil.* Research paper No. 14. Madison, Wisc.: Land Tenure Center.

Ramos, Graciliano. 1965. *Barren Lives.* Translated by Ralph Ellison. Austin: University of Texas Press.

Redfield, Robert. 1960. *Peasant Society and Culture and The Little Community.* Chicago: University of Chicago Press.

Ribeiro, José P. and C. Wharton Jr. 1969. "The ACAR program in Minas Gerais, Brazil." In C. Wharton Jr., ed., *Subsistence Agriculture and Economic Development.* Chicago: Aldine.

Ribeiro, René. 1962. "Brazilian messianic movements." In S. Thrupp, ed., *Millenial Dreams in Action.* The Hague, Mouton.

—— 1972. "The millenium that never came: the story of a Brazilian prophet." In Ronald Chilcote, ed., *Protest and Resistance in Angola and Brazil.* Berkeley: University of California Press.

Riegelhaupt, Joyce F. 1972. "Village non-politics: peasant participation in an established authoritarian system." Paper presented to the Anthropology Department Seminar, February 1972, University of Chicago.

Riegelhaupt, Joyce and Shepard Forman. 1970. "Bodo was never Brazilian," *Journal of Economic History* 30(1):100–16.

Rodrigues, José Honorio. n.d. *Conciliação e Reforma no Brasil: um Desafio Historico-Cultural.* Rio de Janeiro: Editora Civilização Brasileira.

Santos, Adilson Portela. 1961. "Evolução da vida politica no municipio de Picos, Piaui," *Revista Brasileira de Estudes Politicos* 10:160–83.

Santos, Antonio Alves dos. n.d. *O Choro dos Brasileiros por Causa do Imposto e Renda.* Itá, Bahia: Editora Proprietario.

—— n.d. *A Historia da Filha de um Barão Persequida por 3 Vigarios.* Itá, Bahia: Editora Proprietario.

Schattan, Salamao. 1961. "Estrutura economica da agricultura paulista," *Revista Brasiliense* 37:66–101.

Schmitter, Philippe. 1971. *Interest Conflict and Political Change in Brazil.* Stanford, Calif.: Stanford University Press.

—— 1971b. "The Portugalization of Brazil." *Authoritarian Brazil: Origins, Policy, and Future.* In Alfred Stepan, ed., New Haven: Yale University Press, 1973.

Schneider, Ronald. 1972. *The Political System of Brazil.* New York: Columbia University Press.

Schuh, G. Edward. 1970. *The Agricultural Development of Brazil.* New York: Praeger.

Schultz, T. W. 1964. *Transforming Traditional Agriculture.* New Haven, Conn.: Yale University Press.

Schwartz, Stuart. 1973. "Free labor in a slave economy: the lavradores de cana of Colonial Bahia." In Darrel Alden ed., *Colonial Roots of Modern Brazil.* Berkeley: University of California Press.

Scott, James C. 1972a. "Patron-client politics and political change in Southeast Asia," *American Political Science Review* 66:91–113.

—— 1972b. "The erosion of patron-client bonds and social change in rural Southeast Asia," *Journal of Asian Studies* 32(1):5–37.

—— 1973. "How traditional rural patrons lose legitimacy: a theory with special reference to lowland Southeast Asia." Mimeographed. Madison: University of Wisconsin.

Scully, William. 1866. *Brazil: Its Provinces and Chief Cities and the Manners and Customs of the People.* London: Murray.

Shanin, Teodor. 1971. *Peasants and Peasant Societies: Selected Readings.* London: Penguin.

Shils, Edward. 1968a. "Deference." In J. A. Jackson, ed., *Social Stratification.* Sociological Studies No. 1. Cambridge: Cambridge University Press.

—— 1968b. "The concept and function of ideology." In David Sills, ed., *International Encyclopedia of the Social Sciences.* Vol. 7. New York: Macmillan.

Shirley, Robert. 1971. *The End of a Tradition.* New York: Columbia University Press.

Siegel, Bernard. 1955. "Social structure and economic change in Brazil." In S. Kuznets, W. E. Moore, and J. J. Spengler, eds., *Economic Growth: Brazil, India, China.* Durham: University of North Carolina Press.

—— 1959–67. *Biennial Review of Anthropology.* Vols. 1–5. Stanford: Stanford University Press.

Silva, Joaquim N. de Souza de. 1951. *Investigações sobre os recenseamontos da populacão geral do Imperio* (1870). Rio de Janeiro: Conselho Nacional de Estatistica, Serviço Nacional de Recenseamento.

Silva, José Bernardo de. 1963. *Lampião e as Forças Legais.* Joazeiro do Norte; Teará: Tipografia Sao Francisco.

Silva, Manoel. 1961. "I Congresso des trabalhadores rurais do Parana," *Revista Brasiliense* 33:56–62.

Silverman, Sydel. 1965. "Patronage and community-nation relationships in Central Italy," *Ethnology* 4:172–89.

—— 1970. "Exploitation in rural central Italy: structure and ideology in stratification study," *Comparative Studies in Society and History* 12(3):327–39.

Singer, Paulo. 1965. "A politica das classes dominantes." In Octavio Ianni et al., *Politica e Revolucão Social No Brasil.* Rio de Janeiro: Editora Civilização Brasileira.

Skidmore, Thomas. 1967. *Politics in Brazil, 1930–1964: An Experiment in Democracy.* London and New York: Oxford University Press.

Skinner, G. W. 1964. "Marketing and Social Structure in Rural China," *Journal of Asian Studies* 24(1):3–43.

Smith, T. Lynn. 1963. *Brazil: People and Institutions,* rev. ed. Baton Rouge: Louisiana State University Press.

Soares, Glaucio. 1964. "The political sociology of uneven development in Brazil." In Irving L. Horowitz, ed. *Revolution in Brazil.* New York: Dutton.

Sodré, Nelson Wernecke. 1967. *Introdução a Revolução Brasileira.* Rio de Janeiro: Editora Civilização Brasileira.

Sodré, Novais. 1963. *Quem é Francisco Julião.* São Paulo: Redenção Nacional.

SORPE (Service de Orientacao rural de Pernambuco). 1967. "Os trabalhadores rurais querem ser agentes do desenvolvimento do nordeste plantando dois hectares." Mimeographed. Recife.

Souza, Amaury. 1968. "Traditional media and political communication in rural Brazil." Mimeographed. Cambridge: MIT.

—— 1972. "The Cangaço and the politics of violence in Northeast Brazil." In Ronald Chilcote, ed., *Protest and Resistance in Brazil and Angola.* Berkeley: University of California Press.

Souza, Joao G. de. 1956. "Some aspects of land tenure in Brazil." In Kenneth T. Parsons, Raymond J. Penn, and Philip E. Raup, eds., *Land Tenure.* Madison: University of Wisconsin Press.

Souza Barros, Manoel. 1953. *Exodo e Fixação.* Rio de Janeiro: Serviço de Informação Agricola.

Stein, Stanley. 1957. *Vassouras: A Brazilian Coffee Country.* Cambridge: Harvard University Press.

Stepan, Alfred. 1971. *The Military in Politics: Changing Patterns in Brazil.* Princeton, N.J.: Princeton University Press.

Steward, Julian. 1950. *Area Research: Theory and Practice.* New York: Social Science Research Council.

—— 1955. *Theory of Culture Change.* Urbana: University of Illinois Press.

—— 1956. *The People of Puerto Rico.* Urbana: University of Illinois Press.

Tax, Sol. 1953. *Penny Capitalism.* Institute of Social Anthropology, No. 16. Washington, D.C.: Smithsonian Institute.

Torres, João Camillo de Oliveira. 1957. *O Positivismo no Brasil.* Rio de Janeiro: Editora Vozes.

—— 1965. *Estratificação Social no Brasil.* São Paulo: Difusâo Europeia do Livro.

Vallier, Ivan. 1967. "Religious elites: differentiation and developments in Roman Catholicism." In S. M. Lipset and Aldo Solari, eds., *Elites in Latin America.* London and New York: Oxford University Press.

—— 1970. *Catholicism, Social Control, and Modernization in Latin America.* Englewood Cliffs, N.J.: Prentice-Hall.

Vera, Mestor. 1961. "O II congresso componês em Maringa," *Revista Brasiliense* 37:62–65.

—— 1962. "O congresso camponês em Belo Horizonte," *Revista Brasiliense* 39:94–99.

Vianna, Sagadas. 1963. *O estatuto do trabalhador rural e sua aplicação.* São Paulo: Livraria Freitas Bastos.

Vieira da Cunha, Mario Wagner. 1963. *O Sistema Administrativo Brasileiro, 1930–1950.* Rio de Janeiro: Instituto Nacional de Estudos Pedagogicos.

Vilaça, Marcos V. and Roberto Albuquerque. 1965. *Coronel, Coroneis.* Rio de Janeiro.

Vilhena, Luiz Santos. 1921 *Recopilação de noticias soterpolitanas e Brasilicas.* Bahia (1802).

Vinhas, Moises. 1962. "As classes e camadas do campo no estado de São Paulo," *Estudos Sociais* 13(June).

—— 1963. *Operarios e companeses na revolução brasileira.* São Paulo: Editora Fulgre.

Vinhas de Queiroz, Mauricio. 1966. *Messianismo e conflito social.* Rio de Janeiro: Editora Civilização Brasileira.

Wagley, Charles. 1960. "The Brazilian revolution: social change since 1930." In Richard Adams et al., *Social Change in Latin America Today.* New York: Vintage Books.

—— 1963. *An Introduction to Brazil.* New York: Columbia University Press.

—— 1964. *Amazon Town: A Study of Man in the Tropics.* New York: Knopf.

—— 1968. *The Latin American Tradition.* New York: Columbia University Press.

Wagley, Charles et al. 1952. *Race and Class in Rural Brazil.* New York: UNESCO.

Wagley, Charles and Marvin Harris. 1955. "A typology of Latin American Subcultures," *American Anthropologist* 57:428–1.

Warriner, Doreen. 1965. *Economics of Peasant Farming.* 2d ed. New York: Barnes and Noble.

—— 1969. *Land Reform in Principle and Practice.* Oxford: Clarendon Press.

Weffort, Francisco C. 1965. "Politica de massas." In Octavic Ianni et al., *Politica e Revolucão Social no Brasil.* Rio de Janeiro: Editora Civilização Brasileira.

—— 1970. "State and mass in Brazil," In Irving L. Horowitz, ed., *Masses in Latin America.* New York: Oxford University Press.

Wells, Henry, Charles Dougherty, James Rowe, and Ronald Schneider, eds.,

1962. *Brazil: Election Factbook*. Washington, D.C.: Institute for the Comparative Study of Political Systems.

Weil, Thomas E. et al. 1970. *Area Handbook for Brazil*. Washington, D.C.: U.S. Government Printing Office.

Wharton, Clifton R. Jr. 1963. "The economic meaning of 'subsistence,'" *Malayan Economic Review* 8:22–44.

Wiarda, Howard J. 1969. *The Brazilian Catholic Labor Movement: The Dilemmas of National Development*. Boston: University of Massachusetts Press.

Wilkie, Mary W. 1964. *A Report of Rural Syndacates in Pernambuco*. Mimeographed. Madison, Wisc.: Land Tenure Center.

Willems, Emilio. 1947. *Cunha: Tradição e Transição em uma Cultura Rural de Brasil*. São Paulo: Secretaria de Agricultura do Estado.

—— 1966. "Religious mass movements and social change in Brazil." In E. Baklanoff, ed., *New Perspectives of Brazil*. Nashville: Vanderbilt University Press.

—— 1967. *Followers of the New Faith*. Nashville: Vanderbilt University Press.

—— 1970. "Social differentiation in Colonial Brazil," *Comparative Studies in Society and History* 12(1):31–49.

Wolf, Eric R. 1955a. "The Mexican Bajio in the 18th century: an analysis of cultural integration," *Middle American Research Institute Publications*, No. 17::180–99. New Orleans: Tulane University.

—— 1955b. "Types of Latin American Peasantry," *American Anthropologist* 57:452–71.

—— 1956. "Aspects of group relations in a complex society: Mexico," *American Anthropologist* 58(6):1065–78. Reprinted in T. Shanin, *Peasants and Peasant Societies*. London: Penguin.

—— 1966a. *Peasants*. Englewood Cliffs, N.J.: Prentice-Hall.

—— 1966b. "Kinship, friendship, and patron-client relationships in complex societies." In Michael Banton, ed., *The Social Anthropology of Complex Societies*. ASA Monograph 4. London: Tavistock.

—— 1967. "Reflections on peasant revolutions." Paper presented at the Carnegie Seminar on Political and Administrative Development, April 3, 1967, at Indiana University, Bloomington.

—— 1969. *Peasant Wars of the Twentieth Century*. New York: Harper and Row.

Worseley, Peter. 1957. *The Trumpet Shall Sound*. London: Macgibbon and Kee.

Index

Abolition: effects on peasant economy, 22; Liberal Party and, 157; as issue, 159; and elite differentiation, 160; Republican Party and, 161, 162; *see also* Freedmen; Slavery

Absenteeism: among traditional elites, 80, 83, 93, 110; in Itaguaí colony, 131; at ballot box, 179–80

Additional Act of 1834: elevates power of provinces, 156; trade-off for votes began with, 160

Administration vs. politics, 198

Agrarian crisis, 38–39, 121; political solution of, required, 116; and rural–urban migration, 119; and colonization and resettlement schemes, 133; SUDENE as panacea for, 181; re-created in Transamazonian development, 202

Agrarian policy: of Brazilian government, 111, 112, 115, 116, 195, 201, 262n14; limits to, 112; lags behind commercialization, 196

Agrarian reform, 115; Rene Bertholet on, 127; need for, 135; and political promises, 180; demand for, by peasant leagues, 183; and Francisco Julião, 186, 241; Communist Party prefers labor legislation to, 187; Church policy toward, 189, 191; call for, by Second Congress of Rural Workers of Paraná, 191; Bill of 1964, 195

Agreste: mixed farming area in Northeast, 89; spread of peasant leagues in, 184

Agricultural labor, types of, 49 ff., 89; *see also* Peasant types, varieties of

Alagoas, state of, 27; marketing system in, 90 ff., 107–8, 114; population growth in, 93; party structure in, 172–73

Andrade, M. C. de: on numbers of slaves, 22; on sharecropping, 60

Anticlericalism, 278–79n17

Antonil, A. J.: on free labor in colonial period, 21

ARENA (National Renovating Alliance), 196, 197, 198; *see also* Political parties

Armazens, see Warehouses; Wholesaling

Asimow project for rural industrialization, 123

Authoritarian rule, 196

Authority: Submission to, as organizing principle, 74, 76, 80, 83, 206, 217; of landed class, justified, 77, 80, 83, 160, 206; effect of absenteeism on, 83; challenge to, 85, 166, 177, 180; control of legal, by elites, 143; yielding of by landowning elites, 149; on colonial estate, 150–51; of seigniorial class under Pedro I, 155; of Pedro II, 157; of President, increases under Vargas, 169, 171

Azevedo, Thales de, on folk Catholicism, 275n5

Basic Education Movement (MEB), 201, 284n47

Bauer, P. T., on function of middlemen, 105

Belshaw, C.: on development in marketplace, 110; on competition in marketplace, 112